Trajectories of Minority Rights Issues in Europe
The Implementation Trap?

Edited by
Timofey Agarin and Malte Brosig

LONDON AND NEW YORK

First published 2015 by Routledge

2 Park Square, Milton Park, Abingdon, Oxfordshire OX14 4RN

711 Third Avenue, New York, NY 10017

Routledge is an imprint of the Taylor & Francis Group, an informa business

First issued in paperback 2018

Copyright © 2015 Taylor & Francis

All rights reserved. No part of this book may be reprinted or reproduced or utilised in any form or by any electronic, mechanical, or other means, now known or hereafter invented, including photocopying and recording, or in any information storage or retrieval system, without permission in writing from the publishers.

Notice:
Product or corporate names may be trademarks or registered trademarks, and are used only for identification and explanation without intent to infringe.

British Library Cataloguing in Publication Data
A catalogue record for this book is available from the British Library

ISBN13: 978-1-138-79394-1 (hbk)
ISBN13: 978-1-138-37935-0 (pbk)

Typeset in Times New Roman
by Taylor & Francis Books

Publisher's Note
The publisher accepts responsibility for any inconsistencies that may have arisen during the conversion of this book from journal articles to book chapters, namely the possible inclusion of journal terminology.

Disclaimer
Every effort has been made to contact copyright holders for their permission to reprint material in this book. The publishers would be grateful to hear from any copyright holder who is not here acknowledged and will undertake to rectify any errors or omissions in future editions of this book.

Trajectories of Minority Rights Issues in Europe

The interest in minority protection emerged during the period of democratic transition, particularly of ethnically segmented postcommunist societies after the end of the Cold War. Minority issues became prominent as postcommunist states lined up as potential candidates for EU membership as respect for and protection of minority rights was an essential part of the criteria these states had to fulfil before EU accession. Minority rights protection has constituted an important 'gatekeeping' criterion for EU membership. Its monitoring remains a powerful instrument to mediate tensions and to adjudicate discriminations in the present-day Europe. In many countries, minority rights standards have been transposed in domestic legislation, but whether these norms constitute a legitimate background which states accept, sustain and promote is the focus of this book.

This volume takes on the task of analysing the diffusion of minority rights norms across the European continent. It looks specifically at the oft-neglected process of compliance meaning not only the formal adoption of European laws but also their implementation within the domestic context. The contributions analyse the political rhetoric, legal transposition and behavioural compliance in a range of European states, East and West, to assess compliance to norms of minority protection.

This book was published as a special issue of *Perspectives on European Politics and Society*.

Timofey Agarin is a Lecturer in Comparative Politics and Ethnic Conflict in Queen's University Belfast, UK, where he is also the Director of the Centre for the Study of Ethnic Conflict. His research interest is in ethnic politics and their impact on transition from communism in Central Eastern European states. He is interested in the interplay of social and institutional change in postcommunism in issue areas of non-discrimination, minority protection, migration and civil society. Timofey has published in *Ethnopolitics, Perspectives on European Politics and Society, Ethnicities, Nationalities Papers* and *Journal of Baltic Studies*. He authored *A Cat's Lick? Democratisation and Minority Communities in the post-Soviet Baltic* (2010) and edited *Minority Integration in Central Eastern Europe: Between Ethnic Diversity and Equality* (2009, with Malte Brosig) and *Institutional Legacies of Communism: Change and Continuities in Minority Protection* (2013, with Karl Cordell).

Malte Brosig is a Senior Lecturer in International Relations at the University of the Witwatersrand in Johannesburg, South Africa. He received his PhD in 2008 at the Centre for International and European Studies Research at Portsmouth University, UK. He has published widely on questions of norm diffusion and minority protection in Eastern Europe. He is an Associate Editor of European Security and Co-chairing the Human Rights Working Group at the German Political Science Association. His work has been published in accredited journals such as: *Journal of European Integration, International Peacekeeping, European Security, the European Review of International Affairs, the South African Journal of International Affairs*, and the *Journal of International Organization Studies* at which he is also serving as an editorial board member.

Contents

Citation Information   vii

1. Introduction
   Timofey Agarin & Malte Brosig   1

2. No Space for Constructivism? A Critical Appraisal of European Compliance Research
   Malte Brosig   6

3. Exploring the Implementation of Minority Protection Rules in the 'Worlds of Compliance': The Case of Turkey
   Gözde Yilmaz   24

4. Implementation Unwanted? Symbolic vs. Instrumental Policies in the Russian Management of Ethnic Diversity
   Alexander Osipov   41

5. Which is the Only Game in Town? Minority Rights Issues in Estonia and Slovakia During and After EU Accession
   Timofey Agarin & Ada-Charlotte Regelmann   59

6. The (Non) Implementation of Recommendations of the Committee on the Elimination of Racial Discrimination in the Netherlands Explained
   Jasper Krommendijk   78

7. The Implementation of the ECRML in Slovakia under Construction: Structural Preconditions, External influence and Internal Obstacles
   Tanja Mayrgündter   96

8. The Role of NGOs in Promoting Minority Rights in the Enlarged European Union
   Christoph Schnellbach   113

Index   129

Citation Information

The chapters in this book were originally published in the *Perspectives on European Politics and Society*, volume 13, issue 4 (December 2012). When citing this material, please use the original page numbering for each article, as follows:

Chapter 1
Introduction
Timofey Agarin & Malte Brosig
Perspectives on European Politics and Society, volume 13, issue 4 (December 2012) pp. 385-389

Chapter 2
No Space for Constructivism? A Critical Appraisal of European Compliance Research
Malte Brosig
Perspectives on European Politics and Society, volume 13, issue 4 (December 2012) pp. 390-407

Chapter 3
Exploring the Implementation of Minority Protection Rules in the 'Worlds of Compliance: The Case of Turkey
Gözde Yilmaz
Perspectives on European Politics and Society, volume 13, issue 4 (December 2012) pp. 408-424

Chapter 4
Implementation Unwanted? Symbolic vs. Instrumental Policies in the Russian Management of Ethnic Diversity
Alexander Osipov
Perspectives on European Politics and Society, volume 13, issue 4 (December 2012) pp. 425-442

Chapter 5
Which is the Only Game in Town? Minority Rights Issues in Estonia and Slovakia During and After EU Accession
Timofey Agarin & Ada-Charlotte Regelmann
Perspectives on European Politics and Society, volume 13, issue 4 (December 2012) pp. 443-461

CITATION INFORMATION

Chapter 6
The (Non) Implementation of Recommendations of the Committee on the Elimination of Racial Discrimination in the Netherlands Explained
Jasper Krommendijk
Perspectives on European Politics and Society, volume 13, issue 4 (December 2012) pp. 462-479

Chapter 7
The Implementation of the ECRML in Slovakia under Construction: Structural Preconditions, External influence and Internal Obstacles
Tanja Mayrgündter
Perspectives on European Politics and Society, volume 13, issue 4 (December 2012) pp. 480-496

Chapter 8
The Role of NGOs in Promoting Minority Rights in the Enlarged European Union
Christoph Schnellbach
Perspectives on European Politics and Society, volume 13, issue 4 (December 2012) pp. 497-512

Please direct any queries you may have about the citations to clsuk.permissions@cengage.com

Introduction

TIMOFEY AGARIN & MALTE BROSIG

ABSTRACT *The scholarly interest in norm implementation in the area of minority rights protection emerged during the period of the European accession of post-communist societies, which were characterised by persistent cleavage along ethnic lines. These studies have analysed democratic transition of ethnically segmented societies and developed into a broad field that focuses its attention on inter-ethnic relations, the role of history, interstate cooperation and the impact of international organisations on post-communist states' treatment of domestic minorities. All these are usually conducted from a vantage point of the European conditionality research. In our introduction to the special issue we sketch a number of reasons why it is encouraging and indeed, desirable to move beyond the perusal of conditionality into the domain of implementation research.*

Minority rights issues became prominent in European integration studies when post-communist states lined up as potential candidates for the EU membership. In the course of EU enlargement into the post-communist region, the respect for and protection of minority rights was an essential part of the political accession criteria. Protection of minority rights has constituted an important political instrument as a part of the 'gatekeeping' criteria for EU accession, and its monitoring remains a powerful instrument to mediate existing ethnic tensions and racial discrimination in present-day Europe. Today minority rights form an integral part of what constitutes a European normative space. The Council of Europe's (CoE) Framework Convention on the Protection of National Minorities (FCNM) has been signed by all CoE members except France and Turkey, and has only not been ratified by Iceland, Greece, Luxembourg and Belgium. In the case of EU member states, the EU Non-Discrimination Directive applies in addition to the various UN non-discrimination conventions. One can thus rightly claim that minority rights, and in particular non-discrimination clauses, are firmly anchored in European and international law. With the exception of Belarus, no European state can afford to gloss over the application of minority rights norms or avoid international monitoring on the issue. The sheer proliferation of minority rights is indicative of the importance these norms have acquired after the end of the Cold War.

Yet, in the end it is not merely from the prevalence of a norm that its importance is derived, but from its application. This special issue takes on the task of analysing the diffusion of minority rights in various European countries. It specifically looks at the oft-neglected problem of norm implementation, and particularly at the enactment of European minority rights and non-discrimination norms domestically. While normative standards with regard to minority rights issues have been willingly copied in domestic legislation in many countries, whether these norms constitute a legitimate order to which the states subscribe and which they obey is the focus of this special issue. The contributions analyse the encompassing political rhetoric, legal transposition and behavioural compliance in a range of European states, East and West, in order to establish how far the ultimate indicator for effective regulation – i.e., compliance by action – has indeed been successful after the norms of minority rights protection have been legally adopted.

The contributions in the current special issue underline two important perspectives on minority rights issues and norms of non-discrimination, which would seem to represent common sense – at least on the surface – in the contemporary European integration studies. First, norm implementation forms a part of, and upholds, a European and international human rights-based political order. The implementation or non-implementation has thus much to say about the effectiveness of the human rights regime. By exploring the existing variations in compliance, the papers in this collection make statements on the durability, depth and/or political acceptance of this order. These are fundamental qualities of a political regime which often go unnoticed when analysing the issue of minority rights implementation on a country-by-country basis. This is highly unfortunate, as the "implementation trap" strikes right at the heart of the European integration project: the significance of norm implementation is clearly seen when considering the on-going debt-crisis in Eurozone countries. As is widely debated today, much of the headache the current Eurozone leadership endures is easily traced back to a lack of proper implementation of the Euro convergence criteria and/or the lack of strategic steps in policy monitoring by the Eurozone members. Regardless of the fact that economic competitiveness was an agreed norm, deficient implementation and the absence of mechanisms to force those stepping out of line back into the agreed-upon framework have ultimately resulted in the crisis of European economic integration.

Secondly, of course, norm implementation is important because it is the crucial linchpin between an international regulatory governance style and the affected populations. While much of the norm creation process maybe qualified as an esoteric enterprise of far-away international lawyers in Brussels or Strasbourg, it is the application of these norms that really counts. Many legal norms might appear vague in wording, yet in practice they have tangible consequences on the ground: minority rights issues are never trivial or just technical. In contrast to most of the rather technical EU directives and regulations, minority rights norms are often highly political as they touch upon and frame sensitive issues for the affected populations: minority language use, opportunities for self-expression, participation of national and ethnic communities in political process, restriction of misconduct and punishment for discrimination. All of these issues cannot simply be treated as merely functional issues or procedural questions because they strike at the foundations of the project of European societal integration and, decisively, reflect the backdrop of cohesion within an overarching European normative space. As much as the current economic and financial turmoil can reshape the institutional and political contours of Europe, thereby changing its future integration trajectory, minority rights issues have the potential to an important constitute a normative order in their own right.

Our authors look specifically at the record of norm implementation in order to establish whether the accession of post-communist countries in 2004/2007 has led to a deeper, more cohesive Europe for those individual members of the European society who are more often than not the recipients, rather than makers of policies: national minorities and migrant communities. As the papers in this special issue make clear, each and every country in the EU could be singled out for criticism with regard to its record of implementing European norms of minority rights protection and non-discrimination. And yet, the extent of political institutional change over past decades has radically circumscribed opportunities for domestic decision-makers to backslide and renegotiate their countries' obligations vis-à-vis domestic minorities, even when they instead would rather rely on support from their electorates, who are often negatively inclined towards minority issues.

It is an oft repeated truism that the governments of accession states sought to ensure their countries' membership in the EU, and have thus allowed the European Commission and Council to monitor accession countries' political, economic and social institutional performance. As often it is suggested that the EU membership was (and remains) an ultimate 'carrot' for accession states and their societies, as equally rarely it is recognised that following the accession they thereafter become fully-fledged members of the normative community. As such, the new EU member states have means equal to those of old EU member states to sponsor and promote normative standards they have only recently learnt to value, have transposed into domestic legislation under external pressures and were often reprimanded for disregarding in the run up to EU accession in 2004/2007. Even less often are the normative standards adopted in accession states treated as a part and parcel of the wider context of European integration pre-accession and as such, offering immediate rewards and legitimation to policy choices and trajectories incumbent post-communist governments sought to pursue. As the country studies in this issue make clear, even though some norms of minority protection were adopted domestically, many had to be legitimised as crucial, and thus necessary, for societies in accession countries in order to be accepted into the normative community of European nations. Although much ink has been spilt on norm adaptation and incipient policymaking in accession states, the implementation of minority rights protection and non-discrimination in post-accession period has less thoroughly analysed.

Our authors cover this terrain in their papers of country cases and issue areas so as to show that, while in comparison with norm adaptation, implementation is much harder to analyse comprehensively, it is a much more rewarding adventure. Under all circumstances, the rationale of deeper integration into EU structures constrains domestic actors more than otherwise would be the case, and as such opens for a greater variety of policy options, rhetoric and competence in practice. This resurgence of alternative paths in minority rights protection and interpretations of non-discrimination requires a meticulous untangling of the policymaking process into its constituent parts, and implicitly also crosschecking the validity of domestic practices against the European normative framework. The above suggests that although norm implementation in European countries remains wanting, there is a clear potential for positive policy change and even more so, a more coherent European normative space to look forward to in the future.

In their individual contributions, the authors look back at the premises outlined in the European conditionality literature, distilling the impact thereof on the contemporary debate in a united Europe. Malte Brosig looks specifically into the vast array of the research on European compliance, and calls for greater attention to be paid to the role constructivist research agendas can add to the dominant rationalist school. In her contribution on implementation of minority protection rules Gözde Yilmaz further suggests that even the states in the slow lane of accession, such as Turkey, are engaging actively in constituting the rules and practices that are deemed acceptable with regard to minority protection in the wider Europe. Taking the reader beyond the set of EU candidate countries, Alexander Osipov challenges the *bone fide* intention of minority protection policies implemented by the Russian Federation. He claims that being at all times symbolic, minority rights protection should not be seen as token concessions to domestic minorities; rather it is more persuasively treated as an instrument for covert policy objectives of the national governments. Picking up on the similar point, Timofey Agarin and Ada-Charlotte Regelmann query dynamics of Estonia's and Slovakia's minority rights protection policies. Their conclusion is that European norms and policy blueprints were most effectively implemented in the area where they upheld domestic perceptions of sovereignty, demoting minority rights issues to a second-order priority in the process of European norm transposition. Interestingly, similar issues are observed by Jasper Krommendijk in his analyses of the Dutch responses to recommendations of the Committee on the Elimination of Racial Discrimination (CERD). Taking the reader through a number of prominent issues under consideration by CERD, he illustrates that where international normative standards were hardly comparable with domestic practices, these were glossed over and their implementation hampered. Two papers then look specifically at practices of minority rights protection. Using a game theoretical modelling, Tanja Mayrgündter investigates the sustainability of external pressures on Slovakia's implementation record of minority language protection concluding that the domestic opportunities for structural change have not been exhausted yet. Finally, Christoph Schnellbach looks at the transformative power of domestic publics in the process of minority rights protection and discusses the role transnational advocacy networks have played in internationalising awareness of issues regarding Roma in Central Eastern Europe. All our authors conclude that the change in domestic policies of minority rights protection and enforcement of non-discrimination did not come to a halt with the EU membership of states in question. Although pre-accession changes can be to a degree made accountable for by the instrumental response of domestic actors seeking trade-offs (EU membership), only post-accession can we see these responses following their own, unique dynamics. Importantly, contributions to our special issue claim that at all times changes in minority rights protection and non-discrimination spearhead not only the long-standing and well-articulated domestic preferences, they also reflect strategic regional interests shared by many states in the region and beyond, building upon the projected international human rights regime and incipient interests.

Thus, far from painting a dark picture of the implementation of minority rights protection and non-discrimination legislation in contemporary Europe, the contributors and editors of this special issue demonstrate that the root cause for potential instability around minority issues in Europe lies with domestic actors. This is because after EU enlargement supranational organisations only exert limited influence over norm implementation. The EU and CoE enjoy some powers as norm creators and standard setters in the wider Europe, yet both organizations have practically very little means to effectively implement the norms they have created. The actual application of minority norms very much remains the prerogative of domestic players. International actors primarily acquire the role of supervisors and monitors of states with not many sticks on offer. At the end of the day, whether minority rights implementation is trapped by the lack of oversight and domestic opposition remains to be seen as, we hope, this special issue makes it clear.

The editors and authors would like to express their gratitude to the European Centre for Minority Issues (ECMI) in Flensburg, Germany, which facilitated a preparatory workshop in March 2011. The workshop proved to be an extremely stimulating meeting. The editors would like to thank Cameron Ross for providing a publication outlet for a collection of articles on the theme of 'The implementation trap? Trajectories of minority rights issues in Europe'. They would also like to thank all of the anonymous peer reviewers who helped improving the papers appearing here and for their helpful feedback on all the articles, whether they made it to the final publication or not.

No Space for Constructivism? A Critical Appraisal of European Compliance Research

MALTE BROSIG
University of the Witwatersrand, Department of International Relations, South Africa

ABSTRACT *This article aims at critically reviewing the European compliance literature. As this literature is dominated by a rational and positivist understanding of norm adherence primarily emphasizing domestic implementation costs, administrative capacities or external incentives during EU enlargement, this paper reinvigorates a constructivist epistemology of norm compliance in contrast to the analytical limitations of the rational approach.*

Nichts ist ohne sein Gegenteil wahr

(Martin Walser)[1]

Introduction

A burgeoning literature exists examining the compliance performance of EU member states forming an essential part of European integration research. This literature is analyzing which causal conditions are relevant to explain variation in member state compliance performance and variation across different policy areas and has brought to the fore a number of these conditions such as veto players, misfit, administrative capacities, domestic politics (preferences), clarity of norms, socialization, or external incentives. As will be laid down below, most of these concepts either directly subscribe to a rational understanding of norm compliance or have been rationalized within the framework of a positivist research agenda. This literature heavily relies on a consequentialist approach which too often overlooks the value added and advantages constructivist research can offer. Therefore, this paper argues that some of the starting assumptions of the compliance research are unnecessarily narrowing down the analytical focus and thereby largely neglecting constructivist approaches. Moreover, the tendency of the compliance literature to apply a rational logic of norm adherence which is based on individual cost–benefit calculation and functional qualities of domestic actors (administrative capacities, domestic compliance costs) and (inter)national norms (misfit or clarity of norms) reduces the issue of compliance to a mechanistic project in which norm adherence is a matter of calibrating a certain mixture of explanatory variables but politics seem to become a bystander rather peripherally involved in norm adoption and implementation but not driving the process itself.

Often compliance is understood as a question of rather static conformity (Raustiala & Slaughter, 2002, p. 539) of certain domestic and external conditions and the norm which the state is supposed to adhere to. This paper calls for a constructivist revival within compliance research in order to remedy the dominant trend which is over rationalizing compliance. Traditionally the constructivist school has formulated its claims moderately and thus this paper does not operate with a 'constructivism explains all' assumption but was written in the belief that theoretical diversity best matches the existing empirical complexity and bears the greatest potential to explore and further develop theoretical leverage. The paper formulates a critique against the rational prevalence within the field of compliance research in order to instigate reasoning beyond the testing of causal conditions for compliance. The critique formulated comes in different qualities. In some parts it is 'benevolent' in the sense that it does not challenge the principal applicability of a rational/positivist research approach and formulates an internal critique in the form of missing research or calls for a different focus of compliance studies. Constructivism is a multifaceted approach ranging from moderate constructivism (middle ground) applying a positivist research agenda to reflectivist constructivism which applies a strict post-positivist perspective. The critique formulated in this article refers to both streams producing incursions of different depth and reach. Finally it is not the intention of this study to develop a 'ready to use' alternative constructivist toolkit for application, this is a task for future research, but only aims at providing reasoning for doing so by exploring the limitations of the rationalist approach and by formulating an internal (benevolent) and external in some instances more fundamental critique.

The paper proceeds as follows. The first section provides an overview of the most prominent causal conditions featured in the compliance research. It will be shown that most of these conditions have been merged with a rational understanding of cost–benefit calculation of actors. Thereby theorizing rational interests has hardly occurred thus most of these conditions have been applied under utility considerations without exploring the wider normative frameworks in which rational action is played out or exploring the root causes for compliance.

The subsequent section problematizes the functional and static understanding of the concept of norms and compliance. Strangely, the compliance literature is relatively lethargic toward process and interaction not systematically conceptualizing processes of norm construction and enactment. Although norms are at the centre of compliance research they are hardly problematized but assumed to have a more or less fixed meaning and are treated as static social beings. Norms have been 'ontologized as stable factors in world politics' (Wiener, 2003, p. 266). Furthermore, despite their inherently intersubjective nature they have been paired with a positivist epistemology.

The final section is inquiring into methodological concerns of compliance research. While this research has explored a number of causal conditions explaining variance in compliance performance each condition at some point fails the causality test and thus is running the risk of becoming inconclusive (Schwellnus, 2009, p. 127). This section mainly refers to positivist research design but pledges for a move away from competitive theory testing and deterministic causality.

A Short Review of Compliance Mechanisms

The most prominent and straightforward rational assumption of compliance mechanisms can be found in the external incentives model for EU candidate countries in combination with considerations over domestic implementation costs. Especially Schimmfennig and Sedelmeier (2004, 2005) but also Kelley (2004) have detected EU conditionality as the driving force behind candidate states course of *Acquis* transposition during EU enlargement. This stream of compliance research holds that states best adopt new norms if external incentives (EU membership) can offset domestic implementation costs under the condition that their incentives are applied coherently and credibly. In the end, this approach assumes that norms need to be reinforced because states would otherwise not comply. Thus the starting assumption is that states do not comply easily and have to be incentivized for norm adherence.[2] This rational institutionalist approach to norm compliance during EU enlargement is by far the dominant school despite empirical research raising doubts about the effectiveness of conditionality in some instances. Especially research on norm adoption and implementation of minority rights has issued some criticism by pointing at the vague character of minority rights norms or an incoherent promotion of them by the EU Commission (Rechel, 2008 and Sasse, 2008). However, the rationalist reply holds that:

> The limitations of the EU's impact on minority rights... can also be well explained within a rationalist framework, to the extent that they are related to the lack of clear conditions, inconsistent application, or superficial monitoring. (Sedelmeier, 2011, pp. 18–19)

The rational understanding of norm transference is internally coherent and indeed exerts significant explanatory weight when tested against empirical evidence and constructivist concepts of compliance. However, this is hardly surprising as the EU enlargement process was *de facto* not providing the necessary environmental conditions for observing constructivist concepts of norm diffusion as conditionality dominated this process. To this end, constructivist approaches should not be refuted fully as they have been tested under conditions in which constructivists would not assume that their concepts would be most convincing as Europeanization during EU enlargement can indeed be best explained with reference to conditionality.[3]

Still a non-rational based explanation of compliance would add important value by setting interests and incentives in context with the normative surroundings in which they are played out and which they are part and parcel of. By contextualizing interests and incentives we can ask important additional questions. Why was the EU not applying conditionality coherently or why norms lack clarity which is influencing the course of norm adoption and implementation? These aspects remain unaddressed by the rational literature and with it the question what is constituting these political acts?

Under the heading of domestic compliance costs we can summarize a number of prominent assumptions about norm adherence. Traditionally political party preferences (Treib, 2003) or governments political orientation (Mastenbroek & Kaeding, 2007) have been mentioned as key variables steering the norm adoption process. The basic assumption is that conflicting domestic interests can complicate or delay the norm adoption process and thus raise adoption costs. Concepts like misfit or resonance have clear constructivist roots by highlighting the norm construction process (Finnemore & Sikkink, 1998) and understanding normative match and compliance success as a question of appropriateness by analyzing how a norm fits into its surroundings which are shaped by a world of other norms. However, the compliance research has largely promoted a rationalized understanding of this concept. States are assumed to be more likely to comply if their domestically held norms are in match with international norms (Börzel, 2000). In cases in which a significant mis-match is obvious states will adopt and apply these norms much more reluctantly. The underlying logic is one of domestic cost–benefit calculations. Norms are likely to diffuse more easily when domestic adjustment costs are low, the opposite applies if they are high. The poverty of this approach relates to the absence of a social theory on actors and costs. Likewise constructivists have seldom analyzed norm evolution beyond norm emergence (Krook & True, 2010, p. 108) and thereby lost leadership in developing and applying this concept.

The mis-fit and domestic preference approaches inherently assume that actors hold a set of preferences and norms which has a causal impact on the course of norm compliance. In the case of preference congruence with a norm and positive pay offs from norm adoption compliance is assumed to be successful. This requires states to have the ability to formulate these interests and promote them in a rather unitary style as contradictory preferences would dilute attempts to assign it causal significance. While in once off events such as a single decision-making situation actor's interests and cost–benefit calculation might in fact be clear, measurable, come with causal consequences and are not openly contradicting themselves and are thus coherent. However, if we understand compliance as constituting of a chain of events and open-ended long-term process incoherencies in actors preferences and cost–benefit calculations are almost inevitable and would make it difficult to apply a solely rational preference and cost understanding of compliance. In this context we can assume that rational approaches exert a greater leverage when analyzing cases of norm transposition which only require once off action and should be more skeptical toward it explaining norm enactment which is an open-ended process.

What is missing in the perspective of domestic compliance costs is a theoretical framework which conceptualizes political preferences as well as the interaction of existing norms at the international and national level. While the creation of preferences can principally be analyzed within a rational and positivist research design (but compliance research is hardly doing it), treating interests or norms as objective facts and keeping them separate from an overarching world of ideas and discourse is difficult if not artificial from a reflectivist constructivist perspective (Schmidt, 2008, p. 317). Despite prominent rationalists like Duncan Snidal (2002) admitting that rationalism as such is rather a mechanism for action which remains empty without informative knowledge about a normative framework defining rational action, in the compliance research actor preferences often remain under-theorized.

A critique coming from one of the proponents of the rational incentives and domestic costs model weighs equally heavy. In a review article on new member states compliance by Sedelmeier (2011, p. 30) he notes that 'an inductive analysis of domestic costs is not kept separately from the analysis of outcomes, and hence the impact of costs'. In other words, compliance costs are often automatically associated with non- or delayed compliance without showing sufficiently what the real impact of domestic compliance costs are. Beyond this research focusing on domestic compliance conditions is attributing implementation costs causal relevance before inquiring into actor's preference formation. Such a move is delicate as it degrades compliance to a process of just means–ends calculation without having a safe knowledge about the ends. A middle ground constructivist epistemology would exactly aim at analyzing the construction of actor's ends before subduing them to a rational application. In essence good research needs to address how costs come about and alter over time. Additionally the constructivist research agenda would highlight the undesirable effects of keeping intersubjective social kinds static or separate from each other. In fact, during long-term processes of norm compliance we can simple not assume that actor's preferences remain untouched by the norm they are supposed to absorb. Here the problem is not the assumption that actors act rational or calculate costs but that the positivist research approach forces researchers into 'ontologizing' intersubjective kinds such as preferences or norms.

Other prominent domestic conditions steering compliance such as veto players (Haverland, 2000) or administrative capacities encounter similar problems. If separated from their wider normative environment their explanatory leverage remains limited. In the end, the number of veto players may be less informative than the conditions that make actors veto decisions. A constructivist perspective would focus less on veto players as an institution with supposedly causal effects but would inquire into those contextual environments which substantiate veto players and their impact on the course of compliance (Hay, 2006, p. 65). Without understanding the logics that create, sustain and activate veto players, this type of institutional check remains astonishingly empty. Although veto player theory allows theorizing actor preferences, the compliance literature does not make much use of these analytical tools. Nevertheless, the veto player argument is still frequently used as key explanatory variable.

In the case of administrative capacities it is of course convincing that administrative efficiency and government capability (Toshkov, 2007, 2008) impact on norm adherence and can form significant obstacles for norm transposition and implementation. There can logically be no compliance without administrative capacity; it is at least an enabling factor for any kind of compliance. However, the explanatory leverage of government and administrative abilities and its constraints should be examined critically. The management approach to compliance has a tendency to reduce administrative conditions to a question of institutional capacity in which non-compliance is involuntary or accidental but not necessarily intended (Tallberg, 2002, p. 613). Such a perspectives drives out politics of compliance it depoliticizes administrations and assumes them to be throughputs for norms if enough capacity is present. However, the presence or absence of administrative capacity can also be politically induced. Furthermore, it is rather artificial to assume that administrations can be kept separate from domestic political dynamics and wider normative frameworks constituting statehood and denouncing the potential of administrations to be actors in their own right. From a constructivist perspective administrations can only be as influential as those conditions which are constituting them. Constructivist research has put great effort in showing that institutions are not only utility maximizers but are 'subject and focus of political struggle' (Hay, 2006, p. 64). Barnett and Finnemore (1999) have emphasized the dysfunctional and pathological behaviour of institutions. Thus perceiving institutions as 'transmission belts' is neglecting their character as both being shaped by wider normative frameworks and having actorness by themselves.[4] The role of administrations in the implementation process has so far not received the necessary attention as most of the compliance research is analyzing norm transposition in which capacity is fulfilling a functional role.

In contrast to the management approach which assumes involuntary non-compliance as being a consequence of lacking capacities, the enforcement approach argues that the 'harder' the enforcement instruments the better the compliance record. Thus legally binding norms which are enforceable by a court with legal sanctions which impose significant costs on deviant actors will result in more compliant states, while 'softer' enforcement and supervision allows for easy circumvention. In the case of EU compliance research the differentiation between hard and soft enforcement can be ignored in most cases as EU law is generally speaking binding and the European Court of Justice can sanction states with significant fines for non-compliance.

The enforcement argument builds on the assumption that compliance is a question of domestic implementation costs and we can predict a state's behaviour by analyzing the domestic cost–benefit ratio for a given norm. If this is really the case can be doubted. Minority rights pose an interesting example while non-discrimination norms are part of the *Acquis* and are thus enforceable through the European Court of Justice, minority language or cultural rights are not. One can thus assume that states perform better in the area of non-discrimination than in others not directly legally enforceable minority rights. Empirically this is difficult to maintain and some studies have suggested that the full implementation of racial equality norms in Eastern Europe is still problematic and that legal enforceability alone has not remedied this situation (Brosig, 2010). On the other hand, Eastern European countries transposed EU non-discrimination rules on time. Thus the differentiation of transposition vs. implementation is an important one. Drawing a causal relation between effective legal enforcement mechanisms and compliance is thus rather difficult. Furthermore, what is missing in the enforcement approach is informed knowledge about an actor's construction of domestic goals. Again the compliance research assumes states to act out cost–benefit considerations before analyzing a state's preference formation process. Constructivists have argued that such an approach is highly problematic because 'we cannot even describe the properties of social agents without reference to the social structure in which they are embedded' (Risse, 2009, p. 148). While saying this, actors can of course act rational but this is not a given static property but a consequence of social making which should not be essentialized.

A reflectivist constructivist analysis of enforcement instruments would less focus on inflicting costs on states in order to provide for compliance incentives but would primarily address enforcement under the heading of norm validation. A reflectivist view would less focus on the presumed causal consequences of institutional enforcement capacities by arguing that institutions do not directly cause compliance but can play an important enabling role through norm validation (Wiener & Pütter, 2009). Validation means the creation of social recognition and acceptance of a norm. Constructivists have argued that compliance is not only the process which translates 'an international norm... into a legal concept, but into culturally understandable and acceptable' context (Zwingel, 2012, p. 125). It thus requires a different toolkit for analysis. Norm validation is analytically separate from concepts of norm socialization and persuasion in which the burden of adjustment is one sided and only rests with the norms recipient. Validation is driven by the norm promoting institution and the norm absorbers and requires interaction and norm construction through application, discourse and contestation. This rather radical constructivist concept is formulating a fundamental critique against positivist compliance research namely that we cannot analyze norms and their effects separately. The opposite is claimed here, norms and their impact are forming part of one process and they condition each other. This has far reaching consequences for the rational and positivist compliance school. If norms and compliance cannot be separated because norms are not static measuring the impact of certain variables on compliance is basically futile.

Constructivists have argued that the discursive nature of social kinds (including norms and preferences) follows a logic of argumentation in which communicative reasoning structures the discourse (Risse, 2000). While the rational approach to norm compliance uses a concept of fixed norms, norm validation requires a continuous norm construction process entailing discursive elements. The constructivist assumption is that sustainable compliance is less a function of effective sanctioning but much more reliant on the acceptance of norms by the state and communicative leadership by providing supreme reasoning. Exploring conditions for norm acceptation, has so far not figured prominently in the compliance scholarship.

Another condition which has frequently been used is the argument that norms to be transposed and implemented successfully require a certain degree of specificity or determinacy (Legro, 1997; Schimmelfennig & Sedelmeier, 2005). This usually refers to the quality of norms. While specific norms are supposed to be diffused more easily, openly formulated norms are assumed to complicate compliance because the vagueness of norms, which for example entail many escape clauses, opens up opportunities for manipulation and the chance to circumvent strict obligations. In this context European minority rights as formulated by the Council of Europe have been identified as particularly vague and problematic to implement. Here again, a cost–benefit calculation is prevalent as more specific norms are assumed to be easier to adopt and thus entailing only moderate implementation costs while fuzzy or unclear norms or more costly due to their unclear nature.

The problem with the concept of determinacy is that it attributes causal impact to a norm's quality. Empirical research in the area of minority rights and non-discrimination has shown inconclusive though interesting results. On the one hand, on time transposition of the racial equality directive in new member states speaks in favour of the determinacy hypotheses, but at the implementation side both vaguely formulated norms of the Framework Convention on the Protection of National Minorities (FCNM) and the much more strictly formulate EU directive face similar application problems (Brosig, 2010). In the end, the concept of rule determinacy would need further refinement to avoid inconclusive results which is true from both the rationalist and constructivist perspective.

With reference to international norms constructivists have argued that 'norms diffuse precisely because – rather than despite the fact that – they may encompass different meanings, fit in with a variety of contexts, and be subject to framing by diverse actors' (Krook & True, 2010, p. 105). Thus indeterminacy can be an invitation for further norm development which attracts states taking part in norm construction. Here compliance is not a simple domestic alignment process.

Within compliance research constructivist concepts such as socialization found some recognition. In a classical sense scholars working with concepts of socialization have emphasized the process in which institutions induce actors with community norms leading to norm compliance as a consequence of norm internalization. Independent of material incentives an actor complies with norms because they are deemed to represent a legitimate and thereby desirable order following the constructivist logic of appropriateness (Checkel, 2005a, p. 804). Here norm compliance requires actors to be persuaded and receptive against new norms. Compliance is created through a process of persuasion and learning which usually takes a long-term perspective and is accompanied by backlashes and uneven progress. A comprehensive model for norm socialization of human rights norms has been developed by Risse et al. (1999). Compliance research in Europe has been rather sceptical about the influence of socialization on norm transposition. It is often argued that the logic of appropriateness and legitimacy and processes of arguing cannot on their own causally explain observed variations in state compliance (Schimmelfennig & Sedelmeier, 2005) but at times can contribute to explain special cases (Sedelmeier, 2011, p. 23).

A recent criticism to the sociological institutionalist argument about the importance of legitimate norms has been formulated by discursive institutionalists (Schmidt, 2008, p. 320) forming part of the reflectivist stream within the constructivist approach. Independent of the question if socialization and persuasion are effective instruments for creating compliance it has been noted that their understanding of norm socialization equals those of rational compliance approaches. Norms are largely treated as objective facts and are supposed to have a causal impact on states due to their standing as legitimate order. In the end, the importance of socialization is tied to its ability to be causally significant, a very rational and positivist understanding. What is missing here, is a deeper understanding of the constitutive nature of norms and actors during the socialization process. If legitimacy and thus the impact of legitimate norms rely on an intersubjectively created basis, as constructivists claim, and socialization is invoking this very basis to persuade states into compliance, the interactive processes which constitute both legitimacy and norms must be examined thoroughly. The compliance research is, however, only interested in the causal significance of socialization Too easily constructivists have allowed that concepts such as socialization have gone through a rationalization process and have not invested enough effort into applying constructivist methodology alongside the rational one.

In summary, the constructivist position formulated in this section is hardly new. Already two decades ago seminal work by Kratochwil (1989), Onuf (1989) and Wendt (1992, 1999) has commonly highlighted the importance of the constructivist value added spanning from a Kratochwilian post-positivist approach to the Wendtian scientific constructivism which transformed it into a mainstream approach in international relations and European integration research. However, the rise of constructivism has hardly left many traces within the compliance school. The rational approach to compliance fundamentally rests on the assumption that actors calculate the costs and benefits of their action and align themselves accordingly. While this is inherently logical, from a moderate constructivist perspective, the rational approach is missing the answer why actors act the way they do. Cost benefit calculations are relatively meaningless without knowledge about ends and where they come from. In fact, domestic adoption costs are only understood mechanistically, veto players as well as administrative capacities appear as strangely apolitical and concepts such as legitimacy have been merged with a causal logic of impact. But the rationalization of compliance research comes with costs, a certain theoretical stasis and fixation on exploring the causal relevance of individual conditions for compliance without having or aiming at developing an informed theory of actors, norms, and institutions. Instead of clarifying the root causes of compliance phenomena (compliance indeed varies across countries and issue areas) the rationalization of compliance research largely avoids to analyze the construction of preferences, domestic norms and institutions and thus a potential source for variance in the compliance performance ultimately remains exogenous to the theory.

A more fundamental criticism can be formulated with reference to reflectivist constructivism which is questioning the positivist methodology underlying rational compliance research. Often compliance research takes preferences, norms and institutions for granted and treats them as objective facts from which causal inferences can be made. It is the endeavour to ascribe inherently social kinds objective properties which constructivists see as problematic (Zwingel, 2012, p. 116). While domestic preferences, norms and institutions play a pivotal role in concepts such as veto players, administrative capacities and domestic implementation costs, the processes which set these inherently social entities up and make them act the way they do remain underexplored. They do so also because the positivist research agenda tends to privilege the observation of causal inference which often is following a deterministic understanding of causality. Exactly this connection limits the explanatory depth of the compliance literature.

Concepts of norm validation explicitly deny the possibility to separate norms from their effects and therewith challenge the positivist cause effect logic which needs to ontologize norms to test the causal impact of its independent variables. Admittedly, reflectivist constructivists formulated their concerns prominently at the meta-theoretical level but found it much more difficult to reach the mid-range level which certainly has tempted many researchers to follow a rational and positivist research approach.

Nonetheless, the constructivist value added to the compliance research is a fundamental one which still needs further operationalization for application. While the literature dominated by rational approaches aims at singling out conditions which causally impact on a state's compliance record, the constructivist school would highlight the wider social framework which constitutes agents rationales for action and is inducing agents and norms with meaning. The argument is that causal conditions which trigger a certain outcome cannot be more important than those frameworks which constitute actors and their interests. Thus we should not only aim at exploring causal conditions for compliance but also start digging deeper by exploring those environmental conditions which constitute actors, preferences, norms and institutions concurrently and explore those dynamics of interaction between them.

Problematizing Norms, or What is Compliance?

The question what is compliance and how can it be measured is a pivotal one, as any judgement about causal conditions for compliance relies on the ability to clearly measure it. If compliance cannot be measured accurately, exploring the causal impact of independent variables is practically diluted. All the more astonishing is that the compliance literature mostly engages on a technical level with this question. Concerns over the measurability of compliance often results in a debate about the leverage of transposition and infringement data (Hartlapp & Falkner, 2009). Hardly is there a discussion about compliance as a social process of infinite character. Hardly are norms and compliance problematized. Instead they are assumed to be fixed and measurable, an assumption which is contestable.

Compliance is usually understood as domestic alignment toward international norms. States are compliant if their domestic law and practice are congruent with international norms such as EU directives or international treaties. Treib (2008, p. 5) distinguishes between norm transposition, enforcement and application.

Legal transposition refers to the process of domestic norm adoption. Once the EU has passed a directive or a state has ratified an international convention it is usually obliged to bring its domestic legislation in conformity with the international standard. In many cases this requires the adoption or passing of domestic legislation amending or introducing the international standard. Norm enforcement refers to the instruments available to supervise norm application. It focuses on the means and institutions available to enact the transposed norm. Finally norm application refers to state behaviour. It measures to which degree norm transposition is followed by behavioural compliance.

Common to the vast majority of compliance studies in Europe is their focus on transposition. In the case of the EU each adopted act comes with a specific transposition deadline. Thus measuring compliance through transposition is relatively easy. Transposition delays can be analyzed in a quantitative manner for all EU countries and across various policy fields. However, the mere transposition of EU directives might only tell us half the story. At best it is an indicator that a state has transposed something and might be an indicator for rule compliant behaviour later on. How difficult it is to assess the over all norm compliance can be seen at the new EU member states. While there is statistical evidence that new EU member states are outperforming old member states with regard to norm transposition (Sedelmeier, 2008), there are a number of qualitative studies which strongly suggest that new member states do not perform equally well in terms of behavioural compliance (Brosig, 2010; Falkner et al., 2008a; Krizsan, 2009). This example of potentially contradictory results should be taken seriously as inconclusive outcomes may point to a lack of reasoning for those conditions which steer the norm implementation process from those which guide norm transposition. The vast majority of case studies in the compliance literature do not attempt to investigate norm application which in fact is only assessable through intensive qualitative field research thus requiring considerable resources to cover a representative share of European countries and policy areas to provide for results with at least a certain degree of coverage and robustness. In sum, the compliance literature has produced a wealth of case studies using qualitative and quantitative methods across countries and policy fields its measurement of state compliance remains in large parts an assessment based on transposition data which may be or not indicative of coherent norm application later on.

From a constructivist point of view measuring successful compliance against an end state of an action such as legal transposition which is perceived to be a once-off event is not sufficient. Even without recourse to reflectivist thinking which would challenge the assumption that norms are static or objective facts and compliance can be measured accurately, the analysis of transposition rates or infringement data tends to take only a 'snapshot' position as proxy for compliance. Hartlapp and Falkner (2009) argue that these data are not much more than incomplete indicators for compliance. Thus even within the mostly positivist compliance school there is scepticism about the ability to scientifically measure compliance. The problem is twofold: First, transposition does not cover the empirical phenomenon of compliance comprehensively enough as it too often excludes norm implementation. Secondly, examining transposition also serves a methodological purpose to satisfy the positivist need for causal inference which requires researchers to keep norms and compliance stable. It is this methodological requirement which can have distortive effects and should be treated with outmost care. Furthermore, states are often depicted as passive consumers of externally generated fixed norms. Good examples are the enforcement and management schools. These two schools proclaim that norm adherence is primarily a function of either enforcement capabilities of norm generators or are dependent on administrative capacities. In both cases states and norms play a rather passive part as if they are bystanders but not involved in norm transposition and application. Moreover, treating states and norms in such a way artificially reduces compliance to the presence of certain given conditions and fosters tendencies to de-politicize compliance by not allowing actors to shape the compliance process. It seems that the particular governance style of the EU which in large parts is rather bureaucratic and regulatory and less political has tempted research to assume that norm enactment is primarily bureaucratic and apolitical too.

A reflectivist constructivist view to compliance would emphasize the procedural nature of it. This means compliance does not reach a certain end state but is a process of continued interaction between the norm generating entity and the norm addressee in which both norms and compliance are taking different forms. Assessing compliance would thus require examining a chain of accomplishments in a process in which norms can still alter and the sender and receiver of norms shape this process. However, in such as situation the character of a norm is rather fluid not static and thus measuring compliance becomes in itself problematic. Norm creation does not stop with the adoption of a certain legal act. However, the compliance research is primarily interested in what happens after a norm has been issued (Treib, 2008, p. 4) assuming that its fixed nature will allow researchers to trace its course. Assuming norms have a fixed meaning is also important for the positivist research methodology because measuring the causal impact of different independent variables in order to explore their impact on compliance, which is a core undertaking of the compliance literature, works only if norms are stable. If they vary along the transposition and later implementation process the causal chain of explanatory and outcome variable is methodologically impossible to maintain because a change in the meaning of norms is informing the compliance performance. But keeping norms stable just to satisfy methodological considerations is not an innocent move.

In the case of European law there are ample opportunities for norm development during and beyond the formal passing of new legislation. Indeed this is hardly a new phenomenon as for example the consequences of incomplete contracting have been discussed widely in the literature focusing in EU decision-making. Interestingly the EU decision-making and compliance literature which certainly are two of the most well established fields within European integration scholarship appear as rather disconnected. Taking the demanding rule-making process within the EU, which involves the Commission, Council, Parliament and hundreds of comitology committees, the norm construction process has hardly been researched and integrated into compliance studies.

Furthermore, neither the EU nor any other rule-making international organization is actually implementing the norms it is producing. Consequentially, member states are the first to transpose and implement European law. The emergence of deviations in interpretation of new norms across so many nations, languages and cultures is almost unavoidable. In fact, the rule-making process continues beyond the formal passing of new legislation and reaches well into the area of transposition, enforcement and application. International legislation often shows a tendency to formulate vague obligations in order to reach broad acceptance and deliberately leaving space for discretion which has been characterized as soft law. In the EU the Commission has the right to issue implementing acts specifying the meaning and scope of EU law within the comitology system. Thousands of these acts are issued each year and they are not confined to only recently adopted legislation. While it can be debated how hard or soft European law is with varying results across different policy areas a trace of vagueness and a need for interpretation can be found in basically any law. If law would be clear to everyone in any situation at any time we would not need judges and lawyers. There would be no need for interpretation as law would be directly applicable. However, in practice law making or norm creation extends to its application including courtrooms. Again if norms would have a fixed and easy to access meaning lawyers and judges would not need to interpret law or set a precedent their jobs would be disposable. The concept of 'law as integrity' developed by Ronald Dworkin (1986, pp. 176–275) explicitly formulates an interpretative theory of law in which a court's rulings need to be validated through argumentative processes on the basis of textual law but also provide a justification in a wider normative sense of the constituent community in which law is acted out. In a similar vein constructivists hold that norms are not diffused from above but need to be translated into different contexts (Zwingel, 2012, p. 124). Following the idea of 'law as integrity' compliance is not simply a question of alignment to a fixed norm but it is a social practice of norm enactment.

For the compliance research a number of serious questions emerge. If rule-making is not completed at a given point how can we assess compliance? If constructivists are right in claiming that norms are a matter of actors construction beyond the formal legal passing of them ranging into the area of norm application and requiring acts of domestic, local and ultimately individual interpretation diverging interpretations are very likely to emerge with increasing heterogeneity of actors (Wiener & Pütter, 2009, pp. 13–14). This ultimately means that compliance is very difficult to measure collectively. It also means that in order to measure compliance comprehensively research needs to go beyond transposition and enforcement analysis and start recognizing the importance of norm construction through application. More fundamentally, a constructivist understanding of compliance is challenging the positivist notion of it as being clearly measurable overlooking social practices which constitute compliance. In fact, the question of 'how much' compliance is out there and what it has triggered should be substituted with a thorough analysis of which social acts constitute compliance.

Some Methodological Concerns

The dominant stream in compliance research is combining a rational approach to norm adherence with a positivist methodology. Classical comparative small-n case studies have used co-variation in either the independent and/or dependent variable to demonstrate the causal impact of the explanatory condition. The dominant model applied is one of deterministic causality. As mentioned above such an approach has been applied on the assumption that: firstly, norms have a fixed meaning, secondly compliance is a once off event and thirdly preferences are given. All these assumptions can be contested. These incursions are more than second order caveats they are striking at the heart of compliance research because they question the framework in which variables have been tested and attributed causal significance. Besides this fundamental critique research following a positivist methodology can and should be problematized using their own methods. This section primarily attempts to promote a shift in comparative compliance analysis by advocating a move away from competitive theory testing and assumptions about deterministic causality.

The European compliance research has produced sound knowledge of those conditions which influence the course of compliance mostly understood as legal transposition. But what do we actually know about compliance in detail? Despite the very many compliance studies across countries and policy fields there is a profound lack of cumulative results (Treib, 2008, pp. 17–18). We know which conditions are relevant but each independent variable fails to demonstrate causal relevance at some point. There is no master variable which always explains compliance. Small-n studies often apply a deterministic concept of causality. An independent variable which does not cause an outcome continuously does not have causal significance and can thereby be excluded from the analytical analysis. In fact, the positivist research methodology has tempted scholars to test variables in an either/or fashion (see veto player, misfit debate: Haverland, 2000; Bailey, 2002). However, such an approach is inherently problematic because it fosters the search for monocausal relations in a complex empirical world of many inter- and co-dependent variables. George and Bennett (2005, p. 161) argue that the assumption of deterministic causality 'misdirects the attention of the investigator by leading him or her to believe that the task of empirical inquiry is to discover a single causal pattern for cases that have similar values on the dependent variable'. What has been ignored very often in the compliance literature is the search for different explanatory variables for the same outcome.

As a matter of fact the positivist research methodology carries the grain of inclusiveness in cases in which it fosters competitive variable testing and cases in which it values deterministic causality over multiple causality. The question is how to address this problem. So far the compliance research has only started to recognize inconclusiveness as theoretical and methodological challenge. Falkner et al. (2007) speak of only 'sometimes true' theories. In order to avoid the pitfalls of causal inconclusiveness they have started defining the contextual environment in which compliance takes place and thus move to a meta-level. Their exploration of different worlds of compliance (see also Falkner et al., 2008a) moves away from the formulation of causal hypotheses by proposing a typology of compliance types.

The method of congruence might be a feasible alternative to testing hypotheses competitively. Here independent variables are not tested against each other, as they are potentially able to explain a common outcome separately or together, but one only explores to which extent the formulated hypotheses are congruent with empirical observation (George & Bennett, 2005, pp. 181–204). The advantage of this method is that it does not discriminate alternative explanations of the same outcome. It is inherently more geared toward inductively exploring the impact of certain variables but does not seek to demonstrate its causal significance as depending on the failure of other variables. However, it can only do this by providing a plausibility test with limited potential for falsification.

In the case of the compliance research a shift in methodological thinking is particularly desirable as many independent variables are only supposedly independent. Moving away from the assumption that good variables are only those which independently cause a certain outcome and which no other variable can explain would open up compliance research and address existing challenges posed by equifinality and lack of cumulative research results. In this context understanding compliance conditions not as independent variables in a classical sense but recognizing them as causal mechanisms instead can provide some remedy because it allows us to keep the rational reasoning underpinning most compliance variables but also address the contextual environment in which rationality is acted out. This is possible because causal mechanisms can be understood as portable concepts transferable to many cases (Falleti & Lynch, 2009). What a causal mechanism is and how it works, is primarily a matter of context conditions. Context, however, does not have a deterministic impact but only a probabilistic one but is essential to understand how actors act.

As laid down above the compliance research is rather weak when inquiring about constitutive conditions that for example convert actors into veto players or let administrations perform poorly. Thus inquiring about the context and constitutive environment of causal mechanisms (independent variables) will help us to define scope conditions and learn more about when a certain variable can unfold its full potential. Ideally knowledge about scope conditions can produce more cumulative outcomes, if domains of application can be presented in an additive form and thus exert more explanatory leverage than testing individual variables (Jupille et al., 2003, pp. 21–22).

In order to approach the problem of co-determination of independent variables a number of scholars (Schimmelfennig et al., 2006; Schwellnus et al., 2012; Sedelmeier, 2009) have started turn to case oriented instead of variable oriented methodology by using Qualitative Comparative Analysis or QCA. This relatively new methodology which was chiefly developed by Charles Ragin, deviates from the logic of competitive theory testing in which variables are tested against each other and where the 'winner takes it all'. While traditional comparative analysis rejects all those conditions which do not always cause a certain outcome QCA distinguishes between necessary and sufficient conditions and thus allows for the analysis of combinational impact (Schneider & Wegemann, 2007, pp. 73–76). Often the application of QCA is accompanied by an attempt to increase the number of cases within country case studies. This move aims at gathering greater leverage over assumptions of causality by extending the observation basis. QCA can be a viable tool for compliance research because it accepts equifinality of causal conditions, increases the number of observerables through within case analysis and thus better accounts for the existing empirical complexity and plurality of theoretical approaches. However, it cannot be ruled out that QCA will not completely overcome inconclusiveness and might even dilute the search for parsimonious theory building by simply contrasting variation in compliance performance with a complex but unique set of variables whose generalizable impact still needs to be shown.

Conclusion: What Value Added?

This article problematizes the dominant 'rationalist turn' within compliance research. The article has formulated a critique at different levels partly within the positivist school partly outside of it taking into account moderate and reflectivist constructivism. It has been argued that most conditions which have been explored within this sub-field of European integration follow a rationalist logic of calculating costs and benefits of norm adherence. Thereby, mainstream research has been preoccupied with exploring causal conditions for compliance often in a competitive mode. What has been missing so far is a debate discussing often too easily accepted assumptions such as those about the fixed meaning of norms and the measurability of compliance from which the positivist research methodology is dependent. Recent constructivist research on norms in international relations is increasingly challenging this view (Krook & True, 2010; Zwingel, 2012) and is aware that norms to acquire meaning and for being complied with have to undergo a validation process (Wiener & Pütter, 2009). Reflectivist constructivism is breaking with the linear understanding of norms and compliance and indicates alternative ways of assessing compliance.

Another point of criticism is that research tends to explain compliance with the help of rationality without systematically inquiring about those conditions which make actors act rationally. This is important because rationality as such is rather a mechanism for action which is transferrable but not a substantive explanation for action in itself. Consequently, the compliance research has mostly explored causal mechanisms for norm adherence but has largely turned a blind eye toward examining the wider environmental and normative context in which rational behaviour is acted out. The fact that actors act rationally does not tell us very much about why they do so or where rationality is coming from or how it is changing over time. In this context, constructivism has not challenged the importance of rational behaviour per se (preference formation can also be explained with recourse to rational theories) but has argued that those conditions which constitute preferences, norms, and institutions cannot be less consequential than those conditions which directly trigger a certain action.

This article aimed at pointing to the analytical value added of constructivist reasoning within compliance research in a review style manner in order to provoke further debate and provide a basis for further inquiry. It did not formulate 'ready to use' instruments for empirical research. There is much work ahead. Let's start doing it!

Acknowledgments

I thank Guido Schwellnus and Timofey Agarin for their insightful comments on an early draft of this paper.

Notes

[1] 'Nothing is truthful without its counterpart'. Martin Walser is a German novelist. Interview Martin Walser Frankfurter Allgemeine Zeitung 10 Sep. 2007.
[2] In most but not all cases the external incentives model explores the impact of superior external incentives against domestic compliance costs but it also accommodates for cases in which domestic conditions are favourable. These are seen as 'easy' cases of 'self-socialization' (Schimmelfennig, 2000, p. 133).
[3] For a set of conditions under which persuasion is assumed to work see Checkel (2005a, p. 813).
[4] While the compliance research is mostly treating administration as apolitical norm executors the literature on policy implementation has a taken a more sophisticated stance under the rubric of bottom up concepts it does assign implementing agencies a greater role. However, the compliance and public policy implementation literature are only very loosely connected.

References

Bailey, I. (2002) National adaptation to European integration: Institutional vetoes and goodness-of-fit, *Journal of European Public Policy*, 9(5), pp. 791–811.
Barnett, M. & Finnemore, M. (1999) The politics, power, and pathologies of international organizations, *International Organization*, 53(4), pp. 699–732.
Börzel, T. A. (2000) Why there is no 'southern problem': On environmental leaders and laggards in the European Union', *Journal of European Public Policy*, 7(1), pp. 141–162.
Brosig, M. (2010) The challenge of implementing minority rights in Eastern Europe, *Journal of European Integration*, 32(4), pp. 283–301.

Checkel, J. (2005a) International institutions and socialization in Europe: Introduction and framework, *International Organization*, 59(4), pp. 801–826.

Checkel, J. (2005b) It's the process stupid! Process tracing in the study of European and international politics, ARENA Working Paper 26.

Dworkin, R. (1986) *Law's Empire* (London: Fontana Press).

Falleti, T. & Lynch, J. (2009) Context and causal mechanisms in political analysis, *Comparative Political Studies*, 42(9), pp. 1143–1166.

Falkner, G., Hartlapp, M. & Treib, O. (2007) Worlds of compliance: Why leading approaches to the implementation of EU legislation are only 'sometimes-true theories', *European Journal of Political Research*, 46(3), pp. 395–416.

Falkner, G., Treib, O. & Holzleithner, E. (2008a) *Compliance in the Enlarged European Union: Living rights or dead letters?* (Ashgate: Aldershot).

Finnemore, M. & Sikkink, K. (1998) International norm dynamics and political change, *International Organization*, 52(4), pp. 887–917.

George, A. & Bennett, A. (2005) *Case Studies and Theory Development in the Social Sciences* (Cambridge, MA: MIT Press).

Hartlapp, M. & Falkner, G. (2009) Problems of operationalization and data in EU compliance research, *European Union Politics*, 10(2), pp. 281–304.

Haverland, M. (2000) National adaptation to European integration: The importance of institutional veto points, *Journal of Public Policy*, 20(1), pp. 83–103.

Hay, C. (2006) Constructivist institutionalism, in: R.A.W. Rhodes, S.A. Binder & B.A. Rockman (Eds) *Oxford Handbook of Political Institutions*, pp. 56–74 (Oxford: Oxford University Press).

Jupille, J., Caporaso, J. A. & Checkel, J. T. (Eds.) (2003) Integrating institutions: Rationalism, constructivism, and the study of the European Union, *Comparative Political Studies* 36 (1/2), pp. 7–40.

Kelley, J. G. (2004) *Ethnic Politics in Europe: The power of norms and incentives* (Princeton: Princeton University Press).

Kratochwil, F. (1989) *Rules, Norms and Decisions, On the Conditions of Practical and Legal Reasoning in International Relations and Domestic Society* (Cambridge: Cambridge University Press).

Krizsan, A. (2009) From formal adoption to enforcement. Post-accession shifts in EU impact on Hungary in the equality policy field, in: F. Schimmelfennig & F. Trauner (Eds) *Post-accession compliance in the EU's new member states, European Integration online Papers (EIoP)*, Special Issue 2, Vol. 13, Art. 22. Avialable at http://eiop.or.at/eiop/texte/2009-022a.htm.

Krook, M. & True, J. (2010) Rethinking the life cycles of international norms: The United Nations and the global promotion of gender equality, *European Journal of International Relations*, 18(1), pp. 103–127.

Legro, J. (1997) Which norms matter? Revisiting the 'failure' of internationalism, *International Organization*, 51(1), pp. 31–63.

Mastenbroek, E. & Kaeding, M. (2007) Europeanization beyond the goodness of fit: Domestic politics in the forefront, *Comparative European Politics*, 4(4), pp. 331–354.

Onuf, N. (1989) *World of Our Making Rules and Rule in Social Theory and International Relations* (Colombia: University of South Carolina Press).

Raustiala, K. & Slaughter, A.-M. (2002) International law, international relations and compliance, in: W. Carlsnaes, T. Risse & B. A. Simmons (Eds) *Handbook of International Relations*, pp. 538–558 (London: Sage).

Rechel, B. (2008) What has limited the EU's impact on minority rights in accession countries?, *East European Politics and Societies*, 22(1), pp. 171–191.

Risse, T. (2000) 'Let's argue!' Communicative action in international relations, *International Organization*, 54(1), pp. 1–39.

Risse, T. (2009) Social constructivism and European integration, in: A. Wiener & T. Diez (Eds) *European Integration Theory*, pp. 144–160 (Oxford: Oxford University Press).

Risse, T., Ropp, S. & Sikkink, K. (Eds.) (1999) *The Power of Human Rights* (Cambridge: Cambridge University Press).

Sasse, G. (2008) The politics of EU conditionality: The norm of minority protection during and beyond EU accession, *Journal of European Public Policy*, 15(6), pp. 842–860.

Schimmelfennig, F. (2000) International socialization in the new Europe: Rational action in an institutional environment, *European Journal of International Relations*, 6(1), pp. 109–139.

Schimmelfennig, F. & Sedelmeier, U. (2004) Governance by conditionality: EU rule transfer to the candidate countries of Central and Eastern Europe, *Journal of European Public Policy*, 11(4), pp. 661–679.

Schimmelfennig, F. & Sedelmeier, U. (2005) *The Europeanization of Central and Eastern Europe* (Ithaca, NY: Cornell University Press).

Schimmelfennig, F., Engert, S. & Knobel, H. (2006) *International Socialization in Europe: European organizations, political conditionality, and democratic change* (Basingstoke: Palgrave Macmillan).

Schmidt, V. (2008) Discursive institutionalism: The explanatory power of ideas and discourse, *Annual Review of Political Science*, 11, pp. 303–326.

Schneider, C. & Wagemann, C. (2007) *Qualitative Comparative Analysis (QCA) und Fuzzy Sets* (Opladen, Farmington Hills: Verlag Barbara Budrich).

Schwellnus, G. (2005) The adoption of nondiscrimination and minority protection rules in Romania, Hungary, and Poland, in: F. Schimmelfennig & U. Sedelmeier (Eds) *The Europeanization of Central and Eastern Europe*, pp. 51–70 (Ithaca, NY: Cornell University Press).

Schwellnus, G. (2009) The domestic contestation of international norms: An argumentation analysis of the Polish debate regarding a minority law, *Journal of International Law and International Relations*, 5(1), pp. 123–154.

Schwellnus, G., Balazs, L. & Mikalayeva, L. (2009) It ain't over when it's over: The adoption and sustainability of minority protection rules in new EU member state, *European Integration Online Papers*, 13(2), p. 24.

Schwellnus, G., Mikalayeva, L. & Balázs, L. (Forthcoming) Project report: A fuzzy-set qualitative comparative analysis of minority protection rules in ten new EU member states, *European Yearbook of Minority Issues*, Volume 9.

Sedelmeier, U. (2008) After conditionality: Post-accession compliance with EU law in East Central Europe, *Journal of European Public Policy*, 15(6), pp. 806–825.

Sedelmeier, U. (2009) Post-accession compliance with EU gender equality legislation in postcommunist new member states, *European Integration Online Papers*, 13 (Special issue 2) Art. 23. Available at http://eiop.or.at/eiop/texte/2009-023a.htm.

Sedelmeier, U. (2011) Europeanization in New Member and Candidate States, *Living Reviews in European Governance* 6 (1) pp. 1–52.

Snidal, D. (2002) Rational choice and international relations, in: W. Carlsnaes, T. Risse & B. Simmons (Eds) *Handbook of International Relations*, pp. 73–94 (London: Sage Publications).

Tallberg, J. (2002) Paths to compliance: Enforcement, management, and the European Union, *International Organization*, 56(3), pp. 609–643.

Toshkov, D. (2007) Transposition of EU social policy in the new member states, *Journal of European Social Policy*, 17(3), pp. 335–348.

Toshkov, D. (2008) Embracing European law: Compliance with EU directives in Central and Eastern Europe, *European Union Politics*, 9(3), pp. 379–402.

Treib, O. (2003) Die Umsetzung von EU-Richtlinien im Zeichen der Parteipolitik: Eine akteurzentrierte Antwort auf die Misfit-These, *Politische Vierteljahresschrift*, 44(4), pp. 506–528.

Treib, O. (2008) Implementing and complying with EU governance outputs, *Living Reviews in European Governance*, 3(5), pp. 1–30.

Wendt, A. (1992) Anarchy is what states make of it: The social construction of power politics, *International Organization*, 46(2), pp. 391–425.

Wendt, A. (1999) *Social Theory of International Politics* (Cambridge: Cambridge University Press).

Wiener, A. (2003) Constructivism: The limits of bridging gaps, *Journal of International Relations and Development*, 6(3), pp. 253–276.

Wiener, A. & Uwe, P. (2009) The quality of norms is what actors make of it, critical constructivist research on norms, *Journal of International Law and International Relations*, 5(1), pp. 1–16.

Zwingel, S. (2012) How do norms travel? Theorizing international woman's rights in transitional perspective, *International Studies Quarterly*, 56(1), pp. 115–129.

Exploring the Implementation of Minority Protection Rules in the 'Worlds of Compliance': The Case of Turkey

GÖZDE YILMAZ

ABSTRACT *The legal adoption and implementation of minority protection rules in both EU member and candidate countries is a highly contested issue that varies across countries. As the status of European Union (EU) candidate country most debated, Turkey represents relatively a success story in minority rights due to the intensive minority-related legal adoption and increasing implementation in the accession process. The acceleration of the process is puzzling due to the fast transition to the implementation phase in a candidate country, of which the membership prospect has still been debated. Therefore, Turkey represents an interesting case, providing an empirical arena to explore factors that influence the implementation process. Suggesting a revised version of comprehensive 'worlds of compliance' that could be applied to the candidate states as a filter of explanatory factors for implementation, this article argues, that two worlds of compliance matter in Turkey's compliance with minority rights: world of domestic politics for implementation process, influenced by the domestic choice of the Turkish government; and world of law observance for legal adoption driven by the EU's credible conditionality.*

Introduction

Recent developments in EU member states, such as the French dismantling Roma camps, has drawn attention on minority rights in the EU (BBC News Europe, 2010). While often neglecting member states' records concerning minority rights, the EU has paid considerable attention to minority rights in the accession process of Central and East European countries (CEECs). Minority discontent as a potential threat to the stability of Europe in the aftermath of the Cold War has caused the EU to focus on minority rights. Nonetheless, the Europeanization of minority rights in candidate countries remains a highly contested issue that varies across countries.

In comparison to other policy areas, the compliance of candidate countries with minority rights is slower and more problematic. Although the protection of minorities and the improvement of minority rights were included in the Copenhagen Criteria as a pre-condition for accession to the EU, minority rights remain a vague issue within the Union. This is partly because of the fact that there is no minority standard defined in the *acquis* or among the EU member states (Schwellnus, 2005, p. 51). Most importantly, the practical implementation of minority rules in candidate states remains incomplete. The post-accession phase clearly demonstrates the problems of practical application and enforcement in minority rights, such as the unsettled problems of Russian-speakers in Estonia and Latvia or Roma in Slovakia and Bulgaria (Brosig, 2010; Rechel, 2008; Sasse, 2008).

This article aims to explain the variance in Turkey's practical implementation of minority protection rules across time. Therefore, I start the analysis from an empirical puzzle, which is the intensification of minority-related policy implementation in Turkey by 2008. Although the implementation of minority rights is still restricted in the country, the acceleration of the process is puzzling due to the fast transition to the implementation phase in a candidate country, of which the membership prospect to the EU has still been debated. As earlier studies indicated, there is a huge gap between legal adoption and implementation, in which many EU rules are adopted but not properly implemented in the pre-membership phase (Brosig, 2010; Falkner and Treib 2008; Schimmelfennig & Sedelmeier, 2005; Leiber, 2007). Therefore, the case of Turkey represents an interesting case, providing an empirical arena to explore different factors that influence the implementation process, which are in return applicable to the other cases of accession countries.

By focusing under which conditions minority-related rules are implemented in an EU candidate country, the article argues that implementation process is influenced by mainly domestic factors – the domestic choice of the government in the Turkish case – while legal adoption is primarily driven by the EU conditionality. Theoretically framing the argument with the 'worlds of compliance' typology of Falkner *et al.* (2007), which is established to explore how EU member states handle the issue of complying with EU law, the article suggests a revised version of comprehensive 'worlds of compliance' that could be applied to the candidate states as a filter of explanatory factors for implementation.

The article starts with empirical observations to map the variance on the implementation of minority rules with a background of legal adoption in the area due to the puzzle-oriented design of the research. In the second part, theoretical approaches for EU-related implementation research is explored and a revised version of worlds of compliance for accession states is provided. The third part focuses on the explanatory factors for the implementation of minority rules in Turkey.

Empirical Observations: Mapping Minority Rights in Turkey

This part of the article maps minority rights in Turkey via examining the minority-related demands of the EU from Turkey, and minority rights prior to and after the launch of reforms in the country. The analysis relies on three time periods, 2002 and 2004, 2005 and 2007, 2008 and 2010, which are derived through the variation in legal adoption and implementation of minority rules between 2002 and 2010.

Minority-related EU Demands from Turkey

Although minority policies and practices are different in each EU member state, the EU clearly sets some guiding principles for minority protection in the enlargement process (Toktaş, 2006, p. 13). The demands of the EU are clarified as country-specific measures for adoption by candidate countries in the regular reports, progress reports, and Council decisions, which set the priorities for the Accession Partnerships.

The EU's priorities in minority protection, consistently stressed between 2002 and 2010, include the ratification of the CoE Framework Convention for the protection of national minorities; removing the ban on broadcasting and education in languages other than Turkish traditionally used by Turkish citizens and ensuring its implementation; the elimination of the limited interpretation of 1923 Lausanne Treaty;[1] resolving the problems in the southeast of the country, both culturally and socio-economically (including the problems of Internally Displaced Persons (IDPs))[2] and the Kurdish issue; resolving the problems of non-Muslims and their foundations, such as granting property rights or removing the ban on training clergy and opening the Halki seminary for training;[3] and eliminating the problems of non-Sunni minorities (Alevis) (European Commission, 2002, 2003, 2004a, b, c, 2005, 2007, 2008a, b, 2009a, b, 2010a, b).

Set by the EU, these priorities constitute the base for minority-related reforms in Turkey though with a varying emphasis over time. To start with the period between 2002 and 2004, the EU focused on the problems of the southeast of Turkey by stressing the need to lift the emergency rule in the region, the solution to the problem of IDPs and the village guard system.[4] Moreover, the EU widened its demands to include the implementation of the rules adopted in this period, such as the broadcasting in and learning of different languages and dialects traditionally used by Turkish citizens in their daily lives, the measures in regard to the freedom of religion adopted in the area of property rights, and the construction of places of worship (European Commission, 2002, 2003, 2004a).

The problems of non-Muslim religious communities including the legal personality and property rights of their foundations, the training of clergy, minority schools and their internal management, the restrictions on the exercise of cultural rights, and the restrictions on broadcasting in other languages (for television, four hours per week, while not exceeding 45 minutes per day; for radio, five hours per week, while not exceeding 60 minutes per day) all came under increasing pressure from the EU for further improvement (European Commission, 2002, 2003, 2004a).

Between 2005 and 2007, the EU demanded that Turkey needed to remove restrictions further on minorities, such as the use of other languages by political parties, by stressing the duty of the Turkish government to ensure the exercise of the rights provided by the recent reforms for minorities (European Commission, 2005, 2007). Additionally, some specific measures prioritized by the EU included the abolishment of the requirement to indicate religion on ID cards, the solving of the difficulties experienced by non-Muslim minorities in acceding to administrative and military positions and of the problems of IDPs, and the need to eliminate discriminatory language in schoolbooks (European Commission, 2005, 2007).

After the adoption of several minority-related rules by the country, the EU focused, in this period, more on the problems based on the implementation process, mainly on on-going restrictions in a number of minority rights. Moreover, the EU started to seek the active participation of other European organizations in order to improve Turkey's minority protection. For instance, since 2005, the EU has emphasized the necessity of building a dialogue between Turkey and the OSCE High Commissioner on National Minorities (HCNM) on issues such as the participation of minorities in public life (European Commission, 2005, 2007).

Between 2008 and 2010, the EU provided a more detailed roadmap for Turkey to improve its minority rights. The focus was, again, on the implementation of problems in the area. A number of issues raised by the EU, in this period, were the problems of Roma and the necessity of building a strategy by the Turkish government to solve this, the need to cooperate with the OSCE and the need to amend the Law on the Movement and Residence of Aliens, which discriminated against Roma (European Commission, 2008a, 2009a, 2010a). Notably, the period again witnessed the increasing attention of the EU to the Kurdish problem, with an increasing emphasis on solving the problem in each Commission report and document since 2008 (European Commission, 2008a, 2009a, 2010a).

By 2002, the EU insisted each year on the improvement of some specific minority-related issues and detailed its demands from Turkey through time. Three points arose from the analysis of the EU demands of Turkey in regard to minority rights. First, the EU consistently put pressure on Turkey to solve some basic problems, such as eliminating the restrictive definition of minorities in the country or ensuring broadcast and education in other languages used in the daily life of Turkish citizens. Second, the EU has provided Turkey with a very detailed roadmap comprising of recommendations to improve minority protection through time. Since 2008, the EU has detailed the minority-related priorities to be considered by Turkey and how to take action in these areas. Last, the EU has directed its attention more to the problems in the implementation of minority-related rules since 2005. While demanding for further legal adoption in some areas, the EU has begun to pressure Turkey to assure the implementation of the rules adopted.

Minority Rights Prior to the Reforms

The concept of a minority in Turkey is derived from the 1923 Lausanne Peace Treaty, which is still in force today and cited by many as the official policy in regard to minority rights. The treaty defines minorities in Turkey as non-Muslims limited to three minority groups, Armenians, Greeks, and Jews, whose rights are under the protection of the international arena (i.e., the League of Nations at the time the treaty was signed). Therefore, Turkey has rejected the international definition of the minority concept on the basis of racial, linguistic, or religious differences (Oran, 2004, p. 64). As a result, Turkey, from the very emergence of the Republic, has denied the existence of Muslim minorities such as Kurds and Alevis and their rights to preserve their differences (Grigoriadis, 2008, p. 31).

In addition to the restrictive definition, minority rights in Turkey, prior to the launch of reforms in the area, were a restricted policy area, both rhetorically and practically. Both the official and societal stance over minorities were shaped by the denial of minorities and the perception of them as 'threats' to the integrity of the state, as tools of foreign interference to the internal policies of the state and as second class citizens (Grigoriadis, 2008, p. 31; Oran, 2004, p. 64). Furthermore, until the early 2000s Turkey did not have any legal document on minority rights except the Lausanne Treaty. In addition, the Lausanne Treaty, as the only official document for minority protection, has never been fully implemented (Oran, 2009). Reforms of these restricted policies concerning minority rights began to change at the turn of the twenty-first century.

Legal Adoption for Minority Protection

Since 2002, Turkey has launched a number of reforms in minority rights. Many controversial issues, such as broadcasting in languages used in the daily lives of Turkish citizens other than Turkish, or the lack of property rights granted to non-Muslim minorities in the country, have made progress. Although the reforms in minority rights may represent a tremendous step for the Europeanization process of Turkey, the compliance trend in minority rights has fluctuated over time.

Having a progressing trend, Turkey's legal adoption in minority rights varies in the three time periods under consideration. In February 2002, the coalition government started to launch reforms for the legal harmonization of Turkish laws with EU laws, though it did not specifically focus on minority issues. After the 2002 elections, the Justice and Development Party (Adalet ve Kalkınma Partisi – AKP) government continued the reforms in a number of policy areas, including minority rights. Eight reform packages passed parliament between 2002 and 2004. The reform packages included both amendments of some rules restricting minority rights and the adoption of new measures to improve minority protection.

Legal adoption in this period touched on several areas in minority rights, ranging from removing bans on broadcasting in other languages than Turkish (used in the daily life of citizens) to the property rights of non-Muslim foundations (Yilmaz, 2011). The government also granted minorities some legal protection by ratifying international agreements: the 1965 UN Convention on the Elimination of All Forms of Racial Discrimination in 2002, and both the International Covenant on Civil and Political Rights and the International Covenant on Economic, Social and Cultural Rights in 2003 (Secretariat General for EU Affairs of Turkey, 2007, p. 19). The legal reforms in this period, therefore, represent a break from the previous policies, providing a momentum for positive change in minority protection.

Between 2005 and 2007, legal adoption slowed down significantly in the area. Although there were some legal changes, such as the adoption of the ninth harmonization package, legal adoption was inconclusive in this period when compared to the period 2002 and 2004 (Yilmaz, 2011).

The year 2008 represents a revival of legal adoption in minority rights. The government launched a number of legal reforms, including the adoption of new a foundations law, a law on de-mining the Turkish–Syrian border, a minority circular declaring the right of non-Muslim minorities to exercise their cultural rights, and the

Kurdish initiative to solve the Kurdish problem (European Commission, 2009a; Freedom House, 2010; Turkish Official Gazette, 2010).

Although Ankara had adopted and amended a number of legal rules by 2002 in regard to minority protection, legal adoption has been incomplete. For instance, Turkey has not signed the CoE Framework Convention for the Protection of National Minorities nor eliminated the restrictive interpretation of Lausanne Treaty, two things which were consistently demanded by the EU (European Commission, 2009a, p. 28). What we have seen in the case of Turkey is the selective legal approximation of the minority-related rules demanded by the EU.

Implementation of Minority Rules

Implementation of minority rights, which is indicated by the practical implementation of the rules adopted in the previous years, has surprisingly shown a progressing trend.[5] Between 2002 and 2004, the implementation of minority-related rules was very limited. Despite remaining limited, the implementation ranged from the property rights of non-Muslim foundations to broadcasting and teaching in languages used in the daily life of Turkish citizens other than Turkish (Yilmaz, 2011, pp. 17–18; Hammarberg, 2009, p. 4).[6]

Between 2005 and 2007, the implementation process continued to progress, although there was a slowdown in the legal adoption of EU rules (Freedom House, 2007, p. 2). For instance, broadcasting in languages other than Turkish, including Kurdish, moved on in 2007, despite severe restrictions (Freedom House, 2009, p. 3). Consequently, the period represents a limited degree of implementation.

By 2008, many restrictions on the implementation of many minority-related rules were removed and the process intensified (Yilmaz, 2011). Several rules adopted in the previous periods began to be implemented properly, such as broadcasting in other languages or the foundations law. For instance, in the area of broadcasting in languages other than Turkish and following the June 2008 amendments to the relevant law, in January 2009 TRT – the public service broadcaster – started operating channel TRT-6, broadcasting in Kurdish 24-hours a day (Hammarberg, 2009, p. 5). Moreover, more than 10 private companies applied for regional and local broadcasting licenses in Kirmanchi, Zaza and Arabic in January 2010 (UN Human Rights Council, 2010, p. 8).

However, this does not mean that the implementation of minority protection rules in Turkey was without problems. For instance, in spite of the positive developments in the area of broadcasting, the restrictions in the law on the Radio and Television Supreme Council (RTÜK) continued to be applied for private local and regional TV and radio programs (European Commission, 2009a, p. 30). Educational programs in Kurdish were not allowed; several court cases and investigations were launched against GÜN TV – the only private TV channel currently broadcasting in Kurdish (European Commission, 2009a, p. 30).

Nevertheless, the period after 2008 witnessed a series of implementation moves within the country. A considerably tolerant environment was developed in the period, in part due to the debates launched by the government on several issues untouched upon in the past, such as the Armenian issue and Kurdish issue. This period is, thus, one of intensifying implementation.

To conclude, both the legal adoption and implementation of minority rights in Turkey has varied across time. Most importantly, the recent intensification of implementation in Turkey is puzzling, because implementation has often been the most problematic area in the accession process, and the implementation of minority protection rules has been even more problematic in many previous candidate countries (Brosig, 2010; Falkner and Treib 2008). This suggests a need to explore the factors leading to the progress of implementation in the case of Turkey over time, which will be examined in the next sections.

Table 1. Mapping the minority-related legal adoption and implementation in Turkey: 2002–2010

Time period	Legal adoption	Implementation
2002–2004	High	Very limited
2005–2007	Low	Limited
2008–2010	Low–medium	Progressing but still restrictive

Theorizing Implementation? EU-related Implementation Research and Two Worlds of Compliance for Accession Countries

Policy implementation, as Barrett (2004, p. 251) clarifies, refers to the process of 'translating policy into action'. Within the policy cycle, ranging from problem definition to policy formulation or policy implementation, the implementation part is the most problematic one, usually accompanied by long delays (Treib, 2008, pp. 4–5).

Although scholarly attention has recently grown in the field of policy implementation within the EU context, growing literature on the domestic impact of the EU has provided a number of explanatory factors that affects the degree, extent and timeliness of implementation. Most of the EU-related implementation research focuses on three strings of factors: institutional inefficiency, misfit and veto players, and social interest groups (Börzel, 2000; Börzel & Risse, 2000; Duina, 1997; Koutalakis, 2006; Risse *et al.*, 2001; Tsebelis, 2002). Yet, these factors do not provide an encompassing theoretical approach for implementation research and in many cases do not provide explanatory power (see Falkner *et al.*, 2007; Falkner and Treib 2008; Hartlapp & Leiber, 2010).

More recently, testing the afore-mentioned factors in 90 implementation cases in the area of EU social policy, Falkner *et al.* (2007) found that there is no single overriding factor which determines the implementation performance. In order to provide a solution to the different patterns working with different factors in the implementation process of EU member states, Falkner *et al.* (2007) introduce a typology of 'worlds of compliance', each performing as a filter that decides the relevant explanatory factors for different countries. First, in the world of law observance, compliance is the main goal that overrides domestic concerns (Falkner *et al.*, 2007, p. 405). The transposition of EU directives is usually timely and correct, with successful implementation, even if there is conflict with national policy styles (Falkner *et al.*, 2007, p. 405). This pattern is supported by a national 'compliance culture' (Falkner *et al.*, 2007, p. 405). Second, in the world of domestic politics, compliance is one among many goals. In a conflict of interests situation, domestic concerns prevail on the basis of cost–benefit analysis (Falkner et al., 2007, p. 405). The implementation process is not a major problem in this world, while the main obstacle to compliance is political resistance at the transposition phase (Falkner et al., 2007, p. 405). Third, in the world of transposition neglect, compliance is not a goal in itself. A national arrogance signifying the superior domestic standards and administrative inefficiency are typical in this world (Falkner et al., 2007, p. 405). The initial reaction to an EU-related implementation process is most often inactivity with shallow transposition (Falkner et al., 2007, p. 405). Last, Falkner and Treib (2008, p. 308) introduce the world of dead letters, in which transposition works successfully without implementation.

Although the worlds of compliance typology is a good starting point to analyse the implementation process of EU rules in candidate states, the framework is specifically designed for member state implementation of EU rules and directives. Yet, the typology can be applied to the accession countries with some revisions considering the accession process of CEECs. First, as the previous studies (e.g., Schimmelfennig & Sedelmeier, 2005) demonstrate, EU legal adoption in candidate states was successful due to the membership carrot, primarily relying on the credibility of EU conditionality.

Second, the newly adopted EU rules in these countries, in many cases, were not fully implemented and most often remained lagging (see Brosig, 2010; Falkner and Treib, 2008; Leiber, 2007; Rechel, 2008; Sasse, 2008; Schimmelfennig & Sedelmeier, 2005). Minority rights, as the most sensitive issue area for implementation, was among the problematic areas in the CEECs accession process enduring the controversial approach of the EU on the issue, which relies on double standards for member and candidate states, the lack of a common minority standard within the EU, and tendency to accept candidates as members that do not fully implement minority rules (Hughes & Sasse, 2003; Johnson, 2006; Schwellnus, 2005). Nevertheless, research on minority rights in CEECs proves that the legal adoption of minority rules was considerably better than any old member state; however, the problem starts when it comes to the implementation of minority protection rules (Brosig, 2010; Kelley, 2004; Rechel, 2008; Sasse, 2008; Ram, 2003).

This trend of dutiful legal adoption and a lack of or low levels of implementation in the CEEC accession process strongly implies that legal adoption in candidate states, including minority rights, has driven by EU conditionality, remaining in the world of law observance in which the compliance goal overrides domestic concerns. In contrast, the implementation of EU rules would remain in the world of domestic politics, in which domestic concerns, both positively or negatively, prevail in a clash of interests for implementation. The case of Turkey, providing a strong test case due to the decline in credibility of EU conditionality recently, demonstrates the positive impact of domestic factors in the implementation of minority rules.

As a result, there is a necessity to filter factors influencing the implementation process in accession states via an outcome-oriented approach for compliance: the world of law observance for legal adoption and the world of domestic politics for implementation. Although the article relies on only the case of Turkey, this probabilistic framework can be tested across countries and policy areas.

Filtering factors for rule adoption within the world of law observance, the article proposes that legal adoption is likely to be correct and timely where EU conditionality is credible. In regard to the implementation phase, starting with the world of domestic politics, the implementation of EU rules is likely to be correct and timely where the EU's rules tally with the political preferences of the political parties in the government.

It is important to note that the article pursues the path of top-down approaches in implementation research, which emphasizes 'the separation of politics and administration, and co-ordination and control through authority and hierarch' (Barrett, 2004, p. 254). Therefore, I consider the implementation through focusing on central policy-makers. As Barrett stresses, 'policy should be made "at the top", and executed by "agents" in compliance with policy objectives' (Barrett, 2004, p. 254).

The Case of Turkey: From EU's Push of Legal Adoption to Domestic Pull of Implementation

The case of minority rights in Turkey demonstrates a sequential pattern from a high to low degree of legal adoption and from limited to intensifying implementation between 2002 and 2010. The changing trend in the EU's push for minority reforms with credible incentives, decreasing over time, and the recent increase in the domestic pull of minority-related change by the pro-minority government confirms the aforementioned framework to explain the variation in minority-related legal adoption and implementation.

The Credibility of EU Conditionality: No Membership Carrot for Turkey

The credibility of EU conditionality, operating through a carrots and sticks policy, depends on the EU's ability to provide new opportunities and constraints for domestic actors (Kelley, 2004; Schimmelfennig & Sedelmeier, 2005). It is widely recognized that the credibility of EU conditionality has been the most important factor influencing the efficacy of EU conditionality in the enlargement process.

The credibility of EU conditionality stemmed from the linkage of political criteria, which was outlined in the 1993 Copenhagen Summit, to the EU membership.[7] The consistency of references to political criteria and the instances of referring to non-political criteria for accession by EU institutions and member states constitute the primary determinants of the credibility of EU conditionality. Exploring the linkage of membership to political and non-political criteria in Turkey's accession process, the analysis reveals that the credibility of EU conditionality for Turkey had gradually weakened by 2004, due to increasing references by EU institutions to non-political criteria for Turkey's accession to the Union.

Between 1999 and 2004, both the Commission and the Council clearly stated that the membership conditions, which include the same criteria for all candidate countries, for Turkey depended solely on political criteria (European Commission, 2002, pp. 5–8; European Council, 2002, p. 3; European Commission, 2003, p. 15). These remarks delivered a certain signal that Turkey was on the track towards accession negotiations when the country fulfilled the Copenhagen criteria.

By 2004, the credibility of EU conditionality was weakened due to the sharp decrease in references to the political criteria and increase in references to non-political criteria for the membership of Turkey, including the EU's absorption capacity, the open-ended nature of accession negotiations with Turkey, the peaceful settlement of border disputes and good neighbourly relations,[8] the Cyprus problem, and even the high population of Turkey (European Commission, 2004a,b,c; European Council, 2004).

The 2005 'privileged partnership' debate among member states questioning the launch of accession negotiations with Turkey had also a negative impact to the process (Aydın Düzgit, 2006, p. 6). Moreover, the resolution of the Cyprus problem as a non-political criterion for Turkey has become the focal point of Turkey's accession negotiations since 2006 (European Commission, 2006, p. 24; European Council, 2006, p. 22). The EU through its official statements has urged Turkey to find a peaceful settlement for Cyprus problem and recognize the divided island as one entity represented by the Greek side after the membership of the Republic of Cyprus (RoC) to the Union. While the first demand needs to be considered as a non-political criterion outside of Copenhagen criteria, the latter is a valid and legitimate demand of the Union on the basis that 'the recognition and equal treatment of all member states is a fundamental rule of the EU' (Schimmelfennig, 2008, p. 927). Due to the refusal of Turkey to recognize the RoC and its membership to the Union and to implement fully the protocol adapting the Ankara Agreement to the accession of the new EU member states, on 11 December 2006 the EU suspended negotiations with Turkey on eight chapters and restricted the closure of any chapter (European Council, 2006, p. 2).

The recent period from 2008 to 2011 proved even lower levels of credibility due to peaceful settlement of disputes, specifically for the Cyprus issue, and European public support for the enlargement (European Commission, 2009b, p. 21; European Commission, 2010b, pp. 13–22; European Council, 2010, pp. 3–4). Moreover, the issue of Turkey's recognition of the RoC has become a serious obstacle for Turkey's possible membership to the Union (European Commission, 2008a,b, 2009a,b, 2010a,b).

In return, the translation of decreasing credibility of EU conditionality to the domestic arena became evident by 2006. The privileged partnership debate caused a high drop in public support for EU membership in Turkey, from 74 per cent in 2002 to 50 per cent in 2006 (Öniş, 2009, p. 25). The debate strengthened the anti-European coalition in Turkey via the failure of the Cyprus settlement and the demand of the EU and refusal of Turkey to open Turkish ports to the RoC (Aybet, 2006, pp. 532–533).

As a result, the credibility of EU conditionality in the accession process of Turkey had started to weaken by 2004. This, in return, strengthened the Euro-sceptic coalition in the country and significantly limited the impact of the EU on minority rights as one of the most sensitive area for reforms.

The Preferences of the Turkish Government: The AKP as a Domestic Driver of Minority Rule Implementation[9]

> In this country, the problems of my Kurdish and Romani sisters and brothers, of Albanian, Bosnian, Abkhazian, Georgian and my other sisters and brothers

with different ethnic backgrounds were ignored and denied for years. The problems of my Sunni and Alevi sisters and brothers were denied. The problems of minorities and my non-Muslim citizens were denied. (Speech at the AKP Political Group Meeting, 2010a)

The preferences of the single party government of the AKP on minority rights stems from both the political values and election calculations of the party, necessitating pro-minority measures in order to attract votes from minority groups such as Kurds, who comprise 10 to 23 per cent of the whole population. To begin with, as the AKP came to power as a reformist party, 'its political values in general and with regard to minority issues was radically different than the previous parties. At the establishment of the party, the AKP defined itself as 'Conservative Democrat', which consists of a combination of cultural conservatism and political reformism with neoliberal economic views, plus a pro-globalization and pro-EU manner (Taşkın, 2008, p. 61). In the 2002 Election Manifesto (2002), the AKP defined itself as being democrat, conservative, reformist and modern, emphasizing the necessity of democratic governance in Turkey and positioning itself as an agent of change, in order to bring democracy to the country via embracing universal values to guarantee individual rights.

In this context, the stance of the AKP towards minority rights has been affected by its political values, primarily reflecting the aim to consolidate a democratic system in the country. First, the AKP has a more pluralistic notion of democracy (Özbudun, 2006, p. 548). In this respect, tolerance, dialogue and respect for minority rights are constantly stressed by the party, and it specifically refers to diversity as a cultural richness that reinforces solidarity rather than being a source of conflict within society (Özbudun, 2006, pp. 547–548). Second, the AKP adopts a political stance that refrains from any sort of nationalist ideology (Özbudun, 2006, p. 549; Taşkın, 2008, p. 62). The leader of the party, Erdoğan, continuously emphasizes that the AKP is against religious, ethnic, and regional nationalism (Speech at the AKP Political Group Meeting, 2003, 2006, 2008, 2009a). Third, the party adopts a minority approach on the basis of individual rights based on the principle of non-discrimination. The AKP, therefore, promotes an inclusive approach for all citizens, comprising minorities, relying on equality, unity, solidarity and fraternity of the nation. In this context, the party embraces an all-inclusive identity of Türkiyelilik (being from Turkey) on the basis of a geographical–historical notion of identity in contrast to previous official definitions of a restrictive 'Muslim Turk' identity, based exclusively on ethnic and religious history (Oran, 2007, p. 52; Taşkın, 2008, p. 62). In this respect, Erdoğan has stated continuously that citizenship of the Republic of Turkey constitutes a supra-identity for all (Speech at the AKP Political Group Meeting, 2005, 2008, 2009b).

Another factor behind pro-minority position of the AKP is the party's strategic calculations about national and local elections. The AKP government has been under constant pressure to keep its popularity in the elections due to specific domestic factors. First, the AKP is a party attracting votes from various ideological fronts, various regions and various income levels, including protest votes against the poor performance of the previous governments' inactivity on democratization and minority issues (Kumbaracıbası, 2009, p.78, p. 92). The party, therefore, had to keep the support of all of these different groups, including minority groups, in order to consolidate its success in the 2002 elections, in which the party received 34 per cent of the total votes. Second, the electoral nature of the Turkish party system is highly volatile (Çarkoğlu & Kalaycıoğlu, 2007, p. 34). The dramatic expel of the coalition partners of the previous government from the parliament in 2002 elections and the rise of the AKP demonstrates the high volatility (Çarkoğlu & Kalaycıoğlu, 2007, p. 35). Therefore, volatility in the system turns into a cause of vulnerability for the AKP with the possible loss of electoral support in each election. Third, a series of political crisis and polarization between the AKP and the Kemalists, which accelerated in 2007, necessitated the AKP to keep its electoral support to legitimize its position in a period of the AKP's commitment to secular ideals of the Republic questioned (Saatçioğlu, 2011, pp. 31–32).

All these factors contribute to the election considerations of the AKP, which necessitate keeping the party's voter base intact and attracting further votes via targeting reformist groups, including minorities in the country. Most importantly, as Liaras (2009, p. 8) emphasizes, some minority groups, such as Alevis and the Kurds, constitute a considerable population and can affect the overall outcome of a Turkish election. For example, in the 2007 national elections, the AKP raised its share of the vote in the predominantly Kurdish south-eastern regions of the country and even surpassed the share of the pro-Kurdish Democratic Society Party (DTP) in many parts of the region (Polat, 2009, p. 137). The 2007 elections demonstrated that the party's reformist approach including minority rights yielded results via the reward of an increase in the party's votes, this being a 47 per cent share of the total vote. The AKP, thus, seemed to persuade the Kurds with its problem-solving approach, clearly stating the existence of the Kurdish problem, differing from the previous official denial of the problem and providing an approach to solve the problem through the improvement of democracy and human and minority rights (Polat, 2009, p. 137). However, the 2009 elections demonstrated the AKP's loss of votes in the southeast to the DTP (Larrabee & Tol, 2011, p. 147). As Larrabee and Tol (2011, p. 147) emphasize, 'The AKP's poor showing in Kurdish areas served as an important wake-up call and underscored the need to address Kurdish concerns and grievances more seriously'. As a result, the election fever of the party exerted immense pressure on the AKP to keep both its reformist base of votes and attract minority votes.

Due to its political ideology and election calculations, between 2002 and 2010 the AKP focused on minority problems and providing solutions to these problems, with an accelerating trend by 2008 and a particular focus on the implementation of minority rules. After 2008, the party increased their advocacy of minority rights and their implementation, both to keep and attract the votes of reformist and minority groups in the elections and preserve its reformist stance, providing a particular legitimacy to the party, at a time of immense political crises with Kemalists. The increasing focus of the party on minority problems and the propositions for solutions can also be perceived in the discourse of the AKP representatives, focusing exclusively and explicitly on the issue, especially from 2008 onwards:

> We are together and one in this country as Turkish, Kurdish, Laz, Circassian, Georgian, Abkhaz, Bosnian. No ethnic element should and can struggle for superiority over others (Speech at the AKP Political Group Meeting, 2008)

> Everybody in this country with various ethnic origins under the supranational identity of Turkish Republic, as being Turkish, Laz, Kurdish, Circassian, Georgian, is our sisters and brothers... (Speech at the AKP Political Group Meeting, 2009b)

> All, Turkish, Kurdish, Laz, Circassian, Georgian, Abkhaz, Roma, have their own problems. It is wrong to deal with these problems? ... Alevis have their own problems... Christians and Jews more or less have their problems... if you are the state, you will solve these problems; it is your duty to solve. (Speech at the AKP Political Group Meeting, 2010b)

It is important to note that the AKP specifically pushed public institutions to implement minority rules. For instance, in 2010, a minority circular published by the Prime Minister Erdoğan declared the right of non-Muslim minorities to exercise their cultural rights (Turkish Official Gazette, 2010). The circular particularly stressed the problems faced by non-Muslim minorities in public institutions and the necessity of removing any problems caused by the representatives of the public institutions, putting special emphasis on the necessary implementation of minority rights provided by legal adoption in previous years (Turkish Official Gazette, 2010). Another example of this is the implementation of broadcasting in Kurdish 24 hours a day by the state television, TRT 6, without any restriction in January 2009 (Güzeldere, 2009). Erdoğan spoke in once-banned Kurdish at the opening ceremony of the channel, saying: 'TRT şeş bi xêr be' ('May TRT 6 be beneficial') (Güzeldere, 2009). The AKP leaders pushed for the implementation, believing that 'the Kurdish channel of the TRT will further strengthen their senses of belonging' (Speech at the AKP Political Group Meeting, 2009c).

As a result, in contrast to the previous restrictive state policy on minority rights, the AKP represents a movement in favour of change in the official minority policy (Aras & Tokta, 2009, p. 705) the party supported the implementation of minority rules; this was down to its reformist political values and also a strategic calculation to strengthen its voting share in the elections via attracting the support of minority groups.

Concluding Remarks: The Implementation of Minority Rules in a World of Domestic Politics

This article explored the implementation of minority policy in Turkey between 2002 and 2010, with an emphasis on the recent progress on the implementation process. The case of Turkey represents a crucial empirical arena due to two developments. First of all, the implementation of minority policy and the recent intensification of the process represent an interesting development, since earlier studies concluded that there is a huge gap between transposition and implementation in the pre-membership phase (Falkner and Treib 2008; Schimmelfennig & Sedelmeier, 2005;

Leiber, 2007). Therefore, the case of Turkey, demonstrating an acceleration in implementation of minority rights, stands for an important arena to explore different factors that influence the implementation process. Second, the case as the only instance where the credibility of EU conditionality becomes weak enables the researcher to explore different factors than EU conditionality that could lead to progress in the implementation process.

The analysis resulted in two findings, which would facilitate further research in the implementation field within the EU context. First, it reveals that the impact of EU conditionality remains the main impetus for legal adoption of minority rights in Turkey, as was in the case of CEECs. Second, the implementation process, intensified after 2008, is solely influenced by domestic factors, primarily by the policy preferences of the government. The findings suggest that the implementation process needs to be evaluated in the world of domestic politics.

This conclusion suggests that the typology of Falkner *et al.* (2007) needs to be revised for EU candidate states. According to the results of this analysis, there is a need to differ two worlds of compliance according to the outcome of change: either legal adoption or practical implementation. In this logic, a country would not randomly belong to any of the worlds (Falkner *et al.*, 2007, p. 410), but each process would belong to one world: legal adoption in world of law observance and implementation in world of domestic politics. In this case, there would be no need for more than two worlds of compliance since the afore-mentioned worlds comprise both external and internal factors that influence domestic change in accession countries. Nevertheless, the findings of the research need to be explored via other case studies in order to judge the implementation patterns in other candidate countries.

Notes

[1] The concept of minority in Turkey is derived from the 1923 Lausanne Peace Treaty, which is still in force today and constitutes the basis of official minority policy of the country.

[2] The problem of IDPs is caused by the displacement of people in the southeast of Turkey due to the conflict between Turkish armed forces and the Kurdish armed movement – PKK – during the 1990s.

[3] The Halki Seminary is the training college for priests, which was closed by a decision of the Turkish Ministry of National Education on the grounds that the seminary did not have enough students to continue to operate. Since then, it has not been re-opened.

[4] Village guard system is a civil defence force put in place by the state against the PKK in 1985 (Freedom House, 2007).

[5] The progressing trend in the implementation of minority policies in Turkey is surprising due to the limited implementation of legal rules by candidate states. Earlier studies reveal that there is a huge gap between legal adoption and implementation, in which many EU rules are transposed but not implemented in the pre-membership phase (Brosig, 2010; Leiber, 2007; Rechel, 2008; Schimmelfennig & Sedelmeier, 2005).

[6] For further details about the implementation process of minority rules, see Yilmaz (2011).

[7] According to the Copenhagen Criteria, candidate countries need to show 'the stability of institutions guaranteeing democracy, the rule of law, human rights and respect for and protection of minorities' and possess a functioning market economy as well as fulfil the obligations of membership, known as *acquis communautaire* (European Council, 1993, p. 13).

[8] Even though peaceful settlement of disputes and good neighbourly relations has become a criterion to be fulfilled by all candidate states for membership, the EU pressured Turkey on this criterion more than any other candidate state (Saatçioğlu, 2009, p. 567).

[9] Due to the single party government, which held the majority in the parliament, the AKP's policy preferences is relevant in the period between 2002 and 2010.

References

AKP Election Manifesto (2002) Available at http://www.akparti.org.tr/tbmm/belge.asp (accessed 10 June 2010).
Aras, B. & Toktaş, Ş. (2009) The EU and minority rights in Turkey, *Political Science Quarterly*, 124(4), pp. 697–720.
Aybet, G. (2006) Turkey and the EU after the first year of negotiations: Reconciling internal and external policy challenges, *Security Dialogue*, 37(4), pp. 529–549.
Aydin Düzgit, S. (2006) Seeking Kant in the EU's relations with Turkey, *Turkish Economic and Social Studies Foundation (TESEV)* Foreign Policy Program Report, December.
Barrett, S. M. (2004) Implementation studies: Time for a revival? Personal reflections on 20 years of implementation studies, *Public Administration*, 82(2), pp. 249–262.
BBC News Europe (2010) France sends Roma Gypsies back to Romania, 20 August. Available at http://www.bbc.co.uk/news/world-europe-11020429> (accessed 18 June 2011).
Börzel, T. A. (2000) Why there is no 'southern problem'. On environmental leaders and laggards in the European Union, *Journal of European Public Policy*, 7(1), pp. 141–162.
Börzel, T. A. & Risse, T. (2000) When europe hits home: Europeanization and domestic change. *European Integration Online Papers*, 4(15).
Brosig, M. (2010) The challenge of implementing minority rights in Central Eastern Europe, *Journal of European Integration*, 32(4), pp. 393–411.
Çarkoğlu, A. & Kalacıoğlu, E. (2007) *Turkish Democracy Today Elections, Protest and Stability in an Islamic Society* (London: I. B. Tauris).
Duina, F. (1997) Explaining legal implementation in the European Union, *International Journal of the Sociology of Law*, 25, pp. 155–179.
European Commission (2002) Turkey 2002 regular report, SEC (2002) 1412, Brussels.
European Commission (2003) Turkey 2003 progress report, SEC (2003) 1426, Brussels.
European Commission (2004a) Turkey 2004 regular report, SEC (2004) 1201, Brussels.
European Commission (2004b) Issues arising from Turkey's membership perspective, SEC (2004) 1202, Brussels.
European Commission (2004c) Communication from the Commission to the Council and the European Parliament Recommendation of the European Commission on Turkey's progress towards accession, COM (2004)656, Brussels.
European Commission (2005) Turkey 2005 progress report, SEC (2006) 1426, Brussels.
European Commission (2006) Turkey 2006 progress report, SEC (2006) 1390, Brussels.
European Commission (2007) Turkey 2007 progress report, SEC (2007) 1436, Brussels.
European Commission (2008a) Turkey 2008 progress report, SEC (2008) 2699, Brussels.
European Commission (2008b) Enlargement strategy paper, COM (2008) 674 Final, Brussels.
European Commission (2009a) Turkey 2009 progress report, SEC (2009) 1334, Brussels.
European Commission (2009b) Enlargement strategy paper, COM (2009) 533, Brussels.
European Commission (2010a) Turkey 2010 progress report, SEC (2010) 1327, Brussels.
European Commission (2010b) Enlargement strategy paper, COM (2010) 660, Brussels.
European Council (1993) Copenhagen European Council, 21–22 June 1993, presidency conclusions, SN 180/93, Copenhagen.
European Council (2002) Brussels European Council, 24–25 October 2002, presidency conclusions, Brussels.
European Council (2004) Brussels European Council, 25–26 March, presidency conclusions, 9048/04, Brussels.
European Council (2006) Brussels European Council, 11 December 2006, press release 16289/06, Brussels.
European Council (2010) Brussels European Council, 16–17 December, presidency conclusions, Brussels.
Falkner, G., Hartlapp, M. & Treib, O. (2007) Worlds of compliance: Why leading approaches to European Union implementation are only sometimes-true theories, *European Journal of Political Research*, 46(3), pp. 395–416.
Falkner, G. & Treib, O. (2008) Three worlds of compliance or four? The EU-15 compared to new member states, *Journal of Common Market Studies*, 46(2), pp. 293–313.

Freedom House (2007) Countries at the crossroads. Country report – Turkey. Available at http://www.freedomhouse.org/template.cfm?page=140&edition=8&ccrpage=37&ccrcountry=173 (accessed 20 December 2010).

Freedom House (2009) Freedom in the world – Turkey. Available at http://www.freedomhouse.org/template.cfm?page=22&year=2009&country=7722 (accessed 20 December 2010).

Freedom House (2010) Freedom in the world – Turkey. Available at http://www.freedomhouse.org/template.cfm?page=363&year=2010&country=7937 (accessed 20 December 2010).

Grigoriadis, I. (2008) On the Europeanization of minority rights protection: Comparing the cases of Greece and Turkey, *Mediterranean Politics*, 13(1), pp. 23–41.

Güzeldere, E. E. (2009) Turkey: Regional elections and the Kurdish question, *Caucasian Review of International Affairs*, 3(3), pp. 291–306.

Hammarberg, T. (2009) Review report on human rights of minorities, Council of Europe, CommDH (2009)30.

Hartlapp, M. & Leiber, S. (2010) The implementation of EU social policy: The 'southern problem' revisited, *Journal of European Public Policy*, 17(4), pp. 468–486.

Hughes, J. & Sasse G. (2003) Monitoring the monitors: EU enlargement conditionality and minority protection in the CEECs, *Journal on Ethnopolitics and Minority Issues in Europe*, 1(1), pp. 1–36.

Johnson, C. (2006) Use and abuse of minority rights: Assessing past and future EU policies towards accession countries of Central, Eastern and South-Eastern Europe, *The International Journal on Minority and Group Rights*, 13(1), pp. 27–51.

Kelley, J. (2004) *Ethnic Politics in Europe: The power of norms and incentives* (Princeton, NJ: Princeton University Press).

Koutalakis, C. (2004) Environmental compliance in Italy and Greece: The role of non-state actors, *Environmental Politics*, 13(4), pp. 755–775.

Kumbaracibasi, A. C. (2009) *Turkish Politics and the Rise of the AKP* (Routledge: Abingdon).

Larrabee, F. & Tol, G. (2011) Turkey's Kurdish challenge, *Survival*, 53(4), pp. 143–152.

Leiber, S. (2007) Transposition of EU social policy in Poland: Are there different 'worlds of compliance' in East and West?, *Journal of European Social Policy*, 17(4), pp. 349–360.

Liaras, E. (2009) Turkey's party system and the paucity of minority policy reform, *EUI Working Papers, 2009/56*, Florence.

Oran, B. (2004) *Türkiye'de Azınlıklar Kavramlar, Teori, Lozan, İç Mevzuat, İçtihat, Uygulama* (İstanbul: Iletisim).

Oran, B. (2007) The minority concept and rights in Turkey: The Lausanne Peace Treaty and current issues, in: Z. F. Kabasakal Arat (Ed.) *Human Rights in Turkey*, pp. 35–56 (Philadelphia: University of Pennsylvania).

Oran, B. (2009) Western impact and Turkey. Seminar Series in Harvard Kennedy School of Government. Available at http://baskinoran.com/konferanslar.php (accessed 15 June 2010).

Öniş, Z. (2009) The new wave of foreign policy activism in Turkey drifting away from Europeanization? Danish Institute for International Studies, Report 5, Copenhagen.

Özbudun, E. (2006) From political Islam to conservative democracy: The case of the justice and development party in Turkey, *South European Society and Politics*, 11(3/4), pp. 543–557.

Polat, R. K. (2009) The 2007 parliamentary elections in Turkey: Between securitisation and desecuritisation, *Parliamentary Affairs*, 62(1), pp. 129–148.

Ram, M. (2003) Democratization through European integration: The case of minority rights in the Czech Republic and Romania, *Studies in Comparative International Development*, 38(2), pp. 28–56.

Rechel, B. (2008) What has limited the EU's impact on minority rights in accession countries?, *East European Politics and Societies*, 22(1), pp. 171–191.

Risse, T., Caporaso, J. & Cowles, M. G. (Eds) (2001) *Transforming Europe: Europeanization and domestic change* (Ithaca and London: Cornell University Press).

Saatçioğlu, B. (2009) How closely does the European Union's membership conditionality reflect the Copenhagen criteria? Insights from Turkey, *Turkish Studies*, 10(4), pp. 559–576.

Saatçioğlu, B. (2011) Revisiting the role of credible EU membership conditionality for EU compliance: The Turkish case, *Uluslararası İlişkiler (International Relations)*, 8(31), pp. 23–44.

Sasse, G. (2008) The politics of EU conditionality: The norm of minority protection during and beyond EU accession, *Journal of European Public Policy*, 15(6), pp. 842–860.

Schimmelfenning, F. (2008) EU political accession conditionality after the 2004 enlargement: Consistency and effectiveness, *Journal of European Public Policy*, 15(6), pp. 918–937.
Schimmelfenning, F. & Sedelmeier, U. (Eds) (2005) *The Europeanisation of Central and Eastern Europe* (Ithaca and London: Cornell University Press).
Schwellnus, G. (2005) The adoption of non-discrimination and minority protection rules in Romania, Hungary and Poland, in: F. Schimmelfennig & U. Sedelmeier (Eds) *The Europeanisation of Central and Eastern Europe*, pp. 51–70 (Ithaca and London: Cornell University Press).
Secretariat General for EU Affairs of Turkey (2007) *Political Reforms in Turkey*, Ankara. Available at http://egemenbagis.com/wp-content/uploads/2011/09/prt.pdf.
Speech at the AKP Political Group Meeting (2003) 2 December.
Speech at the AKP Political Group Meeting (2005) 22 November.
Speech at the AKP Political Group Meeting (2006) 14 March.
Speech at the AKP Political Group Meeting (2008) 11 November.
Speech at the AKP Political Group Meeting (2009a) 20 October.
Speech at the AKP Political Group Meeting (2009b) 11 August.
Speech at the AKP Political Group Meeting (2009c) 6 January.
Speech at the AKP Political Group Meeting (2010a) 29 June.
Speech at the AKP Political Group Meeting (2010b) 22 June.
Taşkin, Y. (2008) AKP's move to 'conquer' the center-right: Its prospects and possible impacts on the democratization process, *Turkish Studies*, 9(1), pp. 53–72.
Toktaş, Ş. (2006) EU enlargement conditions and minority protection: A reflection on Turkey's non-Muslim minorities, *East European Quarterly*, 40(4), pp. 489–518.
Treib, O. (2008) Implementing and complying with EU governance outputs, *Living Reviews in European Governance*, 3(5), pp. 1–30.
Tsebelis, G. (2002) *Veto Players: How political institutions work* (Princeton: Princeton University Press).
Turkish Official Gazette (2010) No. 27580, 13 May.
UN Human Rights Council (2010) National Report submitted in Accordance with the Paragraph 15 (a) of the Annex to Human Rights Council Resolution 5/1 Turkey, 22 February 2010, A/HRC/WG.6/8/TUR/1.
Yilmaz, G. (2011) Is there a puzzle? Compliance with minority rights in Turkey. *KFG Working Paper Series, No. 23*, January 2011.

Implementation Unwanted? Symbolic vs. Instrumental Policies in the Russian Management of Ethnic Diversity

ALEXANDER OSIPOV
European Centre for Minority Issues (ECMI), Germany

ABSTRACT *The article seeks to suggest a way to explain such cases of minority policies in which deliberate avoidance of implementing certain normative provisions generates no criticism in the given society and goes in combination with the overall silent consent on this state of affairs of all the stakeholders, including minority activists themselves. The author argues that one may regard this as a normal pattern of public politics rather than a deviation, and the lack of implementation as a generally anticipated and accepted outcome rather than a failure. This pattern is labelled as 'systemic hypocrisy', i.e., de-coupling public representation of an organization from its actual functions. It is supposed that diversity policies in general are likely to be prone to systemic hypocrisy since the mainstream group-centric approaches to the management of ethnic diversity are not fully compatible with modern techniques of government. The article exposes and specifies two cases of 'systemic hypocrisy' in minority policies that are non-territorial autonomy and ethnic federalism within the domain of contemporary Russian diversity management. The framework explanation of why systemic hypocrisy demonstrates persistency is that the symbolic policies aimed at ethnic relations become values in themselves as a non-controversial ground of communication for different social and political actors and thus supersede instrumental policies.*

Failure or success of norm implementation pertaining to minority protection can be measured and assessed from different perspectives and according to different sets of criteria. Usually implementation is interpreted as compliance with the existing norms, and compliance is regarded as in principle measurable alignment of the organisation's behaviour and performance with rather static and clearly formalised requirements. In the meantime, compliance does not exist as such beyond norm interpretation and compliance measurement done by some external observer given that both norms and assessment criteria are always context-dependent and are open to interpretations.

Among the incentives for norm implementation is the need to gain acknowledgement and positive reaction of certain external evaluators, whether they were inter-governmental organizations, the voters' majority or certain interest groups. Therefore, convincing the evaluators (or making them pretend that they are convinced) that the demonstrated state of affairs means the desired norm compliance would be the required outcome rather than translation of norms into practice for gaining some material outcome.

EU enlargement process was a clear example of such a sought for a positive external evaluation. The governments seeking accession to the EU first and foremost needed EU's acknowledgement of their countries' compliance with the conditions put forward while in numerous cases they had fewer incentives for the real legislative and political reforms (Cirtautas & Schimmelfennig, 2010, pp. 423–424). In other words, positive evaluation and further accession promised bonuses while new norms and standards implementation entailed costs and political risks (Sasse, 2008). Many Central and Eastern European governments were looking for solutions in separating whenever possible the bargaining with external evaluators from real transformations (Schimmelfennig & Sedelmeier, 2004, pp. 671–684).

This article's main argument is that the strategies of convincing certain target audiences in compliance with or successful implementation of norm pertinent to minority protection by de-coupling 'talks' from 'actions', or, in terms of Nils Brunsson (2007, p. 27; 2009, p. 22), by 'systemic hypocrisy', must be regarded and analysed as a specific type of minority policy. Quite often, domestic minority policies and the respective norm implementation are addressed in terms of failure of a top-down process of norms translation – i.e., negligence, reluctance, or inability to implement. Accordingly, the gap between official representations and performance is assessed as way to circumvent certain requirements and to camouflage this attempt. No doubt, negligence or inability to fulfil certain requirement and then the manoeuvres to justify this may take place.

This article seeks to address another issue and to suggest a way to explain such cases of minority policies in which the alleged lack of implementation turns out to be rather an anticipated and legitimate outcome rather than a failure or deviation. 'Systemic hypocrisy' usually labels a combination of public representation with instrumental activities pursued in the opposite directions (Brunsson, 2009, p. 22; Lipson, 2007).

One may assume that the strategies of policy representation in a way of 'systemic hypocrisy' are pursued notwithstanding whether the target audience was a foreign or domestic one. One should also take into account that attitudes and perceptions of the domestic stakeholders are a more important circumstance than an external evaluation coming from international organisations or academics even if resting on clear formal criteria. Legitimacy of the official policies even among minority spokespersons and a uniform approach to minority issues shared by the rulers and the ruled in a certain country does not represent a unique phenomenon which can be in principle explained by several means, particularly through a Gramscian notion of cultural hegemony (Gramsci, 1971, pp. 245–246; Adamson, 1980). The latter means that the existing social order is discursively framed in a way to persuade the society at large that there is no feasible alternative to the existing social order and that the imposed social norms and the status quo are beneficial to all classes.

My argument here is threefold. First, 'systemic hypocrisy', e.g., the gulf between public representations and actions can be regarded as a widely employed strategy in minority policies and, in particular, an integral component of hegemonic strategies pursued by the ruling elite. Second, a part of representational component in 'systemic hypocrisy' might be so-called 'hidden transcript' – a broad silent agreement within a given society about avoidance of certain issues which can bring about controversies. Third, the very fundamental notions and assumptions of the contemporary minority policies in themselves predetermine 'systemic hypocrisy' and its legitimacy.

'Hypocrisy' is basically about the disjuncture between instrumental and symbolic policies. Symbolic policies can be conceptualized as a sphere where the dominant narrative is produced while instrumental policies are actions resulting in enforcement of concrete strategies and decisions; in the meantime rhetoric can be open to different interpretations while actions may have a symbolic meaning or do not necessarily embody the related rhetoric (Luhmann, 1995). In brief, instrumental policies are viewed as activities having 'resource affects' while 'symbolic' policies have 'interpretative' ones (Schneider & Ingram, 2008, pp. 206–207). Acknowledgement of the very difference between two types of activities often called is nowadays a commonplace for social sciences although there is yet no consent on the definitions and no uniform understanding of how these two areas correspond to each other (Birkland, 2005, pp. 150–151; Schneider & Ingram, 1997, pp. 150–188).

The term 'systemic hypocrisy' was coined by Brunsson (1989) (a similar notion of 'organized hypocrisy' is also introduced by Stephen Krasner, 1999) on the surface means a discrepancy between public representation of an organization (including a state) and its actual functions or/and discrepancies between different units of the same organization. The difference between systemic hypocrisy, on the one hand, and merely intended or unintended incoherence in performances, on the other, is that a certain kind of rhetoric is employed to camouflage and substitute activities completely different in purpose and direction.

> Hypocrisy is a response to a world in which values, ideas, or people are in conflict – a way in which individuals and organizations handle such conflicts. It is a way of trying to satisfy some demands by talk or decisions and others by action. Situations of conflicting demands often make it easier to act in one direction if the decision indicates the opposite. (Brunsson, 2007, p. 9)

> When the Swedish corporation, Ericsson, moved part of its head offices to London, large promotional posters appeared in Swedish cities depicting an enormous Swedish flag with Ericsson as the sender.... And Ericsson would not need to put money into a campaign advertising its Swedishness if it were not moving its head offices abroad. (Brunsson, 2007, pp. 111, 115)

> ... Organizations can reflect inconsistent norms by systematically creating inconsistencies between talk, decisions, and action, i.e., by producing hypocrisy. They can talk in accordance with one set of norms, make decisions in accordance with another, and act according to a third. Hypocrisy easily arises in the political organization, where it is often difficult to implement decisions due to continuous conflict. (Brunsson, 2009, p. 79)

Legal norms and the overall legislative process are belonging to the domain of 'talks' and 'decisions', in Brunsson's terms. One may assume that implementation is not necessarily a condition, when public representation is a value and the goal in itself.

> Organizations embrace specific institutional forms or practices because the latter are widely valued within a broader cultural environment. In some cases, these practices may actually be dysfunctional with regard to achieving the organization's formal goals. Campbell captures this perspective nicely by describing it as a 'logic of social appropriateness' in contrast to a 'logic of instrumentality'. (Hall & Taylor, 1996, p. 949)

Along with this, in practical terms, the creation and existence of certain legal provisions can be employed to camouflage or blur the meaning of certain actions or to divert the public agenda from discussions on unwelcomed issues.

Systemic hypocrisy in some cases goes hand in hand with 'hidden transcript' (the notion introduced by James Scott, 1990), or avoidance of explicit prescriptions or narrations on certain issues in the setup of public representation. In other words, representational component or 'talks' are shaped and designed in a way to increase its discursive appropriateness and the degree of its compliance with public expectations. Although any official text can be interpreted in different ways, its meaning rests on shared knowledge, on linguistic games (in Wittgenstein's terms) and silent consent of the rulers and the ruled. Certain social phenomena, although a common knowledge, may not correspond with the public stance of the government and/or the citizenry; therefore the both chose to keep them offstage and not to address them publicly (Scott, 1990, pp. 51, 105).

One can expect that ethnic, or diversity policies are particularly likely to generate 'hypocrisy' and 'hidden transcripts'. It's a common knowledge that the international (as well as domestic) norms pertinent to minority protection are vaguely formulated (and that became abundantly clear during the EU enlargement and the respective evaluation procedures (Brosig, 2010, pp. 401–408)). Along with this, national governments for a variety of reasons are basically reluctant to go beyond minimal standards. Besides this, the way the issues of ethno–cultural diversity are framed impedes translation of ideas into practice. Modern diversity discourses are resting on the explanatory frames adequately depicted with the term 'groupism'. 'Groupism' is:

> ... the tendency to take discrete, sharply differentiated, internally homogeneous, and externally bounded groups as basic constituents of social life, chief protagonists of social conflicts, and fundamental units of social analysis. (Brubaker et al., 2004, p. 45)

On paper, society can be portrayed as a combination of ethnic groups perceived as internally coherent social units and social actors as such, but one cannot technically act in accordance with this basic assumptions and create a social and political space segregated along ethnic lines.

Therefore, one may look for systemic hypocrisy where an organization (a government in particular) employs the rhetoric of group rights which must be at odd with modern regulatory mechanisms based on individual autonomy and individual rights. Rhetoric of group entitlements and group autonomy is widely employed internationally, basically in 'soft law' provisions without corresponding practical measures (Osipov, 2011). Similar official wording takes place in numerous countries (like Bolivia, China or Ethiopia), which are often far from the ideals of liberal democracy and consistency in minority protection. Below I intend to describe two cases (both are from the Russian Federation) which exemplify how a large-scale manufacture of group rights rhetoric by state and non-state actors turns into 'hypocrisy' and 'hidden transcripts' which become part and parcel of ethnic policies.

The said mass production of group rights rhetoric can be regarded as a long-lasting tradition inherited from the Soviet past. From the very outset of the Soviet rule, the official vocabulary included 'voluntary union of peoples', 'equality and sovereignty of peoples', 'peoples' right to free self-determination', 'free development of national minorities and ethnic groups', and eventually of the 'peoples' (Connor, 1984). All these terms are still widely employed in the official legislation and declarations as well as in the scholarly literature (Karapetian, 2001; Mikhalenok & Melnikova, 2011). The symbolic participation of Russian ethnicities in the state-building rests on the constitutional provision; the 1993 Constitution's Preamble declares the 'principle of peoples' equal rights and self-determination'. Equality is described mostly as securing 'internal self-determination' for all ethnicities (Samoilenko, 2008; Tarasov, 2002; Fomichenko, 2005). Below I intend to describe two frameworks, which pertain both to discursive and institutional territorialisation and deterritorialisation of ethnicity; most scholars traditionally perceive ethnic federalism and supplementary policies labelled as non-territorial autonomy as the core components of the Russian diversity policies (Huttenbach, 1990, pp. 19–20; Laitin, 1998, pp. 67–68; Slocum, 1995; Pain, 1995, pp. 71–87).

Russia is regularly criticized by the Council of Europe institutions for the violation of its standards (Advisory, 2006); simultaneously, Russia as a rule neglects and even objects this criticism (Bowring, 2008, 2009). In the meanwhile, opinions of the international human rights bodies about Russia draw virtually no attention and get no press inside the country. The rhetoric concerning ethnic issues basically targets domestic audiences, and it's important to assess its purposes and effects.

Non-territorial Autonomy

Non-territorial autonomy for ethnic group (usually referred to within the former Soviet Union as 'national–cultural autonomy') and related notions are widely used in the Russian legislation and official statements as well as in academic and popular discourses. Russian officials, ethnic activists and academics regularly mention non-territorial autonomy as an important achievement and a key instrument of the domestic ethno–cultural policy.

> National–cultural autonomy is an important instrument for the identification and satisfaction of citizens' ethno–cultural demands, of achieving inter-ethnic stability and prevention of conflicts on ethnic ground. Being an ex-territorial public entity, national–cultural autonomy without diminishing the rights of the Russian Federation's constituent units safeguarded by the Russian

Federation's Constitution, widens their opportunities and responsibility in the pursuant of the state nationalities policy.[1]

Vladimir Zorin, Chair of the Russian parliamentary Committee on Nationalities Affairs:

> The Law [on national–cultural autonomy] is really unique in the opportunities it gives for the utilization of the peoples' of Russia creative potential, so that it seems that we have not realized this ourselves so far. (Zorin, 1999b, pp. 48–49)

Vladimir Bauer, Deputy Minister of Nationalities Affairs: 'the Law establishes a mechanism for parity-based relations between the state and public movements... an efficient tool of national self-determination' (Bauer, 1999, p.16).

Ramazan Abdulatipov, Minister of Nationalities Affairs:

> The law grants our citizens wide opportunities for the preservation of their cultural uniqueness in the framework of national–cultural self-government, and it also defines the state's responsibility in this sphere of nationalities policy. (Abdulatipov, 1999, p. 4)

Describing and assessing national–cultural autonomy merely as a set of legislative provisions and practices of implementation however does not answer the question about the gap between the high symbolic status and limited instrumental value of the organizations called 'national–cultural autonomies' (Osipov, 2004).

The very idea of national–cultural autonomy goes back to the European liberal and socialist thinkers of the late nineteenth century, who put forward plans for the non-territorial organization of ethnic groups (Renner, 2005, pp. 15–47; Eide et al., 1998, pp. 251–276). National–cultural autonomy was a topical issue in the early twentieth century discussions on the left of Russia's political spectrum'; the idea was rejected and condemned in the Soviet period, but reconsidered and extensively debated in the 1980s and 1990s. The notion of national–cultural autonomy was introduced into Russia's legislation in the aftermath of the Soviet Union's breakdown; the basic act determining the respective policies – the Federal law 'On National–Cultural Autonomy'[2] (hereinafter, 'the NCA Law') – was adopted in 1996.

The term 'national–cultural autonomy' has acquired two basic meanings in the Russian domestic legislation and in the NCA law in particular (Osipov, 2004, pp. 112–150; Stepanov, 2004). The first refers to a general principle by which individuals use various institutional formats to collectively pursue their rights and interests related to their ethnic origin, language, and culture. The second indicates a specific form of ethnicity-based non-governmental organization (hereinafter NGO).

The gaps between public representations and real way the national–cultural autonomy functions manifest themselves in three areas. First, the legislation disadvantages organizations having the formal status of 'national–cultural autonomy' (hereinafter NCA in the meaning of special NGO type) in comparison with other types of NGOs which may also be ethnicity-based. Second, the government has not demonstrated sufficient and coherent efforts to implements the legal provisions concerning NCA. Third, in fact there have been only few limited attempts to treat NCAs differently (in practical, but not symbolic terms) from other NGOs.

In the general meaning of the law, NCAs have two main functions: (a) to carry out their own activities in the promotion of language, education, and culture; and (b) to advise government authorities and official institutions on these issues.

An ordinary non-profit non-governmental organization, while enjoying all the rights that NCAs are granted (including rights in the spheres of culture, mass media, and education), has an advantage *vis-à-vis* NCAs: national–cultural autonomies (a) enjoy fewer rights than ordinary public associations; (b) cannot choose their organizational forms; and (c) face numerous procedural restrictions with respect to their establishment and operation.

The NCA Law contains exhaustive lists of permissible activities (Art. 1) exclusively in the spheres of language, culture, and education. The rights granted to NCAs (Art. 4) are expressly limited to the spheres of 'preserving identities, promoting the language, education, and national [ethnic] culture'. This specification of permissible activities is absent in the general laws on non-profit organizations and public associations.

The 2003 amendments to the NCA Law prescribe only *one* institutional format based on fixed individual membership; less burdensome and more flexible forms have been excluded.

The law does not restrict the number of NCAs established on behalf of a certain ethnic group within a certain territory. For years, however, the territorial departments of justice have, as a rule, denied the registration of parallel NCAs.[3] In March 2004, the Constitutional Court of the Russian Federation ruled that no more than one local or regional autonomy per ethnic community could be set up in a municipality or a region,[4] respectively, thus authorizing the current restrictive practices.

The creation and maintenance of an NCA is more complex in comparison with other kinds of NGOs (Osipov, 2010, pp. 57–60), and this make NCAs dependent (even more than other NGOs) on the discretion of registering and supervisory authorities.

The provisions of the NCA Law that describe relations between NCAs and the government are worded nebulously. Verbs are used in the present tense – e.g., authorities support, assist, consider submitted proposals, take them into account, make resources available, etc. In the existing legal culture, such wording is interpreted to mean that authorities may choose to support and listen to NCAs but have no obligation to do so.[5]

There is no specific obligation for the government to provide funding for NCAs, and the NCA law fails to identify specific mechanisms and criteria for funding allocation as well as specific government bodies empowered to make funding decisions. In fact, the legislation on public associations and non-profit organizations in theory offers ordinary non-profit organizations more forms and grounds on which to request state support. NCAs are financed from public resources on an *ad hoc* and irregular basis; and there have not been any motions to delegate to NCAs any functions or competence with respect to cultural activities or education.

The concept of 'autonomy', nevertheless, sounds attractive to ethnic activists. Despite legislative restrictions and bureaucratic burdens, the number of NCAs has grown over the years. By early 1999, 227 NCAs had been registered, of which 160 were local, 60 regional, and 7 federal (Zorin, 1999a, p. 16). On 1 April 2010, there were 759 organizations, of which 532 were local, 210 regional, and 17 federal.[6] NCAs represent 59 ethnicities including ethnic Russians, even in the regions where Russians constitute the majority, and groups traditionally deemed to be sub-ethnic or ethnographic categories.

The NCA law was amended several times, but the implementation either did not follow or was inconsistent. From late 1990s, governmental official demonstrated concern about NCAs representing ethnic majorities or 'titular' ethnic groups and commented such situations (although rare) as unacceptable anomalies. In 1999–2003, the federal ministries of justice and of nationalities affairs did their best to deny official registration to the newly established federal NCA of ethnic Russians. The amendments of November 2003 imposed a restriction on ethnic ground in terms that an NCA could be set up only on behalf of a group in a position of ethnic minority within the given territory although no law determined what such 'position of ethnic minority' meant. Since the 2003, the law in a formal sense also has not allowed multi-ethnic, coalition-based NCAs.

Nevertheless, very little was done to put these restrictions into practice or the enforcement was contradictory. Most of the existing multi-ethnic NCAs and NCAs of regional majorities (including ethnic Russians) or 'titular' groups were allowed to remain active or were registered anew. For example, in 2008, the local Jewish NCA was officially registered in the Jewish Autonomous Oblast, while the local Buryat NCA in the Republic of Buryatia was denied registration. Until 2009, nothing happened to the regional Karachay NCA in the Karachay–Circassian Republic while the regional NCA of Adygs (who include Circassians) was registered in 2006. Moreover, after 2003, two new multi-ethnic Dagestani NCAs were established in the cities of Kaluga and Tver, and the Turkic NCA (for Azeris and Tatars) was re-established in the Yamalo–Nenetsk Autonomous *Okrug*.

Both government officials and ethnic leaders have repeatedly voiced and endorsed the idea that an NCA should be the single legitimate representative of its ethnic community in relations with the authorities (Drobizheva, 2003, p. 101). The major rationale of the Constitutional Court's ruling on the case of 'parallel' NCAs mentioned above (see Endnote 3) was the argument that an NCA was the only one legitimate representative of its respective ethnic group within the given territorial unit. In practice, however, little has been done to make this principle a reality. The Federal Consultative Council on NCA Affairs, in 1997–2003 under the government, convened irregularly.[7] Re-established in 2007 under the federal ministry of regional development, it has lost most of its significance, because it provides no direct contact between NCA leaders and federal ministers. Seven regions established consultative bodies for NCAs,[8] and of them four have survived to date. The Advisory Committee on the Framework Convention for the Protection of National Minorities repeatedly concluded that the existing mechanisms were falling short of Article 15 requirements concerning participation of minorities in public life (Advisory, 2006, para. 266–269). In general, regional and local authorities interact and communicate with all ethnic minority organizations without any preference to NCAs.

NCAs coexist with other, more numerous ethnicity-based NGOs,[9] and the models of coexistence vary. In practice, NCAs like all other ethno–cultural NGOs are preoccupied primarily with folk arts. Few engage in long-term projects related to education, research, mass media, public advocacy, or inter-regional ties (for an overview see Mukomel, 2003; also Osipov, 2004, pp. 161–224).

Nevertheless, the contradictions in and around the law have drawn no public attention and brought about no protests of the law's potential beneficiaries. Official spokespersons, ethnic activists, and academics basically pay attention to abstract issues (like of which groups should be entitled to create NCAs) and neglect practicalities like NCAs rights and procedures of establishment. The requests of ethnic activists for some public funding do not imply any kind of objection to the fundamentals of the ideology of national–cultural autonomy as the government formulates it.

In the early 1990s, a number of scholars and officials explained that national–cultural autonomy would be a way to depart from the erroneous Soviet tradition of creating hierarchies of peoples; on the contrary, they said, cultural autonomy would mean the acknowledgement of all groups as equal participants in the country's 'nationalities policy' (Pain, 1995, p. 86; Pain, 2004, p. 169). A common position of many authors is that involvement of ethnic groups in dialog with the state, and thus their symbolic recognition, may be expected to pacify public unrest and tensions and, therefore, to contribute to social cohesion and integration.

Alongside this, the very topic of national–cultural autonomy creates substitutions to the agenda of equality on ethnic grounds. Issues of non-discrimination are not salient in Russian public discussions, either in terms of the treatment of individuals or structural conditions for social dynamics and mobility. Public attention is focused on extreme manifestations of ethnic enmity or on cultural policies and thus diverted from equality issues which are overshadowed by such rhetoric figures as 'non-territorial self-determination', 'equal opportunities in cultural development' or just 'development' (Samoilenko, 2008, pp. 2633–2638; Tarasov, 2002, pp. 56–74; Fomichenko, 2005, pp. 35–41).

The idea of NCA for ethnic majorities, or titular ethnicities, was vehemently and almost univocally criticized by public authorities, intellectuals and most ethnic activists. This attitude stemmed from the consideration that such an undertaking would be a violation of equality: majorities and titular groups maintain control over their own structures of government, and the creation of NCAs in addition would give them an unfair advantage in comparison with minorities (Churbakov, 1999, pp. 74–75). Thus idioms of 'autonomy' and 'development' replace the issue of social equality in favour of seeking 'fair' relationships between ethnicities. The organization of social space along ethnic lines means a symbolic assignment of different and unequal positions to various ethnic communities. Although the stakeholders are aware that this imagined status assignment does not relate to resource distribution and to human daily life at large they don't question or dismiss this agenda.

Territorial Autonomy or Ethnic Federalism

Federalism envisaging certain degree of autonomy granted to ethnically defined territorial units are also routinely regarded as a fundament of the Soviet and nowadays Russian model of diversity policies. In numerous official statements the Russian federalism is justified in terms of 'peoples' right to self-determination' while 'peoples' are interpreted as ethnic categories; besides, federalism is often rhetorically merged with and also regarded as partly a synonym to 'nationalities policies'. In formal sense, this approach is stipulated in the Russian constitutional and legal provisions. Article 5, part 3 of the Russian Constitution declares that 'the federal structure of the Russian Federation is based' among other things:

> ... on... the division of subjects of authority and powers between the bodies of state power of the Russian Federation and bodies of state power of the subjects of the Russian Federation, the equality and self-determination of peoples in the Russian Federation.[10]

This official approach goes hand in hand with the common assumption, mostly taken for granted, is that the Russian Federation is built on two pillars: the territorial and the 'national–territorial' (that is, ethnicity-based) principles. Three types of constituent units (referred to as 'federation subjects' in Russia) – republics, one autonomous *oblast* (province), and autonomous *okrugs* (districts) – are considered to be 'national' (that is, 'ethnic') entities; in other words, they are depicted as the 'possession' or forms of organization of specific ethnic groups (Abdulatipov, 2000; Medvedev, 2005; Turovski, 2006, pp. 440–64; Lapidus & Walker, 1995, pp. 218–240; Bremmer, 1993), while the others (*krais*, *oblasts*, federal cities) are seen as purely territorial units.

It is widely believed that Soviet/Russian federalism grants a special status and bestows special advantages on the ethnic groups, possessing statehood or territorial autonomy (Shtromas, 1978, pp. 266, 269), thus creating a formal hierarchy of ethnic communities (Bremmer, 1993, pp. 5–6, 13–17; Roeder, 1991, pp. 204–2008; Slocum, 1995, p. 46).

In the meantime, it remains highly questionable that in fact the Russian ethnicity-based federalism provides institutional framework for the collective organization, participation and social development along ethnic lines as well as for the redistribution of resources in favour of ethnic groups allegedly dominating certain federation units. Even such privileged access to resources and to participation in public life manifests itself, it might be questioned that it is a direct outcome of the ethnicity-based territorial structure. Alongside this, the Russian federalism turns out to be a clear case of 'hidden transcript' when all agents involved steadily refrain from interpreting verbal formulas which lack clarity but are supposed to be legal fundament on one of the key institutions of the Russian statehood.

Even though some federation subjects take the name of their 'titular'[11] ethnic group, neither the constitution nor the legislation explicitly define the republics, autonomous *okrugs* and the autonomous *oblasts* as entities established on ethnic ground. The law neither implies that there is a legal relationship between an ethnic group and a specific state formation nor allows for special treatment of the 'titular' group in any subject of the federation. No references to ethnicity can be found in the major laws concerning the structure of the federation and the vertical division of powers.[12]

At the regional level, the constitutions and charters of republics and autonomous districts often contain ambiguous expressions and internal contradictions that are open to widely different legal interpretations. There is no uniform model that describes the link between ethnicity and the territory, and in some cases the legislation omits any references to such connections. Constitutions and charters adopted in the early 1990s either completely fail to mention the 'titular' groups or speak of 'self-determination of the titular nation' (while at the same time identifying the entire population as the source of political power), or they emphasize the special role reserved to the 'titular' group without any reference to their participation in politics and government.[13] For example, the preamble to the 1994 constitution of Tatarstan states that the constitution expresses 'the will of the *multi-national* people of the Republic of Tatarstan *and the Tatar people*', whereas according to Article 1, part 1, 'the holder of sovereignty and the only source of political power in the Republic of Tatarstan is its multi-national people'.[14]

The constitution of the Republic of Sakha contains no references to the Yakut ethnicity; it uses the term 'national state status' (Chapter 3), but declares that the republic's population, consisting of citizens of all nationalities, is the source of state power and that no one segment of the population can usurp the right to exercise such power (Article 1, part 4).[15]

In total, two regional constitutions contain a reference to the self-determination of their 'titular' ethno-nations; three refer to the self-determination of the 'titular' nations together with all their populations; two posit a special symbolic position of the titular groups; five mention that the specific feature of their statehood relates to the 'titular' people. Eight constitutions fix the regional governments' obligation to secure and promote culture of the 'titular' groups; five declare the government's concern over the 'titular groups' diasporas outside the respective territories. Also eight constitutions have no references to 'titular' ethnicities; of them four mention 'native peoples' in plural without naming them and one (the constitution of Khakassia) mentions the 'native people' in single.[16]

According to some regional constitutions and charters, the government is obliged to support the language and culture of specific groups. However, this obligation can hardly be regarded as a clear sign of 'ethnic' statehood. First, such provisions appear in the constitutions and charters of some constituent republics and autonomous districts, but not in others. Second, charters and laws of some oblasts and *krais* also refer to the specific role of certain ethnic groups or contain pledges to support their cultures and customs. For instance, the charter of Pskov *oblast*'[17]) contains an article that guarantees 'the rights of the Setu people to their original environment, identity, language, self-governance, customs and traditions'.[18]

The charters of all autonomous *okrugs* contain provisions concerning indigenous peoples; in most cases they are referred to in the plural without listing their individual names. Similar formulations appear in the charters of the oblasts where ethnic groups are officially acknowledged as 'small indigenous peoples'. However, unlike the oblasts, autonomous *okrugs* are perceived as 'ethnic' states.

Regional laws of the republics do not contain more specific definitions. Thus, to sum up, in the formal sense there are no clear constitutional or legal provisions in Russia establishing any tangible legal link between specific 'titular' groups and the administrative units to which these groups belong.

In some constituent republics, the languages of 'titular' ethnic groups are declared the state languages, alongside the Russian language, as provided for by Article 68, part 2 of the Russian Constitution. However, such declarations cannot be equated with a special status granted to certain ethnicities, as this rests on the doubtful assumption that a language may always be treated as an attribute of a specific ethnic group. Some constituent republics have no regional state or official languages (examples are Karelia and Dagestan[19]). In other cases, official status has been granted to the languages of groups other than those of the 'titular' ethnicity. Thus, for example, the Republic of Karachay–Circassia recognizes five official languages (the Abazin and Nogai languages alongside Karachay, Circass and Russian).

The mostly important point here is also the lack of a clear correlation between the legal provisions defining the status and the institutions of the republics, the autonomous *oblast* and autonomous *okrugs* and their respective domestic policies, just as in the legal domain there is no uniform model in political and social life. Across the federation there are multiple ways in which ethnic or linguistic differences materialize in public space. The legal status of an 'ethnic' entity does not in itself determine the extent and nature of the protection it offers its 'titular' ethnic group (or groups): there are no uniform political or social policies aimed at 'titular' ethnicities.

In reality, regional governments do things that could be accessed as preferential treatment of 'titular' ethnic groups. This may include granting official status to local languages, support for their public use, symbolic recognition of the special role played by 'titular' groups, funding of cultural and educational institutions, and high visibility of that 'titular' population in the media. However, these elements of domestic policies are not to be found in all republics and autonomous *okrugs*. Regional governments actively promote the teaching of official languages in Tatarstan and Tyva, but neglect this in North Ossetia and Kalmykia. The types of regional linguistic regimes vary substantially. For example, the Tatar language is widely employed in the official sphere in Tatarstan, whereas North Ossetia, Karelia, Komi and Kalmykia are almost exclusively Russian-speaking in both public and private domains.

Noteworthy is the virtual lack of judicial decisions or official comments clarifying the linkage between ethnicity and territory, particularly the meaning of symbolic distinction between 'titular' and 'non-titular' ethnicities. Important things are also a negligible number of public protests against 'ethnic federalism' from within the republics and autonomous *okrug*s themselves and no attempts to challenge it in the Constitutional Court of Russian Federation.

Interestingly, although these questions related to the essence of the Russian ethnic federalism are debated in Russia, but rather as a marginal issue. In particular, the nature and manifestations of what could be called 'ethnic statehood' are rarely debated in the academic literature. Mainstream experts and politicians avoid the issue of contradiction between, ethnic statehood, and the principle of popular sovereignty and equality of citizens before the law. The creation of statehood on ethnic ground turns out to be a self-evident truism, or a cliché, that does not need rationalization. There are very few scholars or politicians who address the issue of disproportions in the ethnic composition of regional parliaments, civil service and business elites in the republics where the so-called 'titular' nationalities are overrepresented. Few authors depict this phenomenon is 'ethnocracy' (Toshenko, 2003; Filippov, 2003; Valentei, 2000), but virtually make no attempt to analyse the existing mechanisms of exclusion.

In sum, the Russian federal system acknowledges certain linkage between ethnicity and territory; the latter is embedded in law although in a blurry way and is commented on officially and unofficially. In the meantime, this symbolic and discursive linkage is not translated into practice or translated in diverse or inconsistent ways. The allegedly fundamental legal principles of the Russian statehood are implemented on the *ad hoc* and selective basis. Also the government and the general public employ 'hidden transcript' avoiding explicit references to the issues which must steer up controversies. Meanwhile, this state of affairs is widely accepted and not contested or criticised at large, and one can hardly speak about a failure in implementation.

Conclusion

The both cases pertain to the key issues of the country's ethnic policies; nevertheless, one can repeatedly notice no attempts of the government within the last 20 years to clarify and instrumentalise the framework norms even through political statements or by pursuing a clear-cut strategy. One can see a set of implications buried in the law rather clearly formulated provisions; these loose ideas are only occasionally formulated in public debated by politicians, mass media and academic experts. The relevance and value of these implications are never contested publicly and are silently taken for granted.

In a nutshell – certain ideas are loudly pronounced and embedded in law, but their instrumental value is doubtful and implementation is insufficient and inconsistent. As in the case of 'ethnic federalism', there is also a 'hidden transcript' – practical drawbacks of the law and its limited practicality are not discussed. Surprisingly, one can observe virtually no public dissatisfaction with this situation; all potential stakeholders and beneficiaries are bonded and constrained with the established agenda and scenarios for addressing the issue in public and very few if any try to violate the rules of the game.

Nothing in the stakeholders' behaviour can be interpreted as a strategy aiming at creating or employing certain regulatory mechanisms. Noteworthy is also the reluctance of other actor including politicians, ethnic activists, mass media and academics to initiate any public discussion. Individual statements or publications raising the issues that one can deem crucial in theory remain isolated occasions resulting in no further repercussions.

The purposes and rationales of 'talk' are different from those of 'actions'; self-representation of an organization (in our case, the state), thus, is not oriented at the achievement of specific instrumental goals; rather, it depends on the perceived external demand for speech of a certain kind. The organization says or omits to say whatever it believes it is expected to say or not to say.

How does 'hypocrisy' work? First and foremost, it allows for avoiding controversies in public domain and the complications. Direct and consistent implementation of the principles pertaining to 'ethnic federalism' would mean discrimination against certain classes of citizenry on ethnic or linguistic ground. In the meantime, the mainstream public figures refrain from debating the essence of 'ethnic statehood' since the opposite would mean a clear emphasis on the existence of first- and second-class citizens on certain territories. Also a clear rejection or criticism of 'ethnic federalism' would be an encroachment on the deeply entrenched moral and ideological justification of the existing statehood. Therefore, all stakeholders resort to 'hidden transcript', avoid implementation of the respective principles and use them selectively and inconsistently for limited purposes.

Likewise, real cultivation of 'national–cultural autonomies' would mean creation of segregated public spaces and discrimination against non-governmental organizations on the ground of their legal status or ethnic affiliation; moreover, this policy may entail growing budgetary expenditures for the support of minority institutions. On the other hand, stressing the instrumental impracticality of cultural autonomy in public would compromise one of the main pillars of the official policies.

Simultaneously, symbolic policies directly unrelated to practicalities create a basic interpretative scheme which establishes a non-controversial ground of communication. It serves as a legitimizing macro-narrative for different social and political actors, a kind of social mythology (in Lyotard's terms) which provides for the general ideological cohesion. All stakeholders who share the same assumptions and expectations and turn out to be bonded and constrained by the same discursive matrix which eliminates demand for practically relevant action. In the meantime, the overt discussion of certain issues do not fit into this protocol of communication and thus avoided; the Russian authorities and the general public resort to 'hidden transcript'.

This basic interpretative frame rests on portraying a given society (Russian in this case) as a combination of ethnic groups as 'collective individuals' brought in some symbolic hierarchical system. The latter means not only recognition of ethnic diversity but also, and even more important, the creation and legitimization of a taxonomy of ethnic groups in Russia. The legislation, along with the other discursive vehicles, reproduces the dominant narrative (with all its figures of preterition), including systematization of ethnic groups and some general ideas concerning protection and promotion of ethnic identities and cultures.

'Ethnic federalism' and national–cultural autonomy seem to be an instrument for the exercise of power, but power should not be understood here as a system of coercion. The state apparatus does not impose these broad ideological repertoires on the public; there are no concurrent and competing agendas in Russia at all. The established symbolic order and the accepted narratives still limit and channel the emerging claims related to the ethnic configuration of society. Government officials, civic activists, academics, and the mass media play the same game and share the same language, perceptions, and hierarchy of priorities. Power functions as a wide range of control and disciplinary techniques embedded in society itself, and it remains invisible, being literally kept out of politics in the narrow sense (Foucault, 2007).

The Russian case cannot be deemed unique. The repertoires of systemic hypocrisy and usage of 'hidden transcript' should be looked for first and foremost when ethnic policies and the respective legislations are analysed. Minds are 'colonised' with ethnicity or, more precisely, with 'groupist' worldview. The ideas of ethnic identity, equality of groups and value of group cultural authenticity have gained global acknowledgement. Meanwhile, there straightforward and consistent implementation is hardly compatible with market-based and individualistic open society. 'Systemic hypocrisy' and 'hidden transcripts' seem to become a tool for reconciling the irreconcilables. 'There is still a lack of implementation, but no implementation *problem*. Instead, hypocrisy is a solution – a solution to several problems' (Brunsson, 2007, p. 116). 'Talks' are generally welcome while actions are neglected by the public; the official policies gain legitimacy and do not entail unwanted protests and claims.

Notes

[1] Kontseptsiia Natsional'noi Politiki Rossiiskoi Federatsii, Ukaz Prezidenta RF 'Ob utverzhdenii Kontseptsii Natsional'noi Politiki Rossiiskoi Federatsii', No. 909, signed 15 June 1996, *Sobranie Zakonodatel'stva Rossiiskoi Federatsii* (SZRF) (1996) No. 25, item 3010. Translated by the author.

[2] Federal'nyi zakon 'O natsional'no-kul'turnoi avtonomii' (with subsequent amendments), No. 74-FZ, signed 17 June 1996, *SZRF* (1996) No.25, item 2965.

[3] This means only NCAs of the same territorial level. Local NCAs are not obliged to join regional NCAs of the same group operating on the same territory. Likewise, regional NCAs are not forced to become parts of federal NCAs.

[4] Postanovlenie Konstitutsionnogo Suda RF ot 3 marta 2004 goda No.5 'Po delu o proverke konstitutsionnosti chasti tret'ei stati 5 Federal'nogo zakona "O natsional'no-kul'turnoi avtonomii" v sviazi s zhaloboi grazhdan A.H.Ditsa i O.A.Shumachera', *SZRF* (2004) No. 11, item 1033.

[5] Russian public officials repeatedly recognized the non-obligatory character of these provisions; see, for instance statements made by the staff of the State Duma Nationalities Committee at an ECMI seminar held in 2001 in Kaliningrad (Martynuk, 2003).

[6] Calculated according to the Ministry of Justice database, Available at: http://www.minjust.ru/common/img/uploaded/docs/2010.03.09_NKA_na_01.01.2010.xls (accessed 26 August 2010).

[7] The Council convened eight times in five years (1997–2001) (Osipov, 2004, p. 193).

[8] Komi Republic, Penza, Tambov, Tula, Tver', Tiumen and Ulianovsk oblasts; the NCA councils in Tambov, Tiumen and Ulianovsk have been reconfigured and renamed.

[9] The total number of ethnicity-based NGOs is unknown and official estimates differ; according to a recent data provided by the Ministry of Justice for Russia's official report on the fulfillment of its obligations under the FCNM, there were approximately 2,600 ethnicity-based NGOs aside from NCAs throughout the country by 1 January 2009 (calculated according to: ANNEXES, 2010, Annexes 2 and 3).

[10] The 1993 Constitution of the Russian Federation. Official translation. Available at http://www.government.ru/eng/gov/base/54.html (accessed 31 March 2012).

[11] The term 'titular' currently denotes ethnic groups that give names to the respective territorial unit which they populate.

[12] For example, in the federal law 'On the General Principles of Organization of the Legislative (Representative) and Executive Organs of the State Power in the Constituent Regions of the Russian Federation' (No. 184-FZ) of 6 October 1999, and the Federal Constitutional Law, 'On the Process of Accession to the Russian Federation and Foundation of a New Constituent Unit of the Russian Federation' (No. 6) of 17 December 2001.

[13] Basically, the compromise approach towards defining the ethnic character of republic statehood has not changed throughout the 1990s and the following decade, but some constitutions of the early 1990s contained a number of radical provisions that were deleted after Vladimir Putin came to power in 2000. For more on the early versions of republican constitutions (see Guboglo, 2000, pp. 154–164).

[14] 'Constitution of the Republic of Tatarstan'. Official portal of the Tatarstan government. Official translation. Available at http://portal.tatarstan.ru/eng/documents/constitution.htm (accessed 9 December 2011; emphasis added).

[15] 'Konstitutsiya (Osnovnoi zakon) Respubliki Sakha (Yakutiya). Official information portal of the government of the Republic Sakha (Yakutia). The authors' translation. Available at: http://sakha.gov.ru/node/17668 (accessed 29 May 2011).

[16] The texts overviewed at the website of the legal information system 'Garant', http://www.constitution.garant.ru/DOC_7000.htm (accessed 29 May 2011).

[17] 'Ustav Pskovskoi oblasti'. Website of the legal information system 'Garant'. The authors' translation. Available at http://www.constitution.garant.ru/DOC_16603701.htm (accessed 12 June 2012).

[18] Setu is an Orthodox Christian group speaking Estonian and living on both sides of the Russian–Estonian border.
[19] The Constitution of Dagestan declared as state languages alongside Russian the languages of unspecified 'peoples of Dagestan'.

References

Abdulatipov, R. (1999) Natsional'no-kulturanaya avtonomiya: u neie bolshoye budushee, *Zhizn' natsionalnostei*, 1(8), pp. 3–11.

Abdulatipov, R. (2000) *Natsionalnyi vopros i gosudarstvennoe ustroistvo Rossii* (Moscow: Slavyanskii dialog).

Adamson, W. L. (1980) *Hegemony and Revolution: Antonio Gramsci's political and cultural theory* (Berkeley and Los Angeles: University of California Press).

Advisory Committee on the Framework Convention for the Protection of National Minorities. Second opinion on the Russian Federation, adopted on 11 May 2006, ACFC/OP/II(2006)004. Available at http://www.coe.int/t/dghl/monitoring/minorities/3_FCNMdocs/PDF_2nd_OP_RussianFederation_en.pdf (accessed 23 October 2012).

ANNEXES 2–6 to the third report submitted by the Russian Federation pursuant to article 25, paragraph 1 of the Framework Convention for the Protection of National Minorities (2010) ACFC/SR/III(2010)005. Strasbourg, 9 April 2010. Available at http://www.coe.int/t/dghl/monitoring/minorities/3_FCNMdocs/PDF_3rd_SR_RussianFed_annexes2-6_en.pdf (accessed 23 October 2012).

Bauer, V. (1999) Novaya forma natsionalnogo samoopredeleniya: problemy i perspektivy, *Zhizn' natsionalnostei*, 1(8), pp. 14–20.

Birkland, T. A. (2005) *An Introduction to the Policy Process: Theories, concepts, and models of public policy making* (Armonk, NY: M.E. Sharpe).

Bowring, B. (2008) Russia and international law, *The EU–Russia Centre Review*, 8, pp. 1–10.

Bowring, B. (2009) Russia and human rights: Incompatible opposites?, *Göttingen Journal of International Law*, 1(2), pp. 257–278.

Bremmer, I. (1993) Introduction. Reassessing Soviet nationalities theory, in: I. Bremmer & R. Taras (Eds) *Nations and Politics in the Soviet Successor States*, pp. 3–26 (Cambridge: Cambridge University Press).

Brosig, M. (2010) The challenge of implementing minority rights in Central Eastern Europe, *European Integration*, 32(4), pp. 393–411.

Brubaker, R., Loveman, M. & Stamatov, P. (2004) Ethnicity as cognition, *Theory and Society*, 33(1), pp. 31–64.

Brunsson, N. (1989) *The Organization of Hypocrisy. Talk, decisions and actions in organizations* (Chinchester, NY: John Wiley & Sons).

Brunsson, N. (2007) *The Consequences of Decision-making* (Oxford: Oxford University Press).

Brunsson, N. (2009) *Reform as Routine. Organizational change and stability in the modern world* (Oxford: Oxford University Press).

Churbakov, A. (1999) Natsional'no-territorial'noe i natsional'no-kul'turnoe samoopredelenie: sootnoshenie poniatii, in: *Gosudarstvenno-pravovye Osnovy Obespecheniia Bezopasnosti v Rossiiskoi Federatsii*, pp. 62–75 (St Petersburg State University: Akademiia Ministerstva vnutrennikh del).

Cirtautas, A. M. & Schimmelfennig, F. (2010) Europeanisation before and after accession: Conditionality, legacies and compliance, *Europe–Asia Studies*, 62(3), pp. 421–441.

Connor, W. (1984) *The National Question in Marxist–Leninist Theory and Strategy* (Princeton, NJ: Princeton University Press).

Drobizheva, L. M. (Ed.) (2003) *Sotsiologiia mezhetnicheskoi tolerantnosti* (Moscow: Institut sotsiologii RAN).

Eide, A., Greni, V. & Lundberg, M. (1998) Cultural autonomy: Concept, content, history and role in the world order, in: , M. Suksi (Ed.) *Autonomy: Applications and implications*, pp. 251–276 (The Hague and Boston: Kluwer Law International).

Filippov, V. (2003) *Kritika Etnicheskogo Federalizma* (Moscow: Rossiiskaya Akademiya Nauk, Tsentr Tsivilizacionnyh i Regional'nyh Issledovanii).

Fomichenko, M. (2005) Natsional'no-kul'turnaia avtonomiia kak forma samoopredeleniia narodov v Rossii, *Natsional'nye interesy*, 8(3), pp. 35–41.

Foucault, M. (2007)   *Security, Territory, Population: Lectures at the Collège de France, 1977–1978* (Basingstoke, Hampshire; New York: Palgrave Macmillan, Houndmills).
Gramsci, A. (1971)   *Selections from the Prison Notebooks* (New York: International Publishers).
Guboglo, M. (2000)   *Mozhet li dvuglavy orel letet s odnim krylom? Razmyshleniya o zakonotvorchestve v sfere etnogosudarstvennyh otnoshenii* (Moscow: TsIMO).
Hall, P. & Taylor, R. (1996) Political science and the three new institutionalisms, *Political Studies*, 44(4), pp. 936–957.
Huttenbach, H. R. (Ed.) (1990) *Soviet Nationality Policies. Ruling ethnic groups in the USSR* (London and New York: Mansell).
Karapetian, L. (2001)   *Federativnoe ustroistvo Rossiiskogo gosudarstva* (Moscow: Norma).
Krasner, S. D. (1999)   *Sovereignty. Organized hypocrisy* (Princeton: Princeton University Press).
Laitin, D. (1998)   *Identity in Formation: The Russian-speaking populations in the near abroad* (Ithaca: Cornell University Press).
Lapidus, G. & Walker, E. (1995) Nationalism, regionalism, and federalism: Center–periphery relations in post-Communist Russia, in: G. Lapidus (Ed.) *The New Russia: Troubled transformation*, pp. 218–240 (Boulder, CO: Westview).
Lipson, M. (2007) Peacekeeping: Organized hypocrisy?, *European Journal of International Relations*, 13(1), pp. 5–34.
Luhmann, L. (1995)   *Funktion und Folgen formaler Organisationen* (Berlin: Duncker und Humbolt).
Martynuk, V. (1999, August) The role of the interethnic factor in the development of the Kaliningrad region. Paper presented at the ECMI conference, Kaliningrad, Russian Federation, 29–30 November 2002, ECMI Report 50. Available at http://www.ecmi.de/uploads/tx_lfpubdb/Report_50_english_edited.pdf (accessed 23 October 2012).
Medvedev, N. (2005)   *Politicheskaya regionalistika* (Moscow: Alfa-M).
Mikhalenok, O. & Melnikova, I. (2011) Samoopredeleniye natsii v sostave federatsii: politicheskii aspekt, *Sotsialno-gumanitarnye znaniya*, 14(1), pp. 255–269.
Mukomel, V. (2003)   *Natsional'nye men'shinstva. Pravovye osnovy i praktika obespecheniia prav lits, prinadlezhashchikh k natsional'nym men'shinstvam, v sub'ektakh Iuga Rossiiskoi Federatsii* (Moscow: CEPRI).
Osipov, A. (2004)   *Natsional'no-kul'turnaia avtonomiia: idei, resheniia, instituty* (St. Petersburg: Tsentr nezavisimykh sotsiologicheskikh issledovanii).
Osipov, A. (2010) National cultural autonomy in Russia: A case of symbolic law, *Review of Central and East European Law*, 35(1), pp. 57–60.
Osipov, A. (2011) Non-territorial autonomy and international law, *International Community Law Review*, 13(4), pp. 393–411.
Pain, E. (1995) Stanovlenie gosudarstvennoi nezavisimosti i natsional'naia konsolidatsiia Rossii: problemy, tendentsii, al'ternativy, *Mir Rossii*, IV(1), pp. 58–90.
Pain, E. (2004)   *Etnopoliticheskii maiatnik. Dinamika i mekhanizmy etnopoliticheskikh protsessov v postsovetskoi Rossii* (Moscow: Institut sotsiologii RAN).
Renner, K. (2005) State and nation, in: E. Nimni (Ed.) *National–Cultural Autonomy and its Contemporary Critics*, pp. 15–47 (London and New York: Routledge).
Roeder, P. G. (1991) Soviet federalism and ethnic mobilization, *World Politics*, 43(2), pp. 196–232.
Samoilenko, O. (2008) Formy samoopredeleniia ravnopravnykh narodov Rossiiskoi Federatsii, *Pravo i politika*, 9(11), pp. 2633–2638.
Sasse, G. (2008) The politics of EU conditionality: The norm of minority protection during and beyond EU accession, *Journal of European Public Policy*, 15(6), pp. 842–860.
Schimmelfennig, F. & Sedelmeier, U. (2004) Governance by conditionality: EU rule transfer to the candidate countries of Central and Eastern Europe, *Journal of European Public Policy*, 11(4), pp. 669–687.
Schneider, A. L. & Ingram, H. (1997)   *Policy Design for Democracy* (Lawrence: University Press of Kansas).
Schneider, A. L. & Ingram, H. (2008) Social constructions in the study of public policy, in: J. A. Holstein & J. F. Gubrium (Eds) *Handbook of Constructionist Research*, pp. 206–207 (New York, NY: Guilford Press).
Scott, J. C. (1990)   *Domination and the Arts of Resistance: Hidden transcripts* (New Haven, CT: Yale University Press).

Shtromas, A. (1978) Legal position of Soviet nationalities and their territorial units according to the 1977 constitution of the USSR, *Russian Review*, 37(2), pp. 265–272.

Slocum, J. (1995) Disintegration and consolidation: National separatism and the evolution of center-periphery relations in the Russian Federation. Cornell University Peace Studies Program: Occasional Paper No. 19. Available at http://www.einaudi.cornell.edu/PeaceProgram/publications/occasional_papers/occasional-paper19.pdf (accessed 12 June 2012).

Stepanov, V. (2004) Natsional'no-kul'turnaia avtonomiia v Rossii kak ideia i pravovaia norma, in: N. Voronina & M. Galdia (Eds) *Pravovye aspekty etnicheskih otnoshenii v Rossii*. pp. 91–117 (Moscow: Delovaia Stolitsa).

Tarasov, A. (2002) Pravo narodov na samoopredelenie kak fundamental'nyi demokraticheskii printsip, *Svobodnaia mysl'-XXI*, 12(9), pp. 56–74.

Toshenko, Z. (2003) *Etnokratiya: Istoriya i Sovremennost' (Sociologicheskie Ocherki)*. (Moscow: ROSSPEN).

Turovski, R. (2006) *Politicheskaya regionalistika* (Moscow: GU-VSHE).

Valentei, S. (2000) Tri vyzova Rossii, *Federalism*, 5(4), pp. 17–32

Zorin, V. (1999a) Etnopoliticheskii faktor v razvitii rossiiskogo federalizma: opyt zakonotvorchestva, *Etnopanorama*, 1(2), pp. 13–18.

Zorin, V. (1999b) Zakon, stavshii proryvom, *Zhizn' natsionalnostei*, 1(8), pp. 46–52

Which is the Only Game in Town? Minority Rights Issues in Estonia and Slovakia During and After EU Accession

TIMOFEY AGARIN & ADA-CHARLOTTE REGELMANN
School of Politics, International Studies and Philosophy, Queen's University Belfast, UK

ABSTRACT *Post-communist transition went hand in hand with the European integration process. Much of the literature on EU accession focuses on the rational decision to implement a set of European norms into domestic legislation pre-accession. It is often concluded that once EU membership is achieved, states succumb their rationality and act on the basis of internalised norms. The paper claims that the past literature overlooks the wider framework within which policy-makers operate before and after the accession, namely domestic sovereignty over policy-making and implementation. Tracing the policy dynamics in the area of minority rights in Estonia and Slovakia, we demonstrate that the European integration ushered greater domestic control over policy implementation on minority issues in two states exposed to a heavy dose of conditionality. As we observe, both states have consolidated their state- and nation-building policies referencing EU conditionality in the course of accession and later EU membership to assert centrality of domestic objectives for policy-making and implementation.*

The end of the Cold War saw the emergence of new polities across Central Eastern Europe. These were often established to serve primarily, at times exclusively, the members of an ethnocultural 'core nation'. Especially where socialist federations fell apart, the new states' ethnic majorities were often running political affairs without involving minority groups (Galbreath & McEvoy, 2011), enforcing 'nationalising' policies (Csergo, 2002; Brubaker, 1996), overemphasising ethnic and cultural differences in public (G. Smith, 1996; Smooha & Järve, 2005), increasing the salience of ethnic differentiation (Jenne, 2004; Guelke, 2010) and overall undermining the incentives for minority political participation (Hale, 2006; O'Dwyer, 2004). Unsurprisingly therefore, the EU was engaged in monitoring relations of most post-communist states with their domestic minorities since the early 1990s.

The EU eastern enlargement, then, is often seen as the pinnacle of the European concern for minorities in post-communism and has led scholars to investigate the role of international organisations in taming nationalisms across Eastern Europe and ensuring peace and stability in the region prior to the EU accession (Galbreath, 2005; Kelley, 2004a). Most studies of accession states corroborate the view that domestic policy-makers toned down their rhetoric in response to cost–benefit calculus about the potential EU membership, complying with EU accession criteria (Bailey & de Propris 2004; Haughton, 2007; Pridham, 2002). Thus, the EU membership had an unprecedented capacity to impact upon domestic policy-making dynamics and accommodation of minority claims (Rechel, 2008; Hughes et al., 2004).

There is no doubt in the fact that comments by international observers have often been followed by compliance with European norms and resulted in changes in domestic policies. International observers have provided critical statements pointing to issues that could potentially hamper accession talks and at times openly reiterating the option of postponed EU accession date (see esp. Hughes & Sasse, 2003; Sedelmeier, 2002). Yet, on many occasions political decisions impalpable to domestic electorate were not implemented. In line with the rational choice argument dominating the literature on European conditionality (Schimmelfennig & Scholtz, 2010; Schimmelfennig & Sedelmeier, 2004), we agree that policy-making in the Central Eastern European (CEE) accession states was geared towards accession, yet we contend that EU membership was a goal to be achieved at all costs. Although there was downloading policy blueprint and taking suggestions from the European monitors into account domestically, many policies were watered down considerably when tailored to local situations. Though states across the post-communist region have shared an understanding of the benefits accrued from the EU accession, each of them responded differently to challenges of transposing *acquis communautaires* into domestic legislation. Policy choices made in each specific context reflected on pre-existing practices of transposition and implementation, interests and agendas of political actors, electorates' expectations and openings in political opportunity structure.

The limited availability of analyses on whether European normative conditionality had any lasting impact on domestic policy regimes leaves a perceptible gap in a qualified estimate of policy compliance in the new EU member states since their accession. This is the case particularly in relation to potential security concerns regarding minority rights issues. Our paper argues that compliance research has to grant greater attention to the process of adopting and implementing new policies in post-communist EU member states to better understand the role of nation state as an autonomous actor during and after European enlargement phase. To do so, we analyse how this norm was validated in two CEE states with considerable tension between the local majority and minority, Estonia and Slovakia. Our analyses of changes in minority rights policies demonstrates that a focus on the 'process' allows comparison of policies' content beyond policy-making (cf. Remmer, 1992) and allows us to uncover more covert goals of domestic policy-makers (see comparatively, Schmidt & Radaelli, 2004; Lynggaard, 2011). We find that 'European integration' was used by domestic policy-makers to justify pre-accession compliance as best choice at hand to ensure longer-term benefits of EU membership as a bulwark against minority claims, as well as a guarantee for domestic sovereignty in decision-making.

We track down the changes in minority policies in but two CEE countries, contrasting conditionality effects on dynamics of minority rights protection and evaluate how these dynamics have impacted minority rights issues after the accession. Both, Slovakia and Estonia were exposed to considerable conditionality pressures throughout the accession period, but as our analyses suggests, these pressures did not translate into greater accommodation of minority rights domestically. We suggest that this incoherence is not due to standards of minority protection, but rather to the mechanisms of European governance. European monitors did not question domestic sovereignty over policy-making, leaving it up to national political actors to devise and implement policies perceived appropriate domestically. We trace these processes throughout the two phases, of consolidation of national policy-making mechanisms first and then during the period when domestic sovereignty in policy-making was validated after the signing of the EU accession agreement. In conclusion, we adjudicate the claim whether post-accession the CEE states contributed to a coherent normative approach to minority issues in the EU.

What Rationale behind Post-communist States' Compliance?

After the demise of state socialism, European Union membership was the major foreign policy objective of the post-communist states in the Eastern Europe. Given the fact that were no formal criteria existed to determine country's eligibility for membership, the European Council meeting in Copenhagen established the requirement of a candidate country to achieve institutional stability 'guaranteeing democracy, the rule of law, human rights, respect for and protection of minorities, the existence of a functioning market economy', as well as the 'ability to take on the obligations of membership'. Provided a country was deemed to fulfil these requirements, it could apply and be granted the status of an EU accession country and would begin the transposition of the *acquis communautaire*, the EU legislative corpus into domestic legislation and eventually become a full member.

In the process, international agreements became institutionalised in domestic legislations (Dimitrova, 2002; Lavenex, 2008). The accession oriented policy development in the CEE states allowed the EU to deploy both carrot and stick in its dealings with national policy-makers, enforcing change in diverse policy areas be means of 'authority, resources, capacity to act and legitimacy' (Friis & Murphy, 1999, p. 214). Successful EU pressures on candidate countries' policy dynamics have only confirmed the central importance of EU membership to post-communist publics, 'accepted by the candidates as an "assymetrical process" of taking over the rules of a club' (Dimitrova, 2002, p. 175). The transfer of EU rules and their adoption by the candidate post-communist states allowed scholarship to perceive of accession states as instrumental actors, responding to rather than anticipating European normative pressures. Norm transfer from the EU and its variant effectiveness have been 'best explained according to the external incentives model and in particular with the credibility of EU conditionality and the domestic cost of rule adoption' (Schimmelfennig & Sedelmeier, 2004, p. 663).

Unsurprisingly maybe, a host of analyses of the impact European conditionality had on outcomes of domestic policy-making emerged during the accession period. Most referred to 'hard' evidence to substantiate the claim that the accession countries were capable of downloading policy blueprints into domestic legislation and were thus attempting to speed up the accession process. The set of criteria, ranging from Copenhagen criteria to start and *acquis* to complete negotiations, provided an intuitive conceptual toolbox to evaluate the progress of 'Europeanisation' across the region (Kelley, 2004a; Vachudova, 2005; Sasse, 2008). Regardless of the existing structural conditions and opportunities for change, policy choices across accession states have been treated if they lay outside of domestic actors' control. Candidate states were looking up to the EU and the Council of Europe because these were guided by normative pressures, regardless of short-term policy decisions (see Kelley, 2004a, p. 4). Much of the literature on pre-accession policy dynamics in post-communist states emphasises the objective of the EU integration as the central driving force underpinning both the actual policy changes and political rhetoric countering anticipated popular reactions. This leads many observers to state that though effects of EU accession were at times unintended and indirect, they tapped 'deeper structural issues' and could also be '"locked-in" through the process of EU involvement' (Sasse, 2008, p. 855).

The analyses of political actors' costs and benefits incurred from adapting to and adapting the reference to European integration has thus become central to understandings of political actors' behaviours in the pre-accession phase. The overtly rationalist perspective on choices in policy transposition and implementation before the EU accession is however counterproductive to understanding post-accession compliance in the new member states. While the conditionality literature identifies obvious trade-offs the states made in relation to EU accession, it faces considerable difficulty in accounting variance in implementation and in compliance. As long as there was considerable political capital to be gained domestically from framing policy-making as being evoked by international demands, policy choices could be analysed as a result of rational decision-making (Lavenex, 2008; Schimmelfennig & Sedelmeier, 2004). When the perspective of the EU membership was secured however, policy choices needed reframing as outcomes of value internalisation, i.e., as normative sets of decisions (Schmidt, 2010; Schimmelfennig, 2001). The turn from rational to normative reasoning in the Europeanisation literature has been criticised increasingly for failing to account for policy misfit between the member state policies and an overarching EU policy framework, and for treating actors acting formerly on rational choice grounds as being increasingly driven by normative considerations after the enlargement.

It seems however that the focus of EU conditionality literature on issues of compliance has something to say about post-accession behaviours of policy-makers. It would seem that policy-makers could usher policy-backsliding when no penalty could be expected from the European monitors, e.g., under the circumstances when accession timeline was already agreed upon and thus the perspective EU membership was certain (Sedelmeier, 2012; Levitz & Pop-Eleches, 2010). Where policy-makers regard EU accession talks as non-reversible and emphasise their objectives which might have postponed accession in the past, we would expect to see a clear overlap of policy objectives inherent to the states and European Union monitors. This is precisely what we find in the literature on EU accession states arguing that the pre-accession period incentivised policy change by spurring policy emulation and application, yet failed to establish domestic mechanisms checking for implementation consistency and compliance (Kelley, 2004b). Although states' compliance with EU pressures post-accession is much less certain then has been anticipated before 2004 (Schimmelfennig et al., 2003; Schwellnus, 2006), some new EU member states have kept high standard in post-accession compliance and implementation (Epstein & Sedelmeier, 2008).

In the past, the European integration literature presumed that the pre- and post-accession rationales in policy-making are inherently different. We claim however, that there was little change in institutions and policies as a result of EU accession, because the EU membership was not an ultimate goal of accession states. Rather, the EU membership was a step on the way to achieving a more covert, yet more subtle policy objective that allows us to explain continuity in policy-making dynamics related to minority issues in Estonia and Slovakia over the past 20 years. Thus, by treating EU accession as but a part of a wider set of states' objective, we are able to explain why post-communist states did not 'backslide' after the EU membership was secured, while remaining rational and independent actors. We claim that the lack of policy backsliding cannot be explained away by reference to internalisation of European norms. Post-communist member states continue to act as rational actors in their own right, following their own preferences which overlapped with those of the European monitors in the past and other EU member states presently. Not only are many policy objectives regarding minority issues shared by the EU member states, they are also superordinate to the objective of the EU membership proper and remained consistent after the accession phase was complete.

The process of policy-making legitimation and rhetoric validation of European accession as a penultimate policy objective, we suggest, is central to understanding policy continuities in post-communist states before and after the accession. Therefore, we see policy choices not as responses to conditionality pressures from European monitors upon the domestic policy-makers, nor do we see these responses as policy choices accurately representing expectations of European demands and norms. Instead, we treat policy-makers' choices as sets of rhetoric actions rationalising their policy choices in the wider context of structural constraints and incentives beyond EU membership. By arguing that post-communist policy-makers contextualised and framed their choices within the wider context of EU membership of their countries, we take stock of previous findings in the literature on importance of politicking in post-communism (Bunce, 2003) and nepotism among the domestic policy-makers (Miller et al., 1997), relative independence of political leadership in setting major societal objectives (Saideman & Ayres 2000) and profiting from lack of opposition to elite driven political projects (Pollack et al., 2003).

In order to establish which principles guided the European policy-making both before and after the enlargement, we argue, it is essential to analyse not the technocratic implementation EU policy blueprint on minority rights issues, but policy-making as a process of framing these principles by domestic political elites in the new member states. Thus, our study is about a much more fundamental norm of

European policy-making, that of sovereign national policy-making regardless international pressures for compliance. In contrast to the rationalist assumptions about the shaming and blaming of candidate countries into compliance, we expect states to come out as more consolidated policy-making entities as a result of policy-makers' framing of national sovereignty. We suggest that the appeal to European norms during the accession phase conjured the dominant role of domestic agency that frames, implements and monitors policies on the ground. This reflects the overarching European norm that domestic policy dynamics and actor preferences developed within the existing opportunity structure also account for breadth and depth of policies implemented. And this is precisely the reason for which the intensity of European conditionality did not challenge the pre-existing notions of accession states' prevalence in policy-making.

The rational choice perspective can view conditionality as either accomplished or failed only, without adding to the understandings of why and in what way selected democratic criteria were adopted and sustained in some countries while remaining irrelevant in others (Hughes & Sasse, 2003; Kelley, 2004b; Lavenex, 2008). In contrast to this causational approach to conditionality impact, our focus is on the strategic enactment of the exigencies of conditionality as a resource generated through policy-makers' discourses on benefits of EU accession. This allows us to conceptualise accession pressures as leading to post-accession norm internalisation, conditionality leading to norm validation and ultimately compliance not in terms of cause and effect, but as dependent on how they were reconciled with states' interests in discourses that frame policy implementation. Fundamentally, to understand how compliance mechanisms operate (and how conditionality pressures are responded to domestically), we must analyse the core assumptions held by the policy-makers as actors invoking 'accession' and 'conditionality' to reconcile the EU pressures with their objectives of domestic sovereignty over policy-making. The superordinate objectives of national sovereignty can be particularly strongly observed in those EU accession states home to large numbers of minorities, whose kin states could be plausibly made responsible to engage in jingoism and influence host state policy-making should the states remain outside the EU (Csergo, 2002; Roe, 2004; Lerch & Schwellnus, 2006).

The impact of European legal corpus on domestic legislations, policies and practices is so complex that of necessity it needs to draw upon selective analyses of states, policy areas or time panel series. In this paper, we conceptualise of European integration as a dynamic process executed by states as heterogeneous, reflexive and strategic actors, responding to pressures emanating principally from domestic policy-makers. By analysing policy-making in only one area, minority rights, we discuss how the opportunity structures available as a result of accession process have been used to strengthen domestic capacity for policy-making against the odds of increased EU monitoring for compliance. Slovakia and Estonia are two excellent case studies to analyse these processes, because political elites in both countries have persistently fallen back on rhetorical rationalisation of their decision to mitigate domestic publics (e.g., European accession, integration into transatlantic normative space) and enact discourse of European integration for their strategic purposes.

Consolidation of National Policy-making

In both Estonia and Slovakia, EU accession was presented as an absolute necessity in order to ensure and protect state sovereignty from national minorities' and their kin states' minority-related claims. Although over the 1990s, some concessions were made to minority communities in terms of their political representation and participation, all these were framed as steps required for the EU membership. In seeking to justify reforms which were likely to prove both politically contentious and socially divisive, domestic political leaders presented their decisions to the respective publics by invoking external constraints. Importantly, the perspective of EU membership provided domestic actors with a reference point to consolidate their domestic interests while referencing Copenhagen criteria and tapping the discourse on European integration to justify their at times unpopular decisions domestically.

Estonia

Estonia regained independence from the Soviet Union in 1991. *De jure* restoration of pre-Soviet independence meant that post-Soviet citizenship was granted automatically only to citizens of the pre-Soviet state and their descendants, disenfranchising around a third of the local population. As a result, no ethnic non-Estonian was represented in the first post-Soviet *Riigikogu* (Parliament) until 1995, granting a *carte blanche* for Estonian-centred state- and nation-building (Kask, 1994). Although parties representing the interests of non-Estonians have at times entered national parliament and were represented in local administrations, their impact on the state's minority policies has been negligible.

Post-Soviet political transition was determined by the initial limitation on political membership for minorities: citizenship policies created a feeling of insecurity among the minority populations, leading Russian-speaking political elites in the north-east of Estonia call for a popular referendum to attain separation from the country and triggering public unrest (D. J. Smith, 2002). Tightened language criteria and other requirements for naturalisation were adopted without minority consultation, and though not lead to public unrest, served to secure majority dominance in the decision-making. Moreover, they ensured political closure by restricting political membership to individuals with 'long-standing ties' with the country and who had vowed their loyalty to the Estonian state (Agarin, 2010).

The situation raised concerns among European actors. Heightened tensions over the Aliens Act in 1993 led to the involvement of the OSCE's High Commissioner on National Minorities (HCNM) to broker a solution, which included the establishment of a Presidential Roundtable for dialogue with minorities and the establishment of a permanent OSCE mission to Estonia. Russian-speakers' protests eventually subsided, when the OSCE came to support the view that the 'position of the Estonian government was largely in conformity with the European standard of minority protection' (European Commission, 1997). Subsequently, the OSCE mission was closely engaged in advising on the draft of the 1995 Citizenship Law and advising on the final version of the 1995 Language Act, largely backing Estonia's approach to national sovereignty.

The Estonian legislative frame grants the right to use minority languages in areas of minority concentrated settlement. Yet, the legal framework makes a clear reference to citizens of the Estonian state who belong to a community that is recognised as a national minority; this does not include Russians or Russian speakers. In the period before Estonia entered accession talks minority provisions were not expanded, nor were the existing regulations implemented. In 1997, the European commission demanded accelerated naturalisation and integration of non-citizens, but did not specify criteria for this (European Commission, 1997). The involvement of European actors was perceived by the Estonian political elites as pro forma interaction aimed at ensuring essential conformity with international obligations without altering policies. Working in a monitoring capacity, the OSCE and other institutions have largely underlined the sovereignty of Estonia's policy-makers to determine the scope of policy-making on their territory. This ushered a remarkable rise of Euroscepticism among the domestic Russian-speaking community in the period prior to opening accession negotiations on 10 November 1997 (Pettai, 2003, p. 97).

Slovakia

The Hungarians in independent Slovakia were not faced with formal exclusion from political membership. Initially, Slovak and Hungarian representatives of the democratisation movement cooperated and even formed a government together (Oltay, 1990). Yet, the ethnonational agenda of post-communist Slovak state- and nation-building meant that the minority was *de facto* excluded from political policy-making and institution-building, during the 1990s further policies were put into place to further restrict minority political participation in the country. The ethnonational agenda took stage with the adoption of the Official State Language law in 1990. The politicisation of ethno-national issues was subsequently adopted as a key strategy of the nationalist wing of the democratisation movement, which later formed the Movement for a Democratic Slovakia (*Hnutie za demokratického Slovensko*, HZDS) and – except for a brief interim government in 1994 – became the dominant party until 1998.

From 1993 onwards, the HZDS engaged in direct anti-minority policies (Wolff, 2001). In reaction to policies restricting language use and curtailing support for minority culture, Hungarian political elites spearheaded regional self-government as a central issue on their agendas (Reisch, 1993). Between 1994 and 1998, HZDS formed a coalition with the notorious Slovak National Party (*Slovenská národná strana*, SNS) openly pressing for Slovakisation, specifically through education (Langman, 2002). The State Language Law (SLL) of 1995 granted Slovak the prominence as the sole state language, significantly restricting minority language visibility in public and prohibiting minority language use in public offices also in areas of concentrated Hungarian settlement (Harlig, 1997). Promoting the principle 'one state – one language', the SLL aimed to establish Slovak ethnonational sovereignty, using 'culture' as the primary tool of state integration.

The controversial language law was one of the reasons for Slovakia's initial rejection from the first round of candidate countries for EU eastern enlargement (Harris, 2007). Slovakia's Europeanisation really only begun with the change in government of 1998, bringing into government a broad coalition of Christian-conservatives, liberal right as well as left parties, and the Hungarian party, SMK. Against the background of worrying backsliding in democratisation, limping economic reforms and diminished cooperation with neighbouring countries, the EU had continuously demanded that the tensions in relation to the Hungarian minority were addressed at the highest policy-making level (Henderson, 2002, p. 92). This enabled the pre-1998 political opposition to argue that 'Slovakia's opportunities for Euro-Atlantic integration were seriously threatened' (Jozef Moravčik, Slovak MP cited in Simon, 2004, p. 157). The European institutions made it very clear that Slovakia had to improve its minority policies if it wanted to become an EU member.

The new government responded to the international and domestic pressure by drafting a Minority Language Law (MLL). Slovakia needed to adopt the MLL in time for the meeting between the government and the European Commission scheduled for July 1999 to discuss the country's prospects for EU accession. The MLL that was eventually adopted closed some, but not all legal gaps that the 1995 SLL had caused for minority language use, but it satisfied the European Commission's expectations. The Commission and the OSCE acknowledged that the law was weak at the foundations and that its enforcement was dependent on further legislation in the spirit of the MLL as well as on the goodwill of government (European Commission, 1999, p. 17).

Since the makeup of Estonia's and Slovakia's political institutions was defined in ethnocultural terms by their constitutions, all policies related to state-building have consolidated majority ethnic communities' dominance in public institutions throughout the first decade of independence. Minority parties, even when they were part of governing coalitions, were largely left out of the political decision-making, particularly in relation to minority matters. European actors closely monitored minority policies in the two countries and already before accession talks began had some influence on decision-making. Overall, during this phase, European actors have largely backed domestic policy dynamics regarding minority issues and supported states' sovereignty in policy-making.

Validation of Domestic Sovereignty over Minority Matters

After Estonia and Slovakia signed Accession Agreements with the EU in 1997 and 1999 respectively, European monitoring and conditionality politics intensified. During this phase, both countries adopted or altered legislation in the issue area of minority rights, framing these as a response to European pressure rhetorically, while essentially continuing policies of state and national sovereignty following early state-building. Concerns about the situation of minorities as raised by European actors concentrated on two broad areas: the rights to enjoy cultural practices of minorities including language use, and minority participation in the political process. Yet, these concerns did not mirror clear European standards or benchmarks for assessment. European actors produced incentives as well as guidance for domestic policy-makers to align minority policies with the recommendations. When the Treaty of Accession was signed between the EU and 10 candidate states, including Slovakia and Estonia at the meeting in Athens of 16 April 2003, it had acknowledged that accession conditions were sufficiently fulfilled (Van Elsuwege, 2008). In the previous section we demonstrated that during the accession phase the content of minority policies had changed only in so far as these supported state capacity to make and implement policies domestically. As this section of our paper shows, during the phase that followed the signing of the Treaty of Accession, Estonia's and Slovakia's sovereignty in legislature and policy-making have further validated European norms that outlook and dynamics of national policies should be determined domestically. Crucially, while both states have corroborated national sovereignty in their approaches to minority accommodation, they did so by contextualising these policies as European and thus not requiring further amendment.

Estonia

The nationalisation policies of the Estonian state had created a difficult situation with regard to political membership, social inclusion and cohesion of the population. Many stateless individuals were opting for citizenship of other states – primarily, the Russian Federation – bringing a potentially powerful external actor into domestic Estonian relations with minorities. Securitising minority policies, the Estonian state restricted and controlled access to Estonian political membership, thereby institutionalising the situation. Increasingly, domestic observers critical of these policies perceived social integration and stability to be threatened due to marginalisation of large parts of population who would not leave the country, as many policy-makers of early state-building had hoped (Järve & Poleshchuk, 2010, p. 6). Moreover, domestic policy-makers were concerned with Estonia 'Europeanness', which was increasingly understood in terms of 'multiculturalism', and thus had consequences for the framing of national sovereignty (Kirch et al., 2006).

In the run-up to European accession, the EU increased the pressure on Estonia to bring its legislation in line with international documents that Estonia had ratified (Järve & Poleshchuk, 2010, p. 8). Additionally, NATO accession and the closure of the OSCE mission to Estonia were conditioned on changes to language requirements for participation in local elections (Järve, 2003, p. 98; Birckenbach, 2000). Interpreted in the literature as a response to these external pressures, citizenship and language policies appeared to become more favourable to minorities. In 1998, naturalisation was eased for children of stateless parents and for students who completed school education in Estonia. Although part of OSCE recommendations since the early 1990s, this policy was adopted only after the EU had included it into its conditionality criteria (Pettai & Kallas, 2009, p. 111). In 2002, an amendment to the language law stipulated the right to use 'foreign languages', including Russian, in official contacts at the local level. With this amendment, Estonia reacted to the repeated criticisms raised in the EC's Regular Reports (European Commission, 2001, 2002).

Domestically, the 'minority-friendly' legislation was framed as a necessary fulfilment of international demands. The accusation that the Estonian government's alignment of its policies with international pressure amounted to 'giving in to Russia' was purported by parliamentary opposition and government members alike (Budryte, 2005, p. 81; Kelley, 2004a, p. 105). Although European conditionality led to the initial expansion of minority rights, these rights' taking effect was in several instances circumvented by follow-up legislation that re-established the earlier restrictive ruling in different form.

Estonia maintained significant leeway in its policy-making, even where responding to international pressure, for example with its strategy to integrate the Soviet-era settlers, for the first time promoting naturalisation and support for 'greater [socio-economic] competitiveness' of everyone living in Estonia (Estonian Government, 2000). However, these objectives were subsumed to the notion of the 'harmonisation of society... around a unifying common core' (defined as the Estonian language and culture) and the 'formation of a population loyal to the Estonian state' (ibid., pp. 17–18). The bulk of activities stipulated in the programme then concerned the teaching of Estonian with up to three quarters of the programme's budget for the years 2000–2003 funded by European funding schemes (Brosig, 2008). The integration programme did not envisage the expansion of minority policies, but it was read as Estonia's compliance with the European Commission's demands to facilitate minority integration and address minority claims for participation in society. Essentially, Estonia's minority policies validated European norm that criteria for political participation should be conditioned upon minority members' cultural adaptation to standards set by the state. European actors' financial support for this approach allowed framing of Estonia's policies of majority dominance as 'European' and coherent with the EU's endorsement of domestic policy choices.

Estonia's post-accession minority policies were largely shaped by the priorities outlined in the first integration strategy, which mirrors the state's concern with sovereignty. Failing to respond to the stagnated situation of interethnic relations in the country, the second integration strategy for the years 2008–2013 was a near copy of the earlier programme. It differed from the first programme in its stronger emphasis on the Estonian concept of 'multiculturalism' (Estonian Government, 2007), designed to provide support for minority culture activities. The understanding of minority culture is very narrow and limits the issues on which minority representatives can be included into the policy process (Malloy, 2009; Agarin, 2010). At the same time, 'Estonian multiculturalism' is used by the policy-makers to buttress majority dominance, such as through co-optation and satisficing without implication for changing minority related policies (Pettai & Hallik, 2002).

Minority and integration policies continue to focus on language sovereignty, promoting 'Estonian language only' in much of public and formal communications. In line with this, in 2007 the parliament reconfirmed the normative centrality of the Estonian language for the state by including the protection of the Estonian language into the preamble of the constitution. Simultaneously, parliament amended the language law to strengthen the role of the language inspectorate, a body that monitors the proficiency in Estonian of employees in professions, where a certain level of Estonian is required (Language Inspection, 2011; LICHR, 2010). This move has increased the pressure on Russian-speaking employees across the country (Kallas, 2008; Poleshchuk, 2009, pp. 99–102). Though the strict control of language proficiency contradicts international and domestic criticism of both the adequacy of the established requirements and the practices of ensuring compliance with these requirements (CoE, 2005), it was not challenged since (Pettai & Kallas, 2009).

The OSCE and the EU refrain from criticising the decisions of the Estonian government towards its minority and decisively took a stance in support of the Estonian government during its domestic disputes with Russian-speaking minority in April 2007 (so-called, Bronze Night riots). Moreover, post-accession minority policies are funded to a significant amount by the EU; for example, around a third of 2010's integration programme budget came directly from EU funds.[1] European financial support mirrors the concern European actors have with regard to majority-minority relations and the simultaneous acceptance that any such policies are in the competence of the nation state alone.

To alleviate the critique that continuous to come from the Council of Europe, Estonia has been eager to align its policies with European standards to show good will and assuage domestic control over minority issues (Eksamikeskus, 2011). Moreover, Estonian officials do not tire of emphasising that their approach to minority protection is commendable in the European context. Estonia presents itself as a modern European state with a large *immigrant* population, comparable to Germany or the United Kingdom. The 'multiculturalism' frame allows for (limited) political inclusion and social participation of minority members on the basis of the 'celebration' of minority cultures. As a result, the framing of Soviet-era settlers as immigrants has made it palatable in the international context not to deal directly with the issue of non-citizens and discuss the matter at the European level.[2]

Overall, the model of Estonian multiculturalism developed by Estonian policy-makers in the context of EU accession, has become the primary tool for domestic validation of European norms pertaining to state sovereignty. These norms however, are not those concerned with the EU-wide policy, but rather build upon nation state sovereignty over domestic decision-making and constitutional right of ethic majority to enjoy protection of their culture and language. Indeed, post-accession minority policies have functioned continuously as a tool for validation of European norms that minority rights issues in Estonia are essentially a domestic policy issue linked to state-building process.

Slovakia

Similar to the situation in Estonia, Slovakia's EU accession negotiations were shaped by the legacies of the nationalisation phase. Besides anti-minority legislation, the HZSD–SNS government had embarked on a reform that introduced the regional level to administration and governance, while drawing the lines to the detriment of the regionally concentrated Hungarian minority. The reform had also increased centralist policy-making and had left long-standing plans for decentralising the Slovak state during post-communism incomplete (Nižňanský & Pilát, 2001). These legacies were of primary concern for international as well as domestic political and civil society actors. In the Accession Agreement of 1999 the EU increased the pressure on Slovakia to make the state fit for membership, with a 'key role' to be played by the public administration reform to reconcile Slovakia's structures of governance with the requirements set out in European documents (European Commission, 1999, p. 14; Klimovsky, 2010). The EU provided PHARE funding in support of the reform, which became a government priority. The envisaged reform touched upon two major issues with an ethno-political dimension. First, territorial–administrative reform bore the chance of redrawing the borders of territorial units and increasing the minorities' share of the respective regional population. Second, the competencies of institutions at the national, regional and local levels had to be redefined, potentially increasing local self-determination on a number of issues, including those especially relevant for minority institutions. While Hungarian representatives saw a chance for renegotiating power division along ethnic lines, the opponents of the reform increased their anti-Hungarian rhetoric, warned against Hungarian irredentism and eventually overturned the bill proposal. In response, the SMK threatened to leave the coalition, if the government failed to guarantee substantial redistribution of political power to bodies of regional and local self-government, as spelt out in the coalition agreement (Slovak Spectator, 1 September 2001).

Concerned with these developments, the EU made the successful continuation of the accession process contingent on the SMK's continued participation in government and on changes to the decision-making competencies of different tiers of governance in line with *acquis* criteria (Brusis, 2003). However it did not issue any policy benchmarks for Slovakia to adhere to. Even though the eventual reform did not foster Hungarian political or functional autonomy, as a combined reform of administrative competencies and boundaries had promised to, minority politicians saw their decision-making authority *de facto* increased thanks to the minority's numerical strength in certain regions and municipalities (Klimovsky, 2010; Nižňanský & Pilát, 2001, p. 228).

The European integration discourse enabled (liberal) political actors to frame their own policy preferences as induced from the outside, satisfying the majority of the population that exhibited a generally very favourable opinion towards EU accession, but who continued to have reservations towards 'minority-friendly' policies (European Parliament, 1999). Slovak parties presented their responsiveness to European pressure to accommodate some of the minority's demands as instrumental for accession; the SMK stayed in government in throughout 2001/2002 (Slovak Spectator, 12 March 2001). At the same time, European conditionality allowed much leeway for domestic policy-makers as the international actors refrained from making accession dependent on specific policies towards minorities. The administrative reform that was eventually adopted confirmed the majoritarian principle of government and strengthened state sovereignty by increasing interethnic stability and improving the situation of the Hungarians, without moving towards ethnopolitical power-sharing or giving in to further reaching minority demands for functional autonomies (Deets & Stroschein, 2005). However, although minimal changes to the legislation during accession negotiations have effectively alleviated minority claims, the European acceptance of status quo minority policies has helped consolidate majority dominance around the notion of national sovereignty during accession period.

Although Slovakia had signed the accession treaty in 2003, European conditionality continued. The fact that Dzurinda government remained in office until 2006 allowed for continuity in dealing with the European recommendations concerning minority protection. Significantly, government had conceded to establish a university with Hungarian as its primary working and teaching language as of 2003 following the suggestion by the European monitors. The act fulfilled an agreement made in the 1995 Basic Treaty with Hungary, and was a late coalition compromise regarding demands from the SMK. The establishment of the 'Hungarian' university should be seen as a minor success for the SMK in government rather than a significant step in Slovakia's minority polices induced from the outside. And yet, the university law did not represent a change in Slovakia's approach to minority protection. Even though the HZDS–SNS government in the mid-1990s had adopted a range of policies that aimed to undermine the well-established system of Hungarian language education, this system remained widely accepted across Slovakia and was constitutionally guaranteed.

The preparedness of the government to finally adopt a law to improve the opportunities for university level education in Hungarian stood in contrast to its reluctance to adopt legislation to follow up the aspects the MLL had left unregulated, and to implement the European Charter for Regional or Minority Languages (ECRML), equally contradicting coalition agreements and international recommendations. In 2009, a Hungarian representative for the SMK still claimed that 'nothing has been implemented from those [international] recommendations. Actually the government said many times... that "now these [are] recommendations not obligations, so we are not going to fulfil them"'.[3] Instead, in 2009, five years after Slovakia's EU accession the Fico government returned to restrictive language legislation with a resurrection of the intermittently abolished SLL of 1995.[4] It was only after the elections of 2010 that the Radičová-government amended the state language law, reducing the potential negative impact on minority language use. In addition, the government moderately expanded the MLL, if with a watered down 'compromise' in light of nationalist opposition claims that the law implemented the 'agenda' of the Hungarian state (Dušan Čaplovič, Education Minister cited in Slovak Spectator, 30 May 2011). Still, the law further validated the primacy of the Slovak legislation over the ECRML.[5]

Even though the European Commission, the OSCE and other European actors had criticised the insufficient provisions of the MLL upon the law's adoption, acknowledging that the MLL's enforcement was dependent on further legislation in the spirit of the MLL (European Commission, 1999), they did not get involved with the amendments of the policy during accession negotiations or post-accession. When between 2000 and 2006 the SMK initiated several draft laws attempting to devise a comprehensive minority law to regulate all questions of minority protection, including those left open by the MLL, these were not supported by the European actors (Regelmann, 2009, p. 194). The hesitation of European organisations of course resonates with their overall reluctance to advise on policy content (Slovak Spectator, 16 September 2009).

Despite the non-involvement of European organisations in post-accession minority policies, Europe remained a framework of reference for majority and minority actors in Slovakia. The law on the 'Hungarian' university in Slovakia triggered a debate in which opposition parties as well as members of government repeatedly referred to their interpretation of what it means to be European (Slovak Spectator, 24 March 2004), with opposition parties calling the establishment of a university a 'provincial and non-European act' and government representatives declaring it a timely policy when the country was 'at the gates of the EU and education is key to success for all nations' (Slovak Spectator, 3 November 2003). Thus, the European framework was used as a rhetorical tool to justify policy preferences and since Slovakia's EU accession, there are even fewer reasons for the political elite to debate those aspects of Slovak statehood that are at the root of interethnic tensions.[6]

Post-accession minority policies in Slovakia and Estonia therefore validated European norms after their own political objectives of nation- and state-building were consolidated. The European conditionality pressure provided an opportunity window to engage in what appeared to be moderately expansionist minority policies, which in post-accession Slovakia and Estonia could be built upon without direct reference to the European framework but in pursuit of enhanced governance and institutional capacity. However, the lack of clear European criteria on minority issues also meant that domestic policies continue to be subject to politicking by various political elites. In this vein, international actors have emphasised the need to protect minority rights and urged Slovakia and Estonia to entrench minority rights issues in domestic policy framework, leaving both states sufficient space to manoeuver when implementing policies on the ground.

Conclusions

Strategic objective of joining the EU was no doubt a shared policy objective among the political elites in the post-communist states. In this paper we have argued that the consensus about the foreign policy objectives (EU accession) across societies in accession states was built on domestic actors' perceptions of *national* sovereignty over policy-making. Domestic institutional design allowed the majority political elites to tap into the conceptual toolbox provided by the discourse on European integration in order to consolidate and ultimately validate policy-making as a penultimate domestic affair.

In our discussion we have outlined how minority issues were reflected in Slovak and Estonian policy dynamics through the lens of the European conditionality pressures. European normative standards, continuously referred to during domestic decisions on addressing minority issues, not only allowed domestic political elites to pursue their interest while anticipating significant pay-offs after EU membership was achieved. The majority political elites specifically, have construed 'European integration' as a bulwark securing national sovereignty in policy-making, while at the same time securitising domestic minorities as a liability for majoritarian decision-making. This underscores the very fact that European accession did exercise pressures on post-communist accession states to reassess minority–majority relations. Yet it did so not so much to strengthen perceptions of participatory decision-making domestically, but to support majoritarian ideals of the incumbent state-bearing majorities.

Our study focused on the effects of European integration on minority rights issues and minority participation in decision-making process. In both case studies we have observed that the perceived pressures to change policy-making in the run-up to the EU accession added to, rather than deconstructed the sovereignty in domestic policy-making as the primary concern of Estonian and Slovak majority political elites. Importantly, perceived pressure to accede the EU constituted crucial nodes to construct domestic policies as being passed as a result of European conditionality. However, policy dynamics and changes in policy-making rationale post-accession suggest that much of these policies changed not to improve relations between the minority and the majority, i.e., debunk security concerns over minority issues.

Rather, the toolbox of European integration provided clear guidelines as to how the majority political elites could entrench ideals of state-ownership in policies and institutions, thus increasing sovereignty perceptions after the EU accession. Thus, the EU accession of Estonia and Slovakia has consolidated and validated perceptions of state sovereignty as national sovereignty, making it less susceptible to change in the future. Essentially, European integration provided the structural resources for domestic actors to stabilise the status quo in interethnic relations through minimal policy change, while strengthening majorities' independence in policy-making on domestic minority issues.

Acknowledgments

The authors would like to thank Malte Brosig and David J. Galbreath for their insightful comments on earlier drafts of this paper.

Notes

[1] Integration and Migration Foundation (MEIS) reports of activity, see http://www.meis.ee/keeleoppe-arendamise-programm (accessed 13 July 2012).
[2] Authors interview with Tänel Mätlik, Head of the Estonian Integration Foundation, Tallinn, 4 December 2009.
[3] Authors interview with József Berényi, Member of the National Council of the Slovak Republic, Bratislava, 30 June 2009.
[4] Bocian and Groszkowski (2009).
[5] Committee of Ministers' Recommendations, 18 November 2009, http://www.coe.int/t/dg4/education/minlang/Report/Recommendations/SlovakiaCMRec2_en.pdf.
[6] Authors interview with László Öllös, Forum Minority Research Institute, Šamorin, 10 September 2009.

References

Agarin, T. (2010) *A Cat's Lick. Democratisation and minority communities in the post-Soviet Baltic* (Amsterdam: Rodopi).
Bailey, D. & de Propris, L. (2004) A bridge too phare? EU pre-accession aid and capacity-building in the candidate countries, *Journal of Common Market Studies*, 42(1), pp. 77–98.
Birckenbach, H. M. (2000) Half full or half empty? The OSCE mission to Estonia and its balance sheet 1993–1999 (Flensburg: European Centre for Minority issues).
Bocian, M. & Groszkowski, J. (2009) The Slovak–Hungarian dispute over Slovakia's language law, *OSW Commentary*, 10. Available at: http://www.osw.waw.pl/en/publikacje/osw-commentary/2009-10-16/slovak-hungarian-dispute-over-slovakias-language-law (accessed 20 November 2011).
Brosig, M. (2008) A plan for the future? The Estonian state integration programme 2000–2007'. *Journal on Ethnopolitics and Minority Issues in Europe*, 7(2), pp. 1–19.
Brubaker, R. (1996) *Nationalism Reframed: Nationhood and the national question in the new Europe* (Cambridge: Cambridge University Press).
Brusis, M. (2003) The European Union and interethnic power-sharing arrangements in accession countries, *Journal on Ethnopolitics and Minority Issues in Europe*, 4(1), pp. 1–21.
Budryte, D. (2005) *Taming Nationalism? Political community building in the post-Soviet Baltic states.* (Aldershot: Ashgate).
Bunce, V. (2003) Rethinking recent democratization: Lessons from the post-communist experience, *World Politics*, 55(2), pp. 167–192.
CoE (2005) Advisory Committee on the Framework Convention for the Protection of National Minorities. Second opinion on Estonia. Adopted on 24 February 2005. http://www.coe.int/t/dghl/monitoring/minorities/3_FCNMdocs/PDF_2nd_OP_Estonia_en.pdf (accessed 30 October 2012).

Csergo, Z. (2002) Beyond ethnic division: Majority–minority debate about the post-communist state in Romania and Slovakia, *East European Politics and Societies*, 16(1), pp. 1–29.

Deets, S. & Stroschein, S. (2005) Dilemmas of autonomy and liberal pluralism: Examples involving Hungarians in Central Europe, *Nations and Nationalism*, 11(2), pp. 285–305.

Dimitrova, A. (2002) Enlargement, institution-building and the EU's administrative capacity requirement, *West European Politics*, 25(4), pp. 171–190.

Eksamikeskus (2011). The National Examinations and Qualifications Centre. http://www.ekk.edu.ee/welcome-to-the-estonian-language-examination/for-whom-is-the-exam-intended (accessed 30 October 2012).

Van Elsuwege, P. (2008) *From Soviet Republics to EU Member States. A legal and political assessment of the Baltic States' accession to the EU* (Leiden: Martinus Nijhoff Publishers).

Epstein, R. A. & Sedelmeier, U. (2008) Beyond conditionality: International institutions in post-communist Europe after enlargement, *Journal of European Public Policy*, 15(6), pp. 795–805.

Estonian Government (2000) *State Programme Integration in Estonian Society 2000–2007* (Tallinn: Estonian Government).

Estonian Government (2007) *Strategy for the Integration of Estonian Society, 2008–2013* (Tallinn: Estonian Government).

European Commission (1997) Regular report from the Commission on Estonia's progress toward accession, Agenda 2000 - Commission Opinion on Estonia's Application for Membership of the European Union. http://ec.europa.eu/enlargement/archives/pdf/dwn/opinions/estonia/es-op_en.pdf (accessed 30 October 2012).

European Commission (1999) Regular report from the Commission on Slovakia's progress toward accession, 1998 Regular Report from the Commission in Slovakia's Progress Towards Accession. http://ec.europa.eu/enlargement/archives/pdf/key_documents/1998/slovakia_en.pdf (accessed 30 October 2012).

European Commission (2001) Regular report from the Commission on Estonia's progress towards accession, ec.europa.eu/enlargement/archives/pdf/key_documents/2001/ee_en.pdf (accessed 30 October 2012).

European Commission (2002) Regular report from the Commission on Estonia's progress towards accession, 2002 Regular Report on Estonia's Progress Towards Accession. http://www.valitsus.ee/UserFiles/valitsus/et/riigikantselei/euroopa/arhiiv/tegevuskavad-ja-eduaruanded/EE_Monitoring_Report_2002.pdf (accessed 30 October 2012).

European Parliament (1999) *Public opinion on enlargement in the EU member states and applicant countries*. Available at http://www.europarl.europa.eu/enlargement/briefings/41a3_en.htm.

Friis, L. & Murphy, A. (1999) The European Union and Central and Eastern Europe: Governance and boundaries, *JCMS: Journal of Common Market Studies*, 37(2), pp. 211–232.

Galbreath, D. J. (2005) *Nation-building and Minority Politics in Post-socialist States: Interests, influence and identities in Estonia and Latvia* (Stuttgart: ibidem Verlag).

Galbreath, D. J. & McEvoy, J. (2011) *The European Minority Rights Regime: Towards a theory of regime effectiveness* (New York and London: Routledge).

Guelke, A. B. (2010) *Democracy and Ethnic Conflict: Advancing peace in deeply divided societies* (Basingstoke: Palgrave Macmillan).

Hale, H. E. (2006) Democracy or autocracy on the march? The colored revolutions as normal dynamics of patronal presidentialism, *Communist and Post-Communist Studies*, 39(3), pp. 305–329.

Harris, E. (2007) Moving politics beyond the state? The Hungarian minority in Slovakia, *Perspectives: Central European Review of International Affairs*, 28, pp. 43–62.

Haughton, T. (2007) When does the EU make a difference? Conditionality and the accession process in Central and Eastern Europe, *Political Studies Review*, 5(2), pp. 233–246.

Henderson, K. (2002) *Slovakia: The Escape from Invisibility* (London: Routledge).

Hughes, J. & Sasse, G. (2003) Monitoring the monitors: EU enlargement conditionality and minority protection in the CEECs, *Journal of Ethnopolitics and Minority Issues in Europe*, 1(1), pp. 1–36.

Hughes, J., Sasse, G. & Gordon, C. (2004) Conditionality and compliance in the EU's eastward enlargement: Regional policy and the reform of sub-national government, *JCMS: Journal of Common Market Studies*, 42(3), pp. 523–551.

Järve, P. (2003) Language battles in the Baltic States: 1989 to 2002, in: F. Dafta & F. Grin (Ed.) *Nation-Building, Ethnicity and Language Politics in Transition Countries*, pp. 75–105. (Budapest: Central European University Press)

Järve, P. & Poleshchuk, V. (2010) *Country Report: Estonia*. Available at http://eudo-citizenship.eu/docs/CountryReports/Estonia.pdf (accessed 30 October 2012).

Jenne, E. (2004) A bargaining theory of minority demands: Explaining the dog that did not bite in 1990s Yugoslavia, *International Studies Quarterly*, 48(4), pp. 729–754.

Kallas, K. (2008) Legal and political integration, in: M. Lauristin (Ed.) *State Integration Programme 2008–2013. Final Report on Needs and Feasibility Research*, pp. 116–189 (Tartu: Estonian Government).

Kask, P. (1994) National radicalization in Estonia: Legislation on citizenship and related issues, *Nationalities Papers*, 22(2), pp. 379–390.

Kelley, J. G. (2004a) *Ethnic Politics in Europe: The power of norms and incentives* (Oxford: Princeton University Press).

Kelley, J. G. (2004b) International actors on the domestic scene: Membership conditionality and socialization by international institutions, *International Organization* 58(3): 425–457.

Kirch, A., Tuisk Y. & Talst, M. (2006) The aspect of culture in the social inclusion of ethnic minorities. Evaluation of the Impact of Inclusion Policies Under the Open Method of Co-ordination in the European Union: Assessing the Cultural Policies of Six Member States. Final Report: Estonia (Flensburg: European Centre for Minority Issues).

Klimovsky, D. (2010) Public administration reform in Slovakia: 20 years of experience with different institutional settings at the local and regional levels, *Analytical*, 3(1), pp. 28–55.

Langman, J. (2002) Mother-tongue Education Versus Bilingual Education: Shifting Ideologies and Policies in the Republic of Slovakia. *International Journal of the Sociology of Language*, 154, pp. 47–64.

Language Inspection (2011) Keeleinspektsioon, *Keeleinspektsioon*. Available at http://www.keeleinsp.ee/?lang=1. (accessed 30 October 2012).

Lavenex, S. (2008) A governance perspective on the European neighbourhood policy: Integration beyond conditionality?, *Journal of European Public Policy*, 15(6), pp. 938–955.

Lerch, M. & Schwellnus, G. (2006) Normative by nature? The role of coherence in justifying the EU's external human rights policy, *Journal of European Public Policy*, 13(2), pp. 304–321.

Levitz, P. & Pop-Eleches, G. (2010) Why no backsliding? The European Union's impact on democracy and governance before and after accession, *Comparative Political Studies*, 43(4), pp. 457–485.

LICHR (2010) *Russian Schools of Estonia. Compendium of Materials* (Tallinn: Legal Information Centre for Human Rights).

Lynggaard, K. (2011) Domestic change in the face of European integration and globalization: Methodological pitfalls and pathways, *Comparative European Politics*, 9(1), pp. 18–37.

Malloy, T. H. (2009) Social cohesion Estonian style: Minority integration through constitutionalised hegemony and fictive pluralism, in: T. Agarin & M. Brosig (Ed.) *Minority Integration in Central Eastern Europe. Between ethnic diversity and equality*, pp. 225–254 (Amsterdam: Rodopi).

Miller, A. H., Hesli, V. L. & Reisinger, W. M. (1997) Conceptions of democracy among mass and elite in post-Soviet societies, *British Journal of Political Science*, 27(2), pp. 157–190.

Nižňanský, V. & Pilát, J. (2001) Public administration reform in the Slovak republic – management of the process, in: G. Péteri (Ed.) *Mastering Decentralization and Public Administration Reforms in Central and Eastern Europe*, pp. 217–232 (Budapest: OSI & LGI).

O'Dwyer, C. (2004) Runaway state building: How political parties shape states in post-communist Eastern Europe, *World Politics*, 56(4), pp. 520–553.

Oltay, E. (1990) Hungarians in Slovakia Organize to Press for Ethnic Rights, RFE/RL, *Report on Eastern Europe* 1 (22).

Pettai, V. (2003) Prospects for multiethnic democracy in Europe: Debating minority integration in Estonia, *Schriften Zur Rechtstheorie*, 215(1), pp. 53–81.

Pettai, V. & Hallik, K. (2002) Understanding processes of ethnic control: Segmentation, dependency and co-operation in post-communist Estonia, *Nations and Nationalism*, 8(4), pp. 505–529.

Pettai, V. & Kallas, K. (2009) Estonia: Conditionality amidst a legal straightjacket, in: B. Rechel (Ed.) *Minority Rights in Central and Eastern Europe*. pp. 104–118 (London: Routledge).

Poleshchuk, V. (2009) *Chance to Survive: Minority rights in Estonia and Latvia* (Tallinn: Foundation for Historical Outlook).

Pollack, D., Jacobs, J., Müller, O. & Pickel, G. (2003) *Political Culture in Post-Communist Europe: Attitudes in new democracies* (Aldershot: Ashgate).

Pridham, G. (2002) The European Union's democratic conditionality and domestic politics in Slovakia: The Me Iar and Dzurinda governments compared, *Europe–Asia Studies*, 54(2), pp. 203–227.

Rechel, B. (2008) What has limited the EU's impact on minority rights in accession countries?, *East European Politics & Societies*, 22(1), p. 171.

Regelmann, A.-C. (2009) Political community, political institutions and minority politics in Slovakia 1998–2006, in: T. Agarin & M. Brosig (Eds) *Minority Integration in Central Eastern Europe. Between Ethnic Diversity and Equality*, pp. 175–198 (Amsterdam: Rodopi).

Reisch, A. (1993) Slovakia's Minority Policy Under International Scrutiny, RFE/RL Research Report 49 (2), pp. 35–42.

Remmer, K. L. (1992) The process of democratization in Latin America, *Studies in Comparative International Development*, 27(4), pp. 3–24.

Roe, P. (2004) Securitization and minority rights: Conditions of desecuritization, *Security Dialogue*, 35(3), pp. 279–294.

Saideman, S. M. & Ayres, R. W. (2000) Determining the causes of irredentism: Logit analyses of minorities at risk data from the 1980s and 1990s, *Journal of Politics*, 62(4), pp. 1126–1144.

Sasse, G. (2008) The politics of EU conditionality: The norm of minority protection during and beyond EU accession, *Journal of European Public Policy*, 15(6), pp. 842–860.

Schimmelfennig, F. (2001) The community trap: Liberal norms, rhetorical action, and the eastern enlargement of the European Union, *International Organization*, 55(1), pp. 47–80.

Schimmelfennig, F., Engert, S. & Knobel, H. (2003) Costs, commitment and compliance: The impact of EU democratic conditionality on Latvia, Slovakia and Turkey, *Journal of Common Market Studies*, 41(3), pp. 495–518.

Schimmelfennig, F. & Scholtz, H. (2010) Legacies and leverage: EU political conditionality and democracy promotion in historical perspective, *Europe–Asia Studies*, 62(3), pp. 443–460.

Schimmelfennig, F. & Sedelmeier, U. (2004) Governance by conditionality: EU rule transfer to the candidate countries of Central and Eastern Europe, *Journal of European Public Policy*, 11(4), pp. 661–679.

Schmidt, V. A. (2010) Taking ideas and discourse seriously: Explaining change through discursive institutionalism as the fourth "new institutionalism", *European Political Science Review*, 2(1), pp. 1–25.

Schmidt, V. A. & Radaelli, C. M. (2004) Policy change and discourse in Europe: Conceptual and methodological issues, *West European Politics*, 27(2), pp. 183–210.

Schwellnus, G. (2006) Reasons for constitutionalization: Non-discrimination, minority rights and social rights in the convention on the EU charter of fundamental rights, *Journal of European Public Policy*, 13(8), pp. 1265–1283.

Sedelmeier, U. (2002) Sectoral dynamics of EU enlargement: Advocacy, access and alliances in a composite policy, *Journal of European Public Policy*, 9(4), pp. 627–649.

Sedelmeier, U. (2012) Is Europeanisation through conditionality sustainable? Lock-in of Institutional change after EU accession, *West European Politics*, 35(1), pp. 20–38.

Simon, J. (2004) *NATO and the Czech and Slovak Republics: A comparative study in civil–military relations* (Oxford: Rowman & Littlefield).

Smith, D. J. (2002) *Estonia: Independence and European integration* (London: Routledge).

Smith, G. (1996) *The Nationalities Question in the Post-Soviet States* (New York: Longman).

Smooha, S. & Järve, P. (2005) *The Fate of Ethnic Democracy in Post-Communist Europe*. Local Government and Public Service Reform Initiative (Budapest: Open Society Institute).

Vachudova, M. A. (2005) *Europe Undivided: Democracy, leverage, and integration after communism* (New York: Oxford University Press).

The (Non) Implementation of Recommendations of the Committee on the Elimination of Racial Discrimination in the Netherlands Explained

JASPER KROMMENDIJK
Maastricht Centre for Human Rights, Maastricht University, The Netherlands

ABSTRACT *This article examines the implementation of the recommendations (COs) of the committee monitoring the Convention on the Elimination of Racial Discrimination (CERD) and the causal mechanisms leading to compliance. It is shown that these non-binding COs for the Netherlands have been ineffective in terms of securing compliance. One reason for this is the limited usefulness, legitimacy and persuasiveness of CERD and the COs. Another more important reason is the absence of domestic mobilisation in relation to CERD's COs. By analysing some effective COs of the committees monitoring the Convention on the Rights of the Child and the Convention on the Elimination of Discrimination Against Women, this article demonstrates that COs might still be effective when other actors than the government, such as parliament and national courts, take action on the basis of COs. It is shown that action and attention of parliament and national courts is dependent upon the lobbying work of NGOs, which is crucial for the effectiveness of COs.*

Racism, discrimination, xenophobia, integration, ethnicity, minority issues and Islamophobia have all been high on the (political) agenda in the Netherlands, especially since the beginning of this new millennium. In 1965, states adopted the International Convention on the Elimination of Racial Discrimination (ICERD), which addressed several of the above issues both directly as well as in a more indirect and implicit way. The implementation of this Convention is monitored by the Committee on the Elimination of Racial Discrimination (CERD),[1] through a process of state reporting and a constructive dialogue between the government and the committee.[2] The dialogue and the resulting recommendations of CERD, the so-called Concluding Observations (COs), for the Netherlands have not focused on racial discrimination alone, but also on, for example, the situation of the only recognised official minority, the Frisians, or the unemployment among ethnic minority groups. Other issues that have been dealt with over the years include racial segregation in schools and neighborhoods, the high number of minority people leaving the police forces, xenophobic, anti-Semitic and Islamophobic incidents, the civic integration examination and the asylum policy in general.[3]

The salience of racial discrimination and minority issues in the Netherlands raises the question of what the impact of the process of state reporting under ICERD is. In particular, this article assesses the effectiveness of the COs, which is understood as the extent to which policy and/or legislative measures have been taken *as a result of* the COs. The latter definition makes clear that it is important to investigate thoroughly whether a causal relationship exists between COs and *subsequent* measures (Raustiala, 2000, p. 394).[4]

This article also concentrates on the factors that influence the state to implement recommendations and take measures on the basis of the COs. In order to do this, state reporting in the context of ICERD will be contrasted with the process of state reporting under the Convention on the Rights of the Child (CRC) and the Convention on the Elimination of Discrimination Against Women (CEDAW).[5] This article, thus, generates insights in the causal mechanisms and factors contributing to the effectiveness and implementation of recommendations of international monitoring bodies.[6] Hence, although this article examines only one country and three UN human rights treaties, its conclusions might be generalizable, since the causal mechanisms are derived from and supported by theoretical and empirical studies.

The theoretical starting point of this article is that there are no external incentives for change on the basis of and in line with COs (Schimmelfennig & Sedelmeier, 2004). This is because COs are legally speaking non-binding and treaty bodies lack instruments to enforce and coerce compliance with their recommendations. This means that compliance depends, first and foremost, upon soft mechanisms of compliance such as persuasion (Checkel, 2005) as well as *domestic* mechanisms of compliance. Firstly, the idea behind focusing on domestic mechanisms of compliance is that involvement and mobilisation of domestic actors eventually affects and is decisive for compliance with non-binding COs (Simmons, 2009; Dai, 2005; Keck & Sikkink, 1998; Risse et al., 1999). The practical and methodological implication is that this article will examine the extent to which domestic actors, such as parliament, NGOs, the media and national courts, have picked up, discussed and utilised CERD's COs to lobby and pressure the government. This examination is based on a documentary analysis of parliamentary papers, court judgements, the printed press and NGO information gathered through systematic database searches.[7]

The second mechanism of compliance revolves around the idea of a normative compliance pull. Crucial for the effectiveness of COs is that governments feel bound to comply with the COs, although they are non-binding. This compliance pull is contingent on the legitimacy, usefulness, persuasiveness and legal quality of the COs, as well as the authority of the committee (Gibson & Caldeira, 1995; Franck, 2004; Kumm, 2004). The view of government officials towards the process of state reporting is considered an important explanation for the incentives to comply (Hakimi, 2009).[8] Based on this theoretical insight, this article will therefore rely on the attitudes and perceptions of Dutch government officials of the process of state reporting, the committee and the COs. For this purpose several interviews were held.[9]

The first section of the article will show that CERD's COs have been largely ineffective. This ineffectiveness is contrasted in the second section with some of the COs of the CEDAW and CRC committee in order to show that the most important factor for COs' effectiveness is domestic mobilisation and especially NGO lobbying. The third section further substantiates the absence of domestic mobilisation in relation to CERD's COs by examining the extent to which domestic actors, such as parliament, NGOs the media and courts, have used and paid attention to CERD COs. The fourth section will take the soft compliance mechanism as a starting point and will focus on the legitimacy, authority, usefulness and persuasiveness of the process of state reporting, CERD and the COs. This section is based on the author's personal observations from the dialogue of CERD with the Netherlands in 2010 and interviews with government officials. The fifth section will give two other (legal) explanations for the limited effectiveness of CERD's COs.

Examining the (In)effectiveness of CERD's COs

First of all it should be stressed that it is difficult to establish the effectiveness of each and every CO of CERD. This is especially because the government has hardly given a reaction to the COs by, for example, sending a letter to parliament. Nor have parliamentary debates about the COs taken place. Only in some periodic state reports have the government responded to the COs in rather general terms by outlining the policies in the respective area. It is, however, difficult to establish a causal relationship between these measures and the COs.

Another important reason why the effectiveness of COs is difficult to establish is that the COs of CERD in particular are rather broad and unspecific and do not prescribe any particular behaviour. This is especially the case where the COs recommend or encourage the state to continue with its policy,[10] and strengthen, intensify or increase its efforts.[11] With these recommendations, the state is left free to consider how it gives meaning and puts flesh to the COs. COs often coincide with measures already in place and reflect what the government is 'constantly doing'. This means that the COs are ineffective since there is no (causal) relationship between the existing policy or legislative measures and the COs. NGO representatives argued that governments can easily claim that they have acted upon the COs, because of their broadness. The scholar Felice also noted that CERD's COs are not very helpful and only endorse a government's current efforts. They are furthermore superficial and are ill-informed, unspecific and void of any content. As a result, these 'flimsy and ineffectual reports from CERD contribute to the sense of futility and cynicism concerning UN human rights efforts' (Felice, 2002, p. 218).

The only substantive governmental reaction to the COs, those of 2010, is nonetheless indicative of the ineffectiveness of COs in the Netherlands.[12] First of all, the government showed its disagreement with some of the concerns and recommendations of CERD. That is to say, in response to the CO concerning the racist speech emanating from 'a few extremist parties' and the tone of the debate, the government pointed to 'the free and open nature of society' and the importance of dialogue in a democratic state governed by the rule of law. It was furthermore stressed that intimidation of politicians is not tolerated also since the latter have more leeway in public debate. Note that the government also disagreed with rather similar recommendations concerning racial discrimination of the European Commission against Racism and Intolerance (ECRI),[13] which address more or less the same concerns.[14]

Secondly, in its reaction to some of the COs of 2010 the government pointed to existing initiatives and measures which were not taken *as a result of* the COs. That is to say, the government referred to an action programme to combat discrimination of which parliament was informed on 13 September 2010. This programme is, however, primarily focused on anti-Semitism and was not the result of the COs, but of a motion passed during an emergency debate on anti-Semitism. Neither CERD, nor the COs, played any role at all during the debate and were not mentioned in the motion.[15]

The limited effectiveness of COs is further shown by interviews with government officials and NGO representatives involved in the process of state reporting concerning CERD. The interviewees could hardly give true examples of COs that had led to measures or a change in policy or legislation. One NGO representative involved in several reporting cycles of different treaties noted that, in comparison with other treaties, hardly anything was done as a result of the COs, if at all. A government official also noted that of the 30 recommendations of CERD, there were usually 28 recommendations without any effect. The official argued that either the government digs one's heels, in or there are already a lot of measures in place. It was said that if there are two recommendations with which you can really do something, then you can count yourself lucky.

The Effectiveness of (some of the) COs of the CRC and CEDAW Committees

Interestingly, several COs of the CEDAW committee and the Committee on the Rights of the Child (CRC committee) have been effective. The following two examples illustrate this.[16] The CEDAW committee already determined three times that the existence of the political party SGP, represented in the parliament, is a violation of Article 7 CEDAW, because this political party excluded women from membership until 2006 and still continues to exclude women from being eligible for election. The CEDAW committee recommended the state to take urgent measures to address this situation through the adoption of legislation.[17] The government initially argued that in spite of the conclusion of the CEDAW committee, the government is of the opinion that the current legislation meets the obligations of Article 7 CEDAW.[18] Only after the Dutch supreme court delivered a judgement, did the responsible minister show a willingness to take measures.[19] The Supreme Court ruled that the fact that a political party excludes women from being eligible for election cannot be accepted in the light of the prohibition of discrimination and Article 7 CEDAW in specific. According to the Supreme Court, the state is obliged to take effective measures to address this situation.[20] What is especially interesting is that this case was initially taken to court by NGOs, who also pointed to the COs during the legal proceedings. As a result, the Court of Justice did refer to the CEDAW committee's 'judgement' by way of confirming its own conclusion.[21] The COs were also reproduced entirely in the advice of the Solicitor General to the Supreme

Court.[22] At the same time, members of parliament have also discussed or mentioned the COs concerning the SGP several times.

The CRC committee also recommended three times the establishment of an Ombudsman for children, monitoring the implementation of the CRC at the national level.[23] The government was again rather dismissive in the beginning. Nonetheless, the first Children Ombudsman took office on 1 April 2011. Its establishment was the result of a legislative proposal by a member of parliament, Arib (PvdA). Arib made clear that her legislative proposal stemmed from the recommendations of the committee and that the proposal was written together with two NGOs, Defence for Children and Unicef.[24]

These two examples show that NGO lobbying, parliamentary action and/or court judgements are essential intervening variables for COs' effectiveness. In other words, the greater effectiveness of COs of the CEDAW and CRC committees is the result of the larger extent of domestic mobilisation. The greater involvement of domestic actors is clearly demonstrated in the table below. The table shows that that there is a considerable *quantitative* difference between CERD and CEDAW and CRC, especially in terms of parliamentary scrutiny and media coverage.

As will be further substantiated in the third section, CERD's COs are hardly paid any attention to by the government, parliament and national courts as well as NGOs and the printed press. One reason for the limited attention to COs is the fact that parliament is poorly informed about the process of state reporting and the COs. This vacuum is not filled by information provided to parliament by NGOs. In fact, CERD's COs are hardly used in NGOs' lobbying and advocacy work, as a result of which parliamentary scrutiny and action is limited as well. Nor have NGOs or other litigants made use of COs in court proceedings. As a consequence, the government can easily ignore or even disregard the COs.

The lack of NGO lobbying with respect to CERD's CO stands in sharp contrast with numerous very active children and women's rights NGOs. These NGOs, of which the most important are the Dutch CEDAW Network and the Dutch Children's Rights Coalition, focus specifically on the implementation of the respective conventions. While the NGOs that prepared shadow reports in relation to ICERD regard the exercise of compiling such a report primarily as an objective in itself, these NGOs see the shadow report and their involvement in the wider process of state reporting merely as a step in a larger process, the primary purpose of which is political lobby at the national level. This means that their lobbying activities are primarily concentrated on follow-up at the national level and the government's implementation of the COs. Both NGOs sent, for instance, commentaries to the government's reaction to the COs to parliament and the responsible minister. They also organised conferences and seminars to discuss follow-up with members of parliament or sometimes even with the responsible minister. In addition, meetings took place between NGOs and governmental officials about the implementation of the conventions and the process of state reporting. With respect to the CRC, there are even structural half-yearly meetings between the Dutch Children's Rights Coalition and the interdepartmental working group on children's rights. Both NGOs have furthermore started legal proceedings on the basis of the conventions and/or relevant COs. Lobbying by these NGOs on the basis of the COs has been effective as well. NGOs' comments are often explicitly mentioned or reacted upon by

Table 1. Domestic mobilisation in relation to CEDAW, CRC and ICERD. This table shows the number of references to the respective treaty and the COs (between brackets) by several actors

	CEDAW COs 2001, 2007, 2010	CRC COs 1999, 2004, 2009	ICERD COs 1998, 2000, 2004, 2010
Governmental informing of Parliament	Very good	Good	Poor
UN documents	On a structural basis	All reports (but some only after request of parliament)	Only some reports
Reaction to COs	Yes	Not always	No
Parliamentary debate COs	Yes	Only COs 2009	No
Government	194	412	58
	(8)	(22)	(7)
Parliament	143	379	31
	(16)	(50)	(6)
National courts	30	>700	12
	(4)	(2)	(0)
NGOs	Active	Active	Lobbying practically non-existent
Media coverage	24 articles	46 articles	8 articles

parliamentarians during parliamentary debates. The NGO lobby is often a major reason for members of parliament to allude to COs or to even put forward a legislative proposal, as was the case with the Children Ombudsman.

Domestic Mechanism of Compliance: The Absence of Mobilisation

The preceding sections have shown that CERD's COs have been ineffective for the Netherlands. That is to say, COs were either unspecific, broad and vague or they were (implicitly) rejected. The experience with CRC and the CEDAW demonstrates that COs might still be effective when other domestic actors, especially the parliament and national courts, act upon them, even though the government itself was (initially) unwilling to comply with the COs. This section will substantiate that both parliament and government hardly discussed, invoked or referred to the process of state reporting in relation to ICERD and CERD's COs in particular. Neither did NGOs and the media pay serious attention to the COs. At the same time, COs are practically absent in legal practice (Table 1).

Government Informing of Parliament

Parliament is hardly informed of the process of state reporting and the COs by the government. Not all periodic state reports submitted to CERD were sent to parliament.[25] More striking, however, is the fact that the government did not always inform parliament about the COs. The COs of 1998 and 2000 were, for example, not sent to parliament. The Minister of Foreign Affairs did send a letter summarising the COs of 2004, but no substantive reaction to the concerns and recommendations was included. The COs of 2010 were sent to parliament as an attachment to a letter about racial discrimination, again without a substantive governmental response. Neither were the COs nor the government's reaction tabled in parliament for discussion.

The government has only referred to the concerns and recommendations of CERD seven times since 1998. This was merely done in rather general terms whereby primarily the positive aspects noted by CERD were highlighted. Never has the government argued that a certain policy or legislative measure was taken in response or in compliance with the COs. Illustrative of the limited scrutiny of COs by the government are the occasions in which the government refrained from referring to ICERD and/or the COs of CERD, although it would have been logical. For example, the National Action Plan against Racism of 2003 did not mention ICERD at all, nor did the note laying down the integration policy for 2007–2011.

Parliamentary Scrutiny and Action

The role of parliament in relation to the COs of CERD is also rather limited. Parliamentarians have very rarely taken action themselves on the basis of the COs. Neither have they urged or pressed the government to do so. Members of parliament referred to the COs in so-called written parliamentary questions (Kamervragen) on four occasions. In these questions, they merely asked the government's opinion about the COs.[26] Interestingly, several of these questions were the result of newspaper articles referring to the COs. This shows that media coverage of the process of state reporting is essential for attention in parliament to the COs.

There were two occasions when the COs had more impact. Firstly, parliament adopted a motion about the accessibility of education, which mentioned the 'reprimand' of CERD in 2000 as one of the reasons 'for consideration of the deficiencies in the accessibility of the educational system'.[27] Note that this motion was only adopted with 73 against 71 votes. Secondly, the COs 2000 were also alluded to in the Explanatory Memorandum of the legislative proposal of the parliamentarians Vos (GL) and Stuurman (PvdA) concerning the extension of the Employment of Minorities Act (Wet SAMEN). The Bill mentioned the 'strong criticism' of CERD concerning the situation in the Netherlands with respect to the big difference in unemployment rates between ethnic minority groups and the native Dutch population and the insufficient protection against discrimination in the labour market.[28] The reference to CERD was, however, one among many other studies and reports covering 17 pages. It, thus, seems that the COs merely served as an additional argument. Further proof for this is that the COs were not mentioned during the rest of the parliamentary discussion. The COs were certainly not decisive, since the Bill was eventually not adopted.

Court Judgements and Legal Practice

National courts have only touched upon ICERD 12 times since December 1999. COs or General Recommendations of CERD have not been considered by national courts. The majority of those 12 cases mentioned ICERD in relation to the interpretation of the notion race or the interpretation of Article 137 (c) and (d) in the Criminal Code, which prohibit public intentional insults and incitement of hatred, discrimination or violence. At other times courts examined the provisions of ICERD more substantively, but often in conjunction with provisions of other human rights treaties such as the ECHR and ICCPR that were discussed in the first place and more extensively. What is more, some courts have even denied the ICERD to have direct effect. This means that individuals cannot directly derive rights from the Convention, nor can they claim their violation in court.

Illustrative of the emphasis on other provisions than ICERD is the judgement of the Court of Justice in Amsterdam ordering the criminal prosecution of the politician Geert Wilders of the PVV for incitement of hatred. ICERD did not play a role at all in the court proceedings. The only treaty law provisions which were considered by the court were Articles 18, 19, 20, 26 and 27 ICCPR, Articles 9, 10, 14 and 17 ECHR and Articles 1 and 7 of the Constitution, besides several provisions in the Dutch Criminal Code.[29] Likewise, a court exclusively considered Article 1 of the Constitution in its judgement that the investigations as to the factual residence and the rights to social security of Somali people in particular is racial discriminatory.[30] These examples show that national courts primarily rely upon the ECHR, ICCPR and the Constitution in relation to racial discrimination.

Media Coverage

Only eight articles have appeared in the printed press about the concerns and COs of CERD since 1 September 1995. The attention and the extent to which the COs were picked up decreased over time. That is to say, the 'reprimand' and concerns of CERD in 1998 were mentioned in four articles, and the COs of 2000 were covered thrice. By contrast, only one article appeared about the COs of 2004, while the dialogue and the COs of 2010 were not dealt with at all in the press. As has been mentioned already, media coverage often leads to questions and discussions in parliament. The limited media attention, thus, partly explains the marginal parliamentary scrutiny of COs and ICERD.

NGOs' Lobbying

NGOs have hardly used COs in their lobby and advocacy. In other words, the extent to which NGOs have exerted pressure on the government and parliament by criticising the policies of government on the basis of COs is limited. Their involvement in the process of state reporting has not gone further than the writing of shadow reports in English for the Geneva-based CERD.[31] Follow-up to COs at the national level has merely consisted of the issuing of press communiqués after the constructive dialogue. These press statements have remained without any result and have almost not been picked up by the media. NGOs have paid little attention to COs and the concerns of CERD in their lobby and advocacy activities and letters to parliament and government. One representative of an NGO acknowledged this and stated that NGOs have not lobbied for the implementation of COs.

There are several reasons why lobbying is practically non-existent in relation to CERD's COs. First of all, there is no NGO which is primarily focused on the (implementation of) ICERD as such.[32] Secondly, the NGOs that have drawn up shadow reports for CERD have limited financial and bureaucratic resources and lack the experience to employ wider lobby and advocacy activities.[33] Thirdly,

CERD's COs are broader and more unspecific than the COs of the other two committees and, as a result, not very useful for lobbying.

Soft Mechanism of Compliance: The Absence of a Compliance Pull

As we have seen in the introduction, crucial for compliance is that governments feel bound to obey COs, although they are non-binding. This compliance pull is contingent on the legitimacy, usefulness, persuasiveness and legal quality of the COs, as well as the authority of CERD. This section will address the functioning of CERD and the COs, based on the author's personal observations from the dialogue of CERD with the Netherlands in 2010 and the perception of government officials rested on several interviews. Both subsections raise, however, doubts about the professionalism and functioning of CERD and, hence, the authority and legitimacy of CERD and quality of COs. This means that a compliance pull is absent, as a result of which the government is not likely to comply with the COs out of its own motion. Note that this article does not aim to criticise expert members individually, especially since some of these small 'errors' are completely understandable given the fact that expert members of CERD fulfil their work voluntarily and without any remuneration, often next to full-time jobs.[34]

As will be discussed below, government officials were almost equally critical about the functioning of the UN human rights treaty bodies. That is to say, they were not significantly more positive about the functioning, quality or authority of the CRC or CEDAW committee and their COs. This insight adds further proof that domestic mobilisation is the major factor or causal pathway leading to COs' effectiveness.

The Constructive Dialogue between CERD and the Netherlands in 2010[35]

The dialogue with CERD started with an opening statement of the government. The Country Rapporteur, Lahiri, gave his view right after the opening statement of the government. He rather easily concluded that the shift in policy concerning the socio-economic integration of immigrant and ethnic communities, whereby the minorities themselves bear principal responsibility, had led to increased anti-immigrant sentiment, hate speech and Islamophobia, without elaborating upon the assumed causal relationship. Likewise, he had already come to the conclusion that the Civic Integration (Preparation Abroad) Act is racially discriminatory, because the overseas integration test only applies to nationals of non-Western countries and had led to a significant reduction of migrants from Morocco and Turkey in particular. He did not raise any questions in his intervention, nor did he ask the government for a reaction to his point of view. In addition, after the answers of the government to the questions of the other experts, he himself did not have any follow-up questions. Remarkably, the preliminary conclusions of the Country Rapporteur at the end of the dialogue were more or less similar to his introductory words.

In general, the dialogue was not structured based on the articles in the Convention, as was for example the case with the dialogue with the CEDAW committee. There were hardly any references to previous COs, nor were the articles of the Convention referred to. Expert member Prosper even said to the government that they might do with the COs what they liked. Remarkably, there was no time limit for expert members of CERD. The consequence of this is, for example, that the expert from Algeria had the chance to take the floor for 18 minutes with a harangue against measures of the Western world against 'countries of Muslim faith' at international airports. He argued that measures against terrorism that punish and humiliate a whole people constitute a violation of ICERD. He also highlighted that he himself is a Muslim and that 'we' (the Muslim world) love art, noting that calligraphy was brought from the Muslim world to Europe. He acknowledged that his concern was not directed at the Netherlands, and that the problem is much larger.[36]

This statement is illustrative of the dialogue in which a lot of experts make statements that were not directly related to the particular situation in the Netherlands, but more generally about Europe and Western countries and the challenges they are facing in light of immigration and integration. Expert member Lindgren made clear that only on rare occasions does CERD have the opportunity to discuss the substance of its work. The second round of questions particularly consisted more of a general philosophical debate about integration, assimilation, the right to identity, diversity and universality of values. Hence, the answers of the government also focused on the broader discussion about integration and assimilation, as a result of which specific questions about the situation in the Netherlands were largely left unanswered. One expert member of CERD explained that the reason for such a broad discussion is that a lot of expert members are from non-Western countries.

What is more, several questions were about issues from years ago. One expert wanted to know again the rationale for the adoption of the Employment of Minorities (Promotion) Act in 1998 and its abolition in December 2003, although this was already addressed in the context of the discussion of the previous reports. Another question dealt with the judgement of the Court of Justice of 29 April 2003 sentencing the Chair of the Nederlandse VolksUnie (NVU) to imprisonment for insulting, racist remarks. Likewise, the government was asked for an explanation as to the assassinations of Fortuijn and van Gogh in 2002 and 2004.

The questions and statements of the expert members not only reflected but also explicitly included personal opinions and backgrounds.[37] Furthermore, in contrast with the CEDAW committee, experts frequently included anecdotes in their statements.[38] The general discussion with a lot of personal reflections might well be the result of the fact that committee members were not that well prepared. One expert asked whether the urban marines would only apply to the Antillean community or to the entire population. It is unclear whether the expert had read the answers of the government to the List of Issues in which it was stated that those urban marines were not specifically created for the Antillean community.

The COs and recommendations of CERD are significantly shorter than those of the CEDAW committee and lack a motivation and reasoning. COs hardly refer to the substantive provisions in ICERD as a result of which it is unclear whether they rest upon legal obligations included in ICERD.[39] We have already seen that the Country Rapporteur had some easy conclusions in his introductory statement. This is striking in light of the sometimes far-reaching recommendations. CERD, for example, recommended reviewing the Civic Integration (Preparation Abroad) Act with a view to abolish its discriminatory application.[40]

Dutch Government Officials' Views on CERD

Research on compliance with COs of the CEDAW committee in the Netherlands concluded that the biggest obstacles for compliance were the not so positive attitudes and ideas of government officials about the usefulness, legitimacy, authority and persuasiveness of the process of state reporting and the CEDAW committee (Krommendijk, 2012). This perception of government officials is reinforced by the – in their eyes inefficient – functioning and working of the CEDAW committee. Issues that came up during the interviews and in parliamentary papers were the idea that the Netherlands is already fulfilling its obligations under CEDAW and that government officials see the dialogue with the CEDAW committee as a matter of defending its report, whereby the main objective is to give 'a good answer'. In relation to the functioning of the CEDAW committee as well as some other treaty bodies, government officials pointed to the basic and limited knowledge of several committee members about the specific national context and the fact that the committee easily relies on information and criticism of NGOs as a result of the limited possibility and time for experts to prepare themselves. In addition, the lack of independence and the political nature of the process were mentioned, as well as the limited usefulness of some COs because of their broadness and unspecifity. Officials also noted the long time span between the submission of the report and the List of Issues, both dealing with a period long before, while a lot of new developments have taken place in the meantime. As a consequence, the usefulness and impact is diminished as well. Similarly, COs are seen as insufficiently motivated and lacking reasoning.

Government officials involved in the process of state reporting under both Conventions made clear in interviews that there were no significant differences between CERD and the CEDAW committee. Both government officials as well as NGO representatives adopted even a more critical attitude towards the dialogue with CERD in 2010 than CEDAW in 2010 and noted that expert members were not (or only poorly) prepared. One government official, who attended several sessions of different committees, observed that especially the expert members of CERD did not understand how the Netherlands exactly works. What is more, CERD hardly listened to and did anything with the replies of the government. Government officials also had the impression that the COs were already completed before the session, because the COs did not reflect the dialogue and did not take into consideration the government's replies. NGO representatives observed that CERD members were ill-informed about details in legislation and current discussions in parliament.

Other Explanations for the Ineffectiveness of CERD's COs

A Fundamental Divergence of Views between CERD and the Government

Another explanation for the limited effectiveness of CERD's COs, is the fundamental divergence of views about the nature of some obligations under ICERD between the government and CERD. This divergence of views essentially boils down to how one views the role and functions of the state in society and the extent to which other fundamental rights and freedoms and multiformity as such should be respected, given the potential clash that exists between state action and, for example, the individual's privacy and freedom of expression, association, religion and education.

During the dialogue with CERD in 2010, the Dutch delegation, for example, stressed that it would be wrong to take measures on specific groups, because this would lead to segregation.[41] The government therefore takes a generic policy targeted at all Dutch citizens, irrespective of their gender, descent or religious and confessional beliefs.[42] Similarly, the government stated that it does not take policies targeting specific forms of discrimination, including racial discrimination. By contrast, CERD has recommended in its COs for the Netherlands to take special measures and policies aimed at specific groups.[43] This example shows that the Dutch government and CERD sometimes take fundamentally different positions. CERD's COs about these issues remain consequently ineffective. This also highlights the dilemma in anti-discrimination policy, which is touched upon by the government in relation to some recommendations of ECRI which are similar to CERD's. ECRI recommended specific policies aimed at Roma, Sinti and Travellers, while it opposed policies targeted at specific groups, such as Antilleans, because it would lead to racial profiling.

The government also disregarded several recommendations, because the issues dealt with in the recommendations not only relate to combating (racial) discrimination but also deal with other – potentially conflicting – interests and human rights which are considered equally or even more important. The government made, for example, clear that the tone of the political and public debate should not only be seen in light of racial discrimination, but also freedom of expression. Likewise, prescribing the way in which human rights are taught at Dutch schools also affects freedom of education. In the context of those conflicting rights, the government seems to adopt a 'justified limitation approach' whereby measures that result in indirect discrimination could, nevertheless, be objectively and reasonably justified when they are legitimate, necessary and proportional. Implicit in the reasoning of the government is the approach by the European Court of Human Rights (ECtHR).[44] It seems that CERD does not adopt such a balancing approach and, hence, pays less attention to other clashing human rights and public interests.[45]

The Dominance of ECHR and EU Obligations

Another explanation for the limited impact and ineffectiveness of CERD's COs is related to the issue of legal overlap and the fact that 'preference' is given to the more precise obligations in the context of the ECHR and the European Union (EU) by national courts and government. As we have seen, national courts have mainly examined other provisions human rights treaties instead of ICERD. Governmental and parliamentary scrutiny, legal practice and scholarly writing with respect to racial discrimination have focused primarily on provisions of ECHR and the jurisprudence developed by the ECtHR.[46] In addition, also the more mandatory and detailed EU rules and jurisdiction of the European Court of Justice (ECJ) in the field of racial discrimination might discourage interest in the noncommittal system of state reporting under ICERD.[47]

Hence, the limited impact and effectiveness of CERD's COs might also be due to the dominance of these other international law regimes. In the instances in which the government gave a reaction to the recommendations of the UN human rights treaty bodies and rejected the COs, the government has sometimes justified its noncompliance with several COs on the basis of other international obligations and jurisprudence of international courts, especially in the context of the ECHR and EU. Noncompliance with recommendations of ECRI in the field of racial discrimination were discarded by pointing to the ECHR and the jurisprudence of the ECtHR.[48] Likewise, the Minister of Justice argued in his response to the recommendation of the Human Rights Committee concerning the use of anonymous witnesses that the government has made use of the margin left in the standard jurisprudence of the ECtHR.[49] In the context of the CEDAW committee's CO about the discrimination part-time workers are facing in relation to overtime, the government mentioned the ruling of the ECJ that 'it was not discriminatory to deny overtime pay to a part-time worker'.[50] There seems to be an idea in government circles that if one complies with the ECHR and EU law, than one also automatically complies with the standards in UN human rights treaties. Such a view, however, neglects that treaty standards and the interpretation of these standards by international courts or committees may differ (Lahuerta, 2009).

The governnment, thus, prefers to have an authoritative statement of the law through a binding judgement by an international or domestic court.[51] During the interviews, several government officials contrasted the UN human rights treaty bodies with the ECtHR and the ECJ. They argued that not only does the legally binding character of the judgements of the ECtHR clearly affect the authority of the court positively, but that the impact of the judgements is also bigger.[52] Hence, government officials are compelled to pay more attention to those judgements, the result of which is that daily activities within a department are oriented towards the jurisprudence of the ECJ and ECtHR. On the other hand, COs are seen as 'advices' or mere 'opinions', whereby it is made clear that the political appraisal is eventually made in the Netherlands. During interviews, government officials noted that due to their non-binding character, COs could easily be rejected and disregarded (Krommendijk, 2011).

Conclusion

In the Netherlands, CERD's COs hardly ever lead to new or additional policy and legislative measures. The government is not eager to immediately act upon and comply with COs. A compliance pull is absent given the not so positive attitudes and ideas of government officials about the usefulness, legitimacy, authority and persuasiveness of the process of state reporting, CERD and the COs. Such a legitimacy deficit is, however, not an insurmountable obstacle for COs effectiveness, as some effective COs of the CRC and CEDAW committee show. COs can be effective when parliament, courts and NGOs take action or pressure the government to adopt or change a certain policy. This article has shown that such domestic mobilisation is absent in relation to CERD's COs. As a result, CERD's COs hardly play a role in policy-making and the government can easily ignore and disregard COs. By contrast, some of COs of the CRC and CEDAW committee have been effective as a consequence of domestic mobilisation. The conclusion that the involvement of domestic actors is essential for the effectiveness of COs and the implementation of UN human rights treaties confirms existing theoretical and empirical studies (Simmons, 2009; Dai, 2005; Keck & Sikkink, 1998; Risse et al., 1999). In sum, the most promising way in which the implementation of recommendations of international monitoring bodies and international treaties could be facilitated or strengthened is through the increased participation of domestic actors such as NGOs, courts and parliament.

Acknowledgements

This research is part of a more extensive PhD research that will be conducted from November 2009 until November 2013 and focuses on state reporting under the six main UN human rights treaties. The author would like to thank Theo van Boven, Malte Brosig, Timofey Agarin as well as the anonymous reviewers for their comments on the first draft. All errors remain the author's sole responsibility.

Notes

[1] CERD is composed of 18 independent experts 'of high moral standing and acknowledged impartiality elected by States Parties from among their nationals, who shall serve in their personal capacity', as Article 8 ICERD provides. The legal basis for the system of state reporting is provided by Article 9 ICERD. Note that CERD is also able to receive state communications (Article 11) and communications from individuals on the basis of Article 14 ICERD.

[2] The system of reporting is based on a so-called constructive dialogue between a treaty monitoring body and representatives of a state party. Input for the dialogue comes from periodic reports submitted by states, plus alternative information presented by non-governmental organisations. Examination of a state report ends with the adoption of COs by the treaty body. COs contain suggestions and recommendations for an improved implementation of the treaty standards by the state concerned.

[3] The focus of this article is on the period after 1995, in which the situation in the Netherlands has been considered four times by CERD, in 1998, 2000, 2004 and 2010. Concluding observations of the Committee on the Elimination of Racial Discrimination, ICERD/C/304/Add.46, 30 March 1998. ICERD/C/304/Add.104, 1 May 2001. ICERD/C/64/CO/7, 10 May 2004. ICERD/C/NLD/CO/17-18, 25 March 2010.

[4] Policies or legislation could be in line with the COs without them having had any role whatsoever in policy decisions. Compliance with COs may, thus, occur without any (additional) policy or legislative measures. For this reason, one has to determine whether COs have led to (an adjustment of) policy or legislative measures. According to Raustiala 'an effective rule is simply a rule that leads to observable, desired behavioural change. Effectiveness is the measure of that change' (2006, p. 394). What distinguishes effectiveness from compliance is the causal impact of legal rules or recommendations on the government's behaviour.

[5] Note that this article does not aim to offer an in-depth and comparative analysis of the effectiveness of the COs of the CERD, CRC and CEDAW committees. The experience with CRC and CEDAW is primarily used to illustrate that the COs of the CRC and CEDAW committees have been more effective because of the greater extent of mobilisation of domestic actors, including parliament, NGOs and courts.

[6] This article has chosen the concept of effectiveness instead of implementation or compliance, because effectiveness also implies a causal relation between (implementing) measures and the COs. See supra note 5.

[7] For the attention of the government and parliament, use was made of the online database for parliamentary papers, Parlando (parlando.sdu.nl). I searched for 'rassendiscriminatie' AND verdrag' (269 results) in the period of 1 January 1995 until 5 April 2010. Additionally, a search was performed with the terms 'IVURD' (one result), 'ICERD' (seven results), 'IVRD' (seven results), 'IVUR' (11 results), 'rassenverdrag' (four results), 'antiracismeverdrag' (four results) and 'ICERD' (79 results). On 23 December 2010 an updated search was performed with the new database zoek.officielebekendmakingen.nl. For court judgements, a search was performed with 'IVURD', 'ICERD', 'IVRD', 'antiracismeverdrag', 'rassenverdrag', 'verdrag ter uitbanning van alle vormen van discriminatie'

and 'VURD' (all 0 results), 'IVUR' (one result), 'internationaal verdrag inzake de uitbanning van alle vormen van rassendiscriminatie' (eight results), 'ICERD' (four results) and 'rassendiscriminatie' AND 'verdrag' (16 results) in the online database www.rechtspraak.nl (30 June 2010). For the analysis of the impact of the COs and ICERD on the media (printed press), use was made of the Lexis Nexis newspaper search engine that provides access to five of the major countrywide newspapers: De Volkskrant, NRC Handelsblad, Trouw, Het Parool and AD/ Algemeen Dagblad. On 30 June 2010 a search was conducted to 'rassendiscriminatie' AND 'verdrag' for the period 1 September 1994 and 30 June 2010 (65 results). Additionally, a search was performed with the terms 'IVURD', 'ICERD', 'IVRD' and 'rassenverdrag' (0 results each), 'antiracismeverdrag' (four results), 'ICERD' (12 results), 'rassendiscriminatie' and 'comite' (42 results). For the lobbying of NGOs, a systematic search of several websites of NGOs was conducted on 30 June 2010 via google with 'ICERD', IVUR, 'ras' AND 'Comité' and 'rassendiscriminatie'. The websites consulted: www.njcm.nl, www.art1.nl (Dutch National Association Against Discrimination (Art. 1 and formerly Landelijk Bureau Rassendiscriminatie (LBR)), www.commissie-meijers.nl (Standing Committee of Experts on International Immigration, Refugee and Criminal law), www.amnesty.nl (Dutch section of Amnesty International) and www.vluchtelingenwerk.nl (Dutch Council for Refugees). Furthermore, www.forum.nl (Institute for multicultural affairs), www.acvz.com (Advisory Committee on Migration Affairs), www.onderwijsraad.nl (Education Council) and www.cgb.nl (Equal Treatment Commission).

[8] Hakimi argued in relation to the experience of the United States before the treaty monitoring bodies in recent years that it is unlikely that states accept as law the norms advanced by actors and institutions, such as the treaty bodies, if they consider them illegitimate or merely aspirational.

[9] Thirty-six interviews were conducted with (former) Dutch government officials from six different ministries involved in the process of state reporting. Note that 12 were involved in the process of state reporting under ICERD. Furthermore, 19 NGO representatives were interviewed, of which five were considerably involved in the process of state reporting and the drawing up of shadow reports in relation to ICERD.

[10] See for example ICERD/C/64/CO/7, 10 May 2004, para. 10: 'The Committee encourages the State party to continue monitoring all tendencies which may give rise to racist and xenophobic behaviour and to combat the negative consequences of such tendencies'. Or para. 11: 'The Committee encourages the State party to continue its efforts to combat this contemporary manifestation of racial discrimination'.

[11] See for example ICERD/C/304/Add.104, 1 May 2001: 'The Committee expresses concern at de facto school segregation in a number of localities and recommends that the State party undertake further measures to reduce de facto segregation'. See also ICERD/C/64/CO/7, 10 May 2004, para. 10: 'The Committee recommends that the State party take adequate policy measures to ensure proper representation of ethnic minority groups in the labour market'.

[12] Information received from Netherlands on the implementation of the concluding observations of CERD, C/NLD/CO/17-18/Add.1, 2 August 2011.

[13] ECRI was established in 1994 as a CoE institution consisting of 47 expert members entrusted with the task of, amongst others, reviewing and monitoring member states' legislation, policies and other measures to combat racism, racial discrimination, xenophobia, antisemitism and intolerance. One of its most important task is the country-by-country monitoring in the context of which ECRI closely examines the situation concerning manifestations of racism and intolerance in each of the CoE member states. Note that ECRI is not a treaty body since it does not monitor the implementation of treaty obligations.

[14] In its response to the report of ECRI that is attached to the report itself, the government stated that it did not share all the conclusions and recommendations of ECRI. Amongst other things, the tone of the political and public debate, the policy for Roma and Sinti, the Antillean Reference Index, the Urban Areas (Special Measures) Act, the scope of the Equal Treatment Act, education and awareness raising. See the response of the government of the Netherlands to ECRI's draft third report 2003–2007 in the annex to ECRI's third report on the Netherlands (CRI (2008) 3), 45–51.

[15] The motion requested the government to draw up an action programme on anti-Semitism. Parliamentary Papers II 2009/10, 32123 VI, no. 111, 24 June 2010.

[16] COs of the CRC committee that have been – partly – effective concern the prohibition of corporal punishment, the amendment prescribing that juvenile offenders would be housed separately from children institutionalised for behavioural problems and the amendment which made it impossible to

impose a life imprisonment on anyone between the age of 16 and 18. COs of the CEDAW committee that have proven to be effective to a certain extent were the Law on Names, in relation to which a working group was established as a result of extensive parliamentary pressure. In addition, attention was paid by the government to the fact that the policy on violence against women is couched in gender-neutral wording.

[17] A/56/38(SUPP), para. 219-220. CEDAW/C/NLD/CO/4, para. 25-26. CEDAW/C/NLD/CO/5, para. 10.

[18] Parliamentary Papers II 2001/02, szw0000961, 2. Fourth periodic report of state parties, CEDAW/C/NLD/4, 47-48. The government also refused to withdraw its appeal against the judgment of the Court of Justice, as recommended by the CEDAW committee, because it considered the matter to be very principal.

[19] During the broadcast of the television programme NOVA on 9 April 2010, the then Minister of the Interior and Kingdom Relations, Ernst Hirsch Ballin, stated that the judgement of the Supreme Court is fully respected and that, thus, new legislation was needed. The political party SGP has, nevertheless, submitted a complaint before the ECtHR. The current government has therefore decided to wait for the final judgement of the ECtHR to take effective measures.

[20] LJN: BK4547, Supreme Court, 08/01354, paras. 4.5.5, 4.6.1 and 4.6.2.

[21] LJN: BC0619, Court of Justice, 05/1725, para. 5.10.

[22] See paras. 1.4, 2.20 and 2.21 of the conclusion by Mr F. F. Langemeijer, LJN: BK4547, Supreme Court, 08/01354.

[23] CRC/C/15/Add.114, para. 12. CRC/C/15/Add.227, para. 8, 20 and 21. CRC/C/NLD/CO/3, para. 8, 16 and 17.

[24] Parliamentary Papers II 2009/10, 31831, nr. 1–3 and nr. 9, 20.

[25] The Minister of Foreign Affairs did send parliament the combined fifteenth and sixteenth periodic state report (2003) and the combined seventeenth and eighteenth report (2008). The thirteenth and fourteenth periodic reports (2000) were, however, not sent to parliament.

[26] Parliamentary Papers II 1997/98, nr. 1148, 10 March 1998. Parliamentary Papers II 1997/98, nr. 1283, 27 March 1998. Parliamentary Papers II 2001/02, nr. 1265, 24 May 2002. Parliamentary Papers II 2000/01, 27412, nr. 3, 6.

[27] The motion was proposed by Lambrechts (D66), Hamer (PvdA) and Rabbae (GL). Parliamentary Papers II 2001/02, 28000 VIII, nr. 71, 29 November 2001.

[28] According to the members of parliament, the Netherlands would not 'be entitled to speak' internationally without an extension of the Act. Parliamentary Papers II 2003/04, 29275, nr. 3, 9 and 14–15.

[29] LJN: BH0496, Court of Justice Amsterdam, K08/0309.

[30] LJN: BA5410, District Court Haarlem, AWB 05-2090 and 05-2093 WWB.

[31] The Dutch section of the International Commission of Jurists (NJCM) and the Dutch National Association Against Discrimination (Art. 1 and formerly Landelijk Bureau Rassendiscriminatie (LBR)) have drawn up separate commentaries to the periodic reports submitted by the Netherlands, so called shadow reports. The Equal Treatment Commission has also given its comments about periodic state reports.

[32] Of the two NGOs most involved in the process of state reporting under ICERD, NJCM focuses on the full spectrum of human rights, irrespective of their source. Art. 1 concentrates on discrimination. Note that its predecessor, LBR, dealt with racial discrimination alone.

[33] NJCM, for example, primarily consists of volunteers, who do their NGOs work in their free time, often besides full time jobs. In addition, most of them are academics, civil servants, lawyers and judges who are not accustomed to lobbying.

[34] It is important to mention that states are responsible for the nomination and election of expert members and for the allocation of sufficient financial resources on the basis of Article 8 ICERD. In that sense, states themselves directly have influence on the functioning of CERD.

[35] This subsection is a purely personal account of the dialogue between CERD and the Dutch delegation about the combined seventeenth and eighteenth report on 23 and 24 February 2010, Geneva. See also the summary records of the 1985th and 1986th meeting, ICERD/C/SR.1985, 3 March 2010 and ICERD/C/SR.1986, 8 March 2010.

[36] See ICERD/C/SR.1985, para. 21. Interestingly, this paragraph is only a very small reproduction of the statement Mr Amir delivered during the dialogue.

37 Amir for example stated that he would like to see culture dominating politics and politics becoming more multicultural. Prosper made clear that he personally agreed with the government's integration policy. Diaconu spoke about his opinion that he expressed during the dialogue, but also in writing about the importance of respecting the principle of equality.

38 Amir spoke about the Netherlands as the maritime power of yesterday. He also referred to the fight of the Helvetians against Caesar and quoted Caesar in this regard. Avtonomov also mentioned the historical role of the Netherlands conquering the sea and emphasised the close ties that exist between Russia and the Netherlands. Ewomsan elaborated upon the fact that the Dutch are well known for trade and that their products are of better quality. Prosper mentioned that he visited the Netherlands and that this visit was reasonably pleasurable and that he had never had any problems.

39 One could even argue that the legal basis of some COs is not only unclear but also questionable from the perspective of ICERD. See for example the recommendation that the state party effectively implement its stated policy of using detention as a measure of last resort or the request to ensure that the asylum procedures are in full conformity with international standards. ICERD/C/NLD/CO/17–18, 25 March 2010, para. 11. ICERD/C/64/CO/7, 10 May 2004, para. 14.

40 ICERD/C/NLD/CO/17–18, 25 March 2010, para. 5.

41 Summary record of the 1985th meeting, ICERD/C/SR.1985, 3 March 2010, para. 3. Furthermore, the government considered that the improvement of the disadvantaged position of women belonging to ethnic minorities is 'their own responsibility to an important extent'. It also held that the focus of emancipation policy must shift from legislation to encouraging initiatives by women and girls themselves. Fourth periodic report of states parties, CEDAW/C/NLD/4, 10 February 2005, 23.

42 Parliamentary Papers II 2009/10, 32123 V, nr. 90, 44. This also means that the government is not very willing to support affirmative action and positive measures. The cabinet Rutte I (2010–2012) even terminated the diversity and preferential treatment policy on the basis of gender and ethnicity althogether.

43 ICERD/C/NLD/CO/17-18, 25 March 2010, para. 6 and 12. CERD's position might result from its focus on equal outcome or obligations of result as the main aim of ICERD instead of equal treatment and obligation of means (Felice, 2002, p. 212; Meron, 1985, pp. 286–287).

44 Timishev vs. Russia, 55762/00 and 55974/00, 13 March 2006 and D. H. and others vs. the Czech Republic, 57325/00, 13 November 2007.

45 From the point of view of CERD this is understandable, since the competence of CERD is limited exclusively to ICERD. CERD furthermore regards the prohibition of racial discrimination as a peremptory norm of international law (*jus cogens* in the sense of Article 53 VCLT). Report of CERD to the General Assembly, A/57/18, 1 November 2002, 107. Thornberry noted that the exceptions to the definition of discrimination are limited under the ICERD. The only limitation clause in Article 1 deals with citizenship (Thornberry, 2005, pp. 249–251). Meron, after pointing to the far-reaching and burdensome obligations under the ICERD, noted that: 'the Convention does not indicate that states can invoke a range of considerations to justify failure to take immediate steps towards implementing the equal achievement goal and can balance that goal with other desired community goals' (Meron, 1985, pp. 289–290 and pp. 298–301). Although CERD has started to adopt more and more a justified limitation approach in its General Comments, this seems not yet visible in its country examination and the resultant COs.

46 Especially with respect to article 14 ECHR and article 1 Protocol 12. This dominance is because the standards in the ECHR are clear and well developed and/or more specific than the ICERD of 1965 given the extensive body of jurisprudence.

47 See the EU Directive 2000/43/EC and FD 2008/913/JHA.

48 Indeed, in response to a recommendation of the European Commissioner of Human Rights, Hammarberg, that mirrors recommendations made by CERD, to ensure that tests, fees and age requirements for family reunification and formation are not a disproportionate obstacle, the government stated that the requirements are in conformity with the EU Directive on family reunification.

49 In this context he mentioned two cases of the ECtHR against the Netherlands. Van Doorson vs. the Netherlands and Van Mechelen. Concluding observations of the Human Rights Committee, CCPR/CO/72/NET, 27 August 2001, para. 12.

50 Summary record, CEDAW/C/SR.512, 6 July 2001, para. 47. CEDAW COs 2001, A/56/38(SUPP), para. 214.

51 For example, the government made clear that it was not willing to definitively give up the Antillean Reference Index ('Verwijsindex Antillianen') based on the third report of ECRI. The government

argued that the 'opinion' of ECRI that the index was not consistent with the ban on racial discrimination is not supported by a court judgement. The ministers also made clear that they wanted to uphold the appeal against the judgement, because they wanted to have a (final) judgement of the Council of State.

[52] Government officials noted that a state could expect to be given a rap over the knuckles by these courts almost on a daily basis. This has an effect on parliamentary scrutiny as parliament is often right on the ball and frequently summons the minister to the weekly question time in parliament concerning those judgements. In addition, judgements of the ECJ and ECtHR are applied by domestic courts who feel obliged to follow legal precedents.

References

Checkel, J. T. (2005) International institutions and socialization in Europe: Introduction and framework, *International Organization*, 59(2), pp. 801–824.

Dai, X. (2005) Why comply? The domestic constituency mechanism, *International Organization*, 59(1), pp. 363–398.

Felice, W. F. (2002) The UN Committee on the Elimination of All Forms of Racial Discrimination: Race, and economic and social human rights, *Human Rights Quarterly*, 24(4), pp. 205–236.

Franck, T. M. (1990) *The Power of Legitimacy and Institution* (New York: Oxford University Press).

Gibson, J. L. & Caldeira, G. A. (1995) The legitimacy of transnational legal institutions: Compliance, support, and the European Court of Justice, *American Journal of Political Science*, 39(2), pp. 459–489.

Hakimi, M. (2009) Secondary human rights law, *Yale Journal of International Law*, 34(2), pp. 596–604.

Keck, M. E. & Sikkink, K. (1998) *Activists Beyond Borders* (Ithaca and London: Cornell University Press).

Krommendijk, J. (2012) The impact and effectiveness of state reporting under the Women's Convention. The case of the Netherlands, in: I. Westendorp (Ed.) *The Women's Convention Turned 30: Achievements, setbacks, and prospects* pp. 487–512 (Antwerpen: Intersentia).

Krommendijk, J. (2011) The effectiveness of non-judicial mechanisms for the implementation of human rights, *Human Rights and International Legal Discourse*, 5(2), pp. 264–293.

Kumm, M. (2004) The legitimacy of international law: A constitutionalist framework of analysis, *European Journal of International Law*, 15(5), pp. 907–931.

Lahuerta, S. B. (2009) Race equality and TCNs, or how to fight discrimination with a discriminatory law, *European Law Journal*, 15(6), pp. 738–756.

Lindgren Alves, J. A. (2008) Race and religion in the United Nations Committee on the Elimination of Racial Discrimination, *University of San Francisco Law Review*, 42(4), pp. 941–982.

Meron, T. (1985) The meaning and reach of the International Convention on the Elimination of all forms of Racial Discrimination, *The American Journal of International Law*, 79, pp. 283–318.

Raustiala, K. (2000) Compliance and effectiveness in international regulatory cooperation, *Case Western Reserve JIL*, 32(2), pp. 387–440.

Risse, T., Ropp, S. C. & Sikkink, K. (1999) *The Power of Human Rights. International norms and domestic change* (Cambridge: Cambridge University Press).

Schimmelfennig, F. & Sedelmeier, U. (2004) Governance by conditionality: EU rule transfer to the candidate countries of Central and Eastern Europe, *Journal of European Public Policy*, 11(4), pp. 669–687.

Simmons, B. A. (2009) *Mobilizing for Human Rights. International law in domestic politics* (Cambridge: Cambridge University Press).

Thornberry, P. (2005) Confronting racial discrimination: A ICERD perspective, *Human Rights Law Review*, 5(2), pp. 239–269.

The Implementation of the ECRML in Slovakia under Construction: Structural Preconditions, External influence and Internal Obstacles

TANJA MAYRGÜNDTER*

ABSTRACT *In the early 1990s, the young Republic of Slovakia, fearing threats of devolution, embarked on an ethno-centric nation-state building, triggering a conflict structure between the majority and the minorities that can be illustrated in the game theoretic model of a 'Pure conflict'. Even under these unfavourable structural conditions, EU conditionality prompted the state to fulfil the Copenhagen Criteria and to adopt the necessary European legislative package, but inducing formal changes in the legislative mainly. Before accession, the European Charter for Regional or Minority Language was also adopted, but appropriate measures necessary for its implementation did not implicitly follow. Nevertheless, medium-term effects show that due to the strong entrenchment with the international institutions involved, such as the European Council, social ties could be created. Consequently, social practice generated reciprocal collective meanings on minority language rights and proved to have a constitutive impact on Slovakia's identity profile in the post-accession period. However, externally induced progress has overlapped with the alternating political elites in power, dominated by populist and nationalistic rhetoric or moderate centre-right parties, finally hampering a more comprehensive implementation of Slovak minority language protection until today.*

Introduction

In the interests of preserving their national integrity, states tend to be attached to their own ethnic basis. This national self-assertion of 'one state-one nation' may lead to cultural, religious, social, economic as well as political dominance of the majority group over minorities, when, for instance, only one language is elevated to official language status. To the degree that the dominant culture is promoted and institutionalized, the survival of other ethnic identities is likely to be threatened. When unity is seen as uniformity, the democratic majority rule can lead to an existential menace to minorities, such that their basic rights in education, employment and economic participation are abrogated.[1] Therefore, *unless* minority protection becomes a *collective* national *interest*, it is in general difficult for minority groups to avoid being outvoted on substantial issues.

This problematic relationship between the majority and the weaker minority relates to issues of the actors' preferences (De Varennes, 2000, p. 9) and can therefore be demonstrated by game theoretic models. As assumed by game theory, each actor pursues his own interests while implicitly imposing a binding constraint on the other actor. Consequently, an interaction takes place, which results in a distinctive situation that can either lead to cooperation, if mutual gains can be achieved, or to a conflict, if this is not feasible. The archetype of a minority conflict can be identified as a *pure conflict*, namely a zero-sum game, characterized by a strong asymmetric structure (Mayrgündter, 2012), where one actor, the majority, assumes total control over the ethnocentric oriented state, while minorities remain in constant struggle for their identity. In zero-sum games, any best response to the actions of the adversary triggers a result in which the gains of one player correspond exactly to the losses of the other one. As a consequence, the outcome represents a result with no chance of a win-win situation. Deadlocked situations that bear a high potential for escalation are typical of minority conflicts belonging to this group of strict competitive games. Due to the unfavourable conflict structure, no incentive for cooperation is offered *unless* the *interest profiles* of the actors and, consequently, the conflict structure *change*. To be more precise, even under regulative constraints imposed subsequent to the interaction in the down-stream phase of conflict building, it is not possible under such conditions to accommodate both parties. In contrast to other types of conflicts where incentives for cooperation can be institutionalized to secure relative gains and stabilize the outcome for mutual convenience, this does not apply to such a type of minority conflict, where the incentive to deviate from the stipulated agreement is stronger than the will to accommodate. However, *before* an interaction takes place, that is, in the up-stream phase of conflict building, norms, ideas and institutions have the potential to affect and shape the preferences of the decision-makers. Interests are neither exogenously given, nor can they be taken for granted, but are subject to the constant change in underlying motivational preferences. This is where the potential to tackle minority conflicts in general lies and this is the reason why all efforts, in order to be successful, have to be targeted towards the up-stream phase of conflict building. The characteristic position of a national minority vis-à-vis a state majority can be illustrated by the pure conflict in Figure 1.

In this conflict type, the state has the clear dominant strategy of protecting its ethno-national integrity, while, correspondingly, the interest of the national minority lies in maintaining its identity, which they want to see protected. These basic preferences of the actors are highly conflictual and, determined by the only existing Nash equilibrium $(-2, 2)$, inevitably provoke an outcome in which the interests of both actors clash without any chance of cooperation. As there is only one Nash equilibrium in the game, this outcome is further aggravated by the fact that the powerful position of the state majority constantly triggers a *strong asymmetric*

State \ National minority	Ethnocentrism	No Ethnocentrism
Scarce or no Engagement for minority rights	- 4, 4	1, -1
Engagement for minority rights	-2, 2	2, -2

Figure 1: The archetype of a minority conflict: a *pure conflict*.

relationship at the expense of the minority. Furthermore, as a Nash equilibrium always represents the best response to each other, no incentive is given for either party to deviate in its choices, the reason why, in principle, the conflict becomes deadlocked and, therefore, lasting long into the future.

One advantage the European Charter for Regional or Minority Languages, scrutinized hereafter, offers is its capacity to side-step this central state's concern about national integrity . The Charter's approach, which attributes rights, not to individuals, but to languages, benchmarks a paradigm change in the post-war minority protection tradition, which is usually based on individual rights (Boysen, 2011, p. 41). As languages and not individuals are beneficiaries of the commitments by the state, minority members cannot automatically enforce these rights. This allows the state to indirectly make concessions to the minorities without the risk of losing its integrity.

EU-conditionality - limited impact of regulative norms

Norms, as understood by Giddens (1979), are 'regulative rules' that can be seen as injunctions establishing an intervening variable, taken into account by the anticipatory calculations of the (collective) actors. Regulative rules satisfy the requirement of being a constraint and might trigger compliance, but are often weak in their impact in terms of immediate behavioural change. In pure conflicts, for instance, norms may lead to formal changes, but have no real impact on state behaviour and, as Kratochwil (1993, p. 459) puts it, thus, do not automatically function as 'problem-solving devices': 'The rules of chess or football neither cause the game to be played nor cause any particular move within the play.'

Scholars confirm that the EU-conditionality policy designed to foster the integration process has actually led to domestic change in nearly all candidate states and new member-states. In anticipation of EU membership, states have adopted fundamental legislative changes in order to meet the membership requirements. But this process does not mean that formal changes are followed by substantial behavioural shifts and the discrepancy between formal rule adoption and real institutional and policy change has been observed by many scholars (e.g. Dimitrova, 2010; Sedelmeier, 2008; Kizilkan-Kisacik, 2010). With respect to minority rights, a top-down 'Europeanization' concentrated on the down-stream phase of conflict building, has therefore led to changes mainly at the institutional and legislative levels, while the fundamental antagonism between majority and minority groups has often remained untouched (Börzel & Risse, 2000; Risse, 2001).

> [...] Europeanization of policies limited to formal changes does not lead automatically to Europeanization of national identities and beliefs on minorities, giving rise to harmonious coexistence. (Kizilkan-Kisacik, 2010)

In order to enhance effectiveness, an endogenization of preferences becomes crucial (Kratochwil 1993, p. 464), thereby increasing the chance to gain greater influence over the actors' values and beliefs. Sovereignty, for instance, would not have any regulative effect without a normative internalization of shared understanding and acceptance by the participants. Social order is not produced by centralization and hierarchy, but by legitimacy and the acceptance of participants.

The constitutive effects of norms and discursive interventions in the pre- and post-accession period

Norms, besides having a formal impact, potentially provide also a *constitutive function* as having a secondary influence on the beliefs and identity of the actors. Consequently, preferences become subject to change, inducing a new social world, which is interpreted by others accordingly. In social-constructivist terms, a mutually determining exchange between actor and structure takes place (Wendt, 1987).

The behaviourist understanding of strategic interaction suggests government behaviour to be the dependent variable, understood as the reaction to particular norms (Katzenstein, 1996; Finnemore & Sikkink, 1998). The aim is then to establish norms that regulate behaviour and trigger compliance. 'Socialization' is thereby a key strategy aimed at obtaining norm recognition through social ties within a liberal community to bring about shared identities (Schimmelfennig, 2001).

An adequate definition of Europeanization, the process whereby a transfer from the European core to other jurisdictions, institutions, rules, beliefs and norms takes place, that concentrates primarily on the constitutive and not on the regulative capacity of norm compliance is offered by the concept of *Societal Europeanization* (Kizilkan-Kisacik, 2010, p. 17). 'Societal Europeanization' is understood as a strategy that, through the construction of collective meanings, aims at producing an impact on the perception, beliefs and values of the actors in order to foster behavioural change. Such a strategy aims at provoking a deeper impact on 'the way actors see themselves', influencing their preferences and finally also their attitudes (Kizilkan-Kisacik, 2010, p. 18).

Third parties, such as the EU, the Council of Europe or the Organization for Security and Cooperation in Europe (OSCE), in order to achieve success in tackling minority issues, therefore, need to aim at the empowerment of the state and the social actors, while relying on the constitutive effects that norms implicitly provoke. Consequently, human rights, even if neglected by the majority, may provide a discursive opening that challenges their beliefs. If provisions of minority protection are incorporated into the legislation, people and politicians may start questioning: Why, if human rights are accepted by and incorporated in the state, are they still not regarded (Risse & Sikkink, 1999)? The adoption of human rights and minority protection rules might open a discourse, challenging relevant actors' identities and beliefs. This *could* lead to an increased value being placed upon minority protection, although there is an immanent risk that increased public exposure of the minority question would lead to more intense nationalist discourse and increased hostility between majority and minority groups, as, for instance, becomes evident in the case of Turkey (Kizilkan-Kisacik, 2010).

Especially in the post-accession phase, after norms were incorporated into the legal framework of the new member-states, socialization effects have become crucial in the implementation process. The European Charter for Regional or Minority Languages (ECRML) is a legal instrument, which contributes in different ways to the enhancement of constitutive European socialization effects:

1. The Charter encourages states to take concrete measures of internal law applicable to the state's distinctive regional or minority languages situation. So, to a great extent, it depends on each state (especially for the substantial Part III of the Charter) which provisions it is going to adopt and which measures it will concretely take. This 'á la carte' character of the Charter brings about a great flexibility of legal rule adoption and implementation with respect to regional or minority languages, which, within the given legal framework, encourages the state to take decisions with which it actually identifies.
2. The ECRML requires very concrete and precise commitments by the state, which, in turn, are subject to a monitoring mechanism that provides for precise and practical measures. The periodical recommendations by the Committee of Ministers contain advice on how a state can further improve the situation of the languages. This contributes to the empowerment of the state actors on issues with which they are often not familiar enough.
3. Throughout the whole process of ratification and implementation of the Charter, social ties with state and social actors have been intensified by the Council of Europe and other international organizations. Especially during the monitoring process, the bodies of the Council of Europe collaborate with national, regional and local authorities and the most relevant non-governmental minority organizations as, for instance, during the 'on the spot' visits of the Committee of Experts. These exchanges enhance the creation of social ties with all the relevant actors.

The secondary effect of norms and institutions on minority rights is further enhanced by the discursive intervention provided through social practice. While the 'behavioural approach' focuses on the immediate reaction to norms, the 'reflexive approach' takes additional account of the discursive interventions of social practice that entail reconstructing the meaning of norms (Wiener, 2004). The reflexive approach suggests an understanding of norm constitution that goes beyond a unilateral and fixed internalization of regulations by the recipient. The meaning of norms is seen as the dependent variable, in terms of being contextually embedded. Correspondingly, social change is seen as being brought about by changes in the relationship between structure/institution and agency. A norm consists then of a collective expectation concerning the proper behaviour of the actors (Katzenstein, 1996), while having a twofold quality manifested by its ability to structure and be restructured. Thus, actors contribute through practice to the (re)construction of norms, while at the same time being guided by them (Wiener, 2004). If, according to the behaviourist approach, norms entail 'standards of behaviour' (Finnemore & Sikkink, 1998), according to the reflexive approach, the 'structural properties of social systems are both the medium and the outcome of the practice that constitute those systems' (Giddens, 1979, p. 69), opening up space for interpretation and reconstruction. Put differently, 'social change occurs as a result of discursive interventions uttered by both norm setters and norm followers' (Wiener, 2004). Those types of norms, which are more vaguely articulated than other norms (Goldstein & Keohane, 1993), permit a wider range of interpretation and are therefore more prone to be reflexively reconstructed.

Both pillars of EU conditionality, the 'non-discrimination' principle as well as other minority rights, by being vaguely formulated, allow a certain openness for discourse and interpretation by the state. Because in the case of minority protection conditionality, clear instructions that can easily be adopted are not offered to the state, norms inevitably become subject to discussion and interpretation. This has the advantage that norms can be shaped according to need and, therefore, represent a constitutive element. In fact, the latest empirical findings attest to the fact that it is only at first glance that EU conditionality may be seen to be fixed and constant. Medium-term effects have revealed it to have 'chameleon-like' characteristics instead, turning the minority problem into a dynamic process, such as in the case of Latvia and Estonia (Sasse, 2008, p. 843). New studies of the post-enlargement period suggest compliance with the *aquis* to be primarily a question of administrative capacity and political will (Sedelmeier, 2008). Minority rights, as defined by the Copenhagen Criteria (such as in the case of the European Charter for Regional or Minority Languages), instead offer the EU limited leverage in the post-accession period. Implementation and proactive engagement depend, therefore, mainly on the involvement and the ties that have been created with domestic actors before the candidate states acceded to membership (Sasse, 2008, pp. 855–6). This momentum is further enforced by other international actors, such as the Council of Europe or the OSCE, with their particular expertise in minority issues.

In the specific case of the Charter for Regional and Minority Languages, due to its á la carte character, the aim is not a fixed and unilateral internalisation of legal provisions, rather a reflexive approach is adopted, which, through political discourse, leads to the adoption of provisions on which both the norm setter and the norm follower are agreed. This social practice is further advanced by the specific monitoring system of the Charter where a constant exchange takes place between the parties on concrete policies and measures. Due to the behavioural and reflexive approach, the ECRML is a unique instrument within the field of minority protection, which particularly focuses on socialization effects. The potential of the Charter is going to be measured in the case of Slovakia, a state where the underlying conflict structure between majority and minorities corresponds to the difficult pure conflict type assessed in the first section.

The European Charter for Regional or Minority Languages (ECRML)

The aspect of norm relevance for the minority in question is a reason why language rights are important. Language is the fundamental basis of cultural identity and if minorities are not permitted to use their own languages, both the language and the ethnic identity will cease to exist in the long run. Language rights offer also the advantage that the level of implementation becomes measurable, because of its public visibility (e.g., on public signs, in courts, in the administration and in the education system). If the implementation of minority language rights is examined in terms of (post) EU conditionality, the European Charter for Regional or Minority Languages (ECRML) is seen to provide a substantive document. The Charter was one of the crucial legal instruments to ensure the protection of minority languages in the candidate states, which, in order to get full membership, were obliged to comply with its principles. The adoption of the ECRML was considered a political condition of the Copenhagen Criteria and, therefore, had to be fulfilled before accession.

The ECRML is the European legal frame of reference for the protection and promotion of languages used by traditional national and ethnic minorities. Its main objectives are to ensure respect of regional or minority languages within the territories in which the languages are used. The policies, legislation and practices within the state should therefore be based on the recognition and promotion of regional and minority languages so that their survival in oral and literary form in both public and private life is guaranteed (ECRML Part II, Art. 7). The measures that must be taken in order to guarantee the implementation of these principles cover virtually all domains of public life, such as education, judicial authorities, administration and public services, media, cultural activities and facilities, economic and social life and transfrontier exchanges with other states of the same language (ECRML, Part II, Art. 8–14)

The ECRML was particularly important to those European states that had envisaged EU membership in 2004 and 2007, as the Charter, enforced in 1998, automatically became part of the Copenhagen Criteria and, so, a condition of membership. Therefore, the Eastern Enlargement brought about a new wave of adoption of the ECRML in this period, such as in the case of Slovakia, which signed and ratified it in 2001.

Slovakia is one of the new member-states that joined the EU in 2004. For the young nation, the issues of sovereignty and state integrity have become central political concerns, given the risk, that a weak centre could have troubles maintaining the state's unity (Kemp, 2002, p. 8). The main principle and political cognition of the political elite and the public is, therefore, the notion of minorities as a security threat

(Chudžíková, 2011, p. 10). Under such unfavourable conditions, the impact of the ECRML on the state's behaviour is scrutinized hereafter.

Slovakia's minority language protection before and after EU accession

a. The root causes of national ethnocentrism before accession

An historical retrospective of Slovakia allows one to grasp the country-specific problematic of forces tending to national integrity on the one hand, and the counter-dynamic of ethno-political centrifugal forces on the other. From the 10th century until the end of World War I, Slovakia as presently constituted belonged first to the Hungarian kingdom and then to Austria-Hungary. The Slovaks, sharing a multi-ethnic environment with other Slavs, Germans and Jews, lived in the Upper Hungarian counties. In the Kingdom of Hungary, the Law on Minorities of 1868 allowed for regional and local use of minority languages, but under the Austro-Hungarian Empire, the Slovaks suffered from the 'Magyarisation' policy (or 'Hungarianisation'), which was a strongly nationalistic policy aimed at assimilating the Slovak population. The Roma became marginalized within the territory as well.

After World War I, most of Upper Hungary became part of Czechoslovakia and minority protection was promised under the Treaties of Trianon (1919) and Saint-Germain (1920). Despite the legal provisions incorporated in the Constitution and the Language Law of 1920, the implementation of minority rights was limited. Slovaks suffered uneven treatment so that their position never equalled that of the Czechs. Despite being recognized as an official language in the Slovak part of the country, Slovak language rights were undermined, and, conversely, the development of the Slovak language towards Czech was in practice promoted (Gramma, 2006, p. 7). Under the Language Law, the minority language could be used in the courts, but only once the German, Hungarian or Polish minorities in the municipalities reached the level of 20 per cent of the population as a whole,[2] a condition that applied also to the right to maintain a German school system and to provide for public minority libraries. Far worse was the situation of the Roma, who suffered discrimination throughout the inter-war period in Czechoslovakia. By contrast, the Hungarians rejected the Trianon treaty entirely and asserted the right to re-establish their old status by returning to Hungary. Czechoslovakia's government response was the initiation of a 'Slovakization' strategy with respect to the minority group.

At the end of World War II, the Beneš Decrees caused a general deterioration of the situation of minorities in the newly established Czechoslovak Republic, but affected Germans and Hungarians particularly. In fact, Germans and Hungarians were deprived of their civil rights and removed from their economic foundations, except those with an active anti-fascist past (Beneš Decrees No. 33/1945). In the aftermath, the deportation of more than 44,000 Hungarians to Bohemia and a population exchange between 90,000 Hungarians and around 73,000 Slovak volunteers from Hungary was forced.[3] In order to keep Slovakian citizenship, people belonging to these groups had to declare themselves Slovaks officially. The situation of the Germans was especially seriously affected, with more than two million people being expelled from the country.[4] Due to this nationalistic policy, the minority landscape underwent a profound change in these years: The Hungarian population halved and, according to official declaration, the German minority was reduced to a few thousand members.[5] The Communist regime that came into power in 1948 officially moderated this policy, but, despite legal provisions permitting minorities to have their own education, media and cultural facilities, these rights were actually never enforced. Only as late as the Socialist Constitution of 1960 could Czechoslovak citizenship be partially gained back by Germans and Hungarians and concessions started to be reintroduced, so that education and cultural activities in the mother tongue were again gradually granted to citizens of Hungarian, Ukrainian and Polish nationality (Gramma, 2006, pp. 11–12). Constitutional Law no. 144/1968 benchmarked a considerable improvement in the legal status and rights for minorities, but, once again, due to external constraints, only the use of the mother tongue in oral communications in administrative offices was implemented (Gramma, 2006, p. 12). The efforts of the Communist regime to integrate the Roma into the labour market and society more generally, in practice, amounted to an assimilation policy, given that they actually deprived them of their cultural heritages. In fact, the Communist regime constituted a menace to the very existence of the Roma.

After decades of repression by Austria-Hungary and Czechoslovakia, the regime change of 1990 might have opened a new prospective, but, in fact, led to increased Slovak national consciousness, finally resulting in the division of the country into the separate Czech and Slovak Republics in 1993. The struggle for national integrity proved to be incompatible with the demand for minority protection, which was perceived as presenting the immanent risk of destabilization and decentralization of the newly established national entity. Thus, despite the multi-ethnic character of the country, official recognition was not granted to any minority language other than Czech. National self-consciousness was indeed expressed in the Constitution in terms of Slovak ethnicity only[6] and, according to Article 6 (1), Slovak is stipulated as the only state language of the Slovak Republic, even though the constitution officially provides for the possibility to recognize national minorities or ethnic groups as well as their educational, linguistic and cultural rights.[7] But the first democratic parliamentary elections brought about a governing populist-nationalistic party coalition (Movement for a Democratic Slovakia - HZDS and the Slovak National Party – SNS), which polarized ethno-political differences and acted as a brake on attempts at multicultural nation-state building. The 1990s saw the reduction of minority protection, especially for Hungarians, provoking domestic and international criticism. The adoption of the Bilateral Agreement on Good Neighbourliness and Friendly Cooperation of 1995 was no more than a minimal pragmatic response to satisfy international demands and the law was not respected accordingly later.[8] What followed instead was the adoption of a new regulation, the State Language Law in 1995, which, based on Article 6 (1) of the Constitution, entailed further restrictions in the public use of minority languages. This discriminatory law aimed at giving unilateral priority to the state's majority language in every sphere of public life and in all official spoken and written communications, and failure to comply was met by severe fines. The law was internally motivated by fear of political mobilization by the Hungarians, which could have provoked a re-annexation to Hungary of the areas where Hungarians were living (Gramma, 2006, p. 15).

b. EU conditionality and Hungarian government participation as a driving force for minority language rights adoption before accession

The relations between the majority and minority communities of the young Slovak state in the early 1990s is characterized by a pure conflict structure, bearing a high potential for conflict. Minority protection demands clashed with the aims of the state in terms of national integrity. However, Slovakia had a great interest in becoming an EU member-state. Therefore, it presented its official request for EU membership in 1995, but, according to the EU Commission report of 1997, the state was not ready for accession because of failure to fully satisfy the political prerequisites and the official membership talks were denied (Commission's Opinion, 1997, p. 22). Most criticism focused on the non-implementation of minority language rights as stipulated by the Slovak constitution. Discriminatory practices, especially with regard to the Hungarian community, came in for criticism, given that subsidies to Hungarian cultural associations were reduced and bilingual school reports in Hungarian schools abolished. Furthermore, the Roma continued to suffer from considerable discrimination in daily life.[9]

In 1999, however, the Law on the Use of Minority Languages was adopted by a slim majority of the new government coalition, which ruled from 1998 to 2006, and minority languages were accepted in official communications with public administrative organs and organs of local self-administration where the minority counted for at least 20 per cent of the population at the municipal level (Regular Report on Slovakia, 1999, p. 17). This provision reflects a return to standards prior to World War II and the Habsburg legislation, but can be fairly interpreted as a pragmatic response to the external demands of the EU. From a domestic point of view, these developments were a reflection of the increased bargaining power of the Hungarians, the largest minority group of the country, enhanced by the role of the newly elected Hungarian Coalition Party (SMK) in the Dzurinda government, which, after 1998, put the minority language issue on the national agenda.[10] Progress towards accession was acknowledged for the first time in the Regular Report of 1999 the Laws on the Use of Minority Languages came into force. Furthermore, the Deputy Prime Minister for Human Rights, National Minorities and Regional Development was appointed, a government advisory body, the Council for National and Ethnic Minorities[11] was created, and, in order to reintroduce bilingual school certificates, the legislation on education was amended (Regular Report, 1999, p. 16). However, shortcomings were still expressed with respect to the lack of appropriate measures taken to ensure the integration of the Roma (Regular Report, 1999, pp. 17–18). These developments and, among others, the ratification of the European Charter of Regional and Minority Languages in June 2001 finally led to a positive evaluation of Slovakia (Regular Report, 2001, p. 22), which can be considered a direct response to the pressure applied by the EU: 'Few will dispute the claim that the EU pressure on minority rights played a crucial role in positive developments that started in the late 90s.'[12]

Additionally, EU support helped to launch the Hungarian minority agenda that favoured prioritization of the minority issue and allowed for more state measures to follow (Sasse, 2005, p. 17). However, the speedy adoption of the EU-requested legislation had also harmful trade-offs in terms of the quality of implementation and showed the prevailing emphasis on formal rule adoption expected by the EU (McDonagh, 2011, p. 12–13).

c. The implementation of the ECRML in the post-accession period

Before accession, under the auspices of the EU, Slovakia opted for a very ambitious instrument of ratification in 2001, covering all regional or minority languages spoken in Slovakia (1st Report of the Committee of Experts, 2005, p. 134). The implementation of these difficult undertakings have primarily been monitored by the Council of Europe, which, without any enforcing lever in hand, has successfully been creating strong social ties with the actors involved, which have allowed the Slovak minority language issue to be tackled through a constructive dialogue throughout the post-accession period. However, not only has external influence played a key role during the implementation process until today, but internal government constellations have also added much to the developments which can be characterized by changes between unfavourable nationalistic rhetoric and practice under the Fico government from 2006 to 2010, and more supportive undertakings by coalition governments with (Hungarian) minority participation through the SMK until 2006 and through its liberal successor, Most-Hid, in the Radičová government from 2010 to Spring 2012.

The primary issue, a general problem affecting all languages whose course of change is most directly linked to the momentum of the political constellation in government, is the State Language Law. After accession, the Fico coalition government amended the State Language Law in June 2009 and, by fulfilling the recommendation of the OSCE High Commissioner to address the problematic provisions, it also released the Principles for the implementation of the law on 16 December 2009 (Györy, 2011, p. 50). According to the Venice Commission, which examined the State Language Law of 2009 in conjunction with the Principles of the government upon request by the state authorities, the laws contain several restrictive provisions which hamper the proper implementation of some crucial minority language rights and they have a disproportionate impact of the state language in relation to the minority languages. While the aims of the government to protect and promote the state language are considered to be legitimate (Venice Commission 2010, p. 27, para 135), its 'ambiguous and contradictory' relationship to the Minority Language Law of 1999 is considered a matter of concern (Venice Commission, 2010, p. 5, para 17). As a result, certain provisions appear to be incompatible with the international obligations undertaken, such as the duty to use the state language in official communication in areas where the minority population does not reach the threshold of 20 per cent and the non-recognition of contracts drafted in minority languages. Other undertakings, instead, should be re-examined and possibly revised, such as the strengthened punitive approach of imposing fines for incorrect use of the Slovak language by institutions.

From 2010 to 2012, once again, a minority party, Most-Hid, was included in the moderate centre-right government coalition led by Radičová. Intended to correct the undertakings of the previous government according to its Manifesto, the government set key priorities concerning minority issues. However, compared to its initial draft, the amended State Language Law of February 2011 represents a clear compromise constrained by the opposition parties' resistance (Advisory Committee on the FCNM, 2011, pp. 4–5). Thus, only one of the four main recommendations of the Venice Commission has virtually been addressed, finally recognizing the contracts drafted in minority languages, whereas several restrictions supposed to have been removed according to the draft amendment in September 2010 have been disregarded (Commissioner for Human Rights, 2011, p. 2 and Advisory Committee on the FCNM, 2011, p. 4). The unsolved ambiguity between the State Language Law and the Law on the Use of Minority Languages, however, prompted the government to opt also for a new amendment of the Minority Language Law.

Indeed, the Minority Language Act of 1999 is the second general problem affecting all languages in the implementation of the Charter, as the 20 per cent threshold barrier represents a serious obstacle limiting the applicability of the provisions under Article 10 (administration) of the ECRML (1st Report of the Committee of Experts, 2005, p. 13). Under the supervision of the Deputy Prime Minister of the Slovak Republic for Human Rights and National Minorities, Rudolf Chmel (Most-Hid representative), in the draft amendment of 2011, the threshold for the use of minority languages was significantly lowered from 20 per cent to 15 per cent. Despite this progress, which owed much to the active engagement of the Deputy Prime Minister, once again due to the final Slovak National Council's decision, the threshold may only be applied beginning 2021 (Deputy Prime Minister, 2011). Furthermore, the new provision extends the use of minority languages also in oral official communications to the whole Slovak territory, but, still, the new amendment does not reach legal conformity with the State Language Law.

These latest commitments of the government reveal the Slovak Republic to be on a 'pro-active track', willing to enhance the protection and promotion of language diversity in Slovakia (Commissioner for Human Rights, 2011). Besides the intention to lower the 20 per cent threshold, the approval of a long-term national minority policy in November 2011 and a proposed amendment to the Education Act aiming at reaching a unifying and complementary adjustment in the field of national minority education also underline these developments (Deputy Prime Minister, 2011). However, this progress has been hampered by the persisting obstruction of populist-nationalistic parties and the early elections of March 2012 weakened the position of the Radičová government so that further measures could not be put into practice. Roberto Fico's social-democratic party, Smer, won absolute majority in the March elections of 2012, which is why it has not had to deal with nationalist coalition partners as it did in the past. However, as several MPs of the Smer party are contrary to the minority policy of the Radičová government with respect to the two corner language laws, a more restrictive approach can again be expected in the next legislation period (Gažovičová, 2011).

Considering each language and field separately, the implementation of the provisions of the ECRML depends mainly on three factors: first on the historically evolved position of the language itself, second on the provisions of the State Language Law that might hamper the implementation of further language rights, and third on the party constellation in the government and the National Council. According to the First Report of the Committee (2005), the fewest problems are related to the Czech language, a fact that owes much to its special status, but the Ukrainian language also finds itself in a relatively favourable situation. Hungarian, the strongest minority language, is especially affected by the general problems caused by the restrictions of the State Language Law; nevertheless, the position of the Hungarian language in the education system is strong. The German language is in a very weak position because it suffers from serious shortcomings in the administration, the judicial system, the media as well as in education at all levels. The situation of the Ruthenian language is also problematic: it suffers from insufficient recognition vis-á-vis the Ukrainian language, despite its significant presence in parts of the territory. Shortcomings are especially noted in the whole field of education. There are very few and dispersed Bulgarian, Croatian and Polish language speakers in the territory, notwithstanding the protection they enjoy under the Charter, but due to the lack of information, the implementation of the respective rights can only be hypothesized to be insufficient.

If each field of language protection under the Charter is scrutinized, it becomes evident that the restrictive regulations of the State Language Act have a negative impact in the field of media. Even though, in general, broadcasting time on public television and radio has increased for most minority languages due to the obligation to provide subtitles in the state language, private television programmes in minority languages are still virtually absent from broadcasting. The latest amendments to the State Language Law have loosened this restriction with regard to private radio programmes. New provisions by the government aim at increasing and distributing the broadcasting time for minorities corresponding to national and ethnic structure with respect to public broadcasting (Act No 532/2010 Coll. on the Radio and Television of Slovakia). After newspapers having been practically absent for nearly all minorities, the government's 'National Minorities Culture 2011' programme now supports the publication of the minority periodical press in the form of grant schemes and it has incentivised the creation of several new newspapers for nearly all minorities. Education as the most striking realm lacks appropriate and systemic measures with regard to many languages, and especially for the German language, where it needs considerable improvements (2nd Report of the Committee of Experts, 2009). In the field of justice, the absence of specific legal rules regarding the use of minority languages has been criticized, but some degree of use in practice has been observed. With regard to administration, as a result of the restrictions in the State Language Law, there are still shortcomings concerning the use of regional or minority languages within and in relation to the regional and local authorities. What has improved during the second monitoring cycle is the administrative practice guaranteeing women the right to adopt or use their family names in regional or minority languages, which, until 2005, was reserved unconditionally only for men. Slovak authorities have also strengthened the support for cultural activities to raise awareness of minority cultures vis-á-vis the majority population (e. g., a network of minority culture museums has been funded by the Slovak authorities), but there is a noticeable lack of history teaching (1st Report of the Committee of Experts, 2005). A particular achievement is a series of steps that have been undertaken concerning the sensitive question of the use of the Romany language. These undertakings have resulted in the development of a curriculum for Romany language education, which has helped to achieve a standardization of the Slovak variant of the Romany language. These measures have been evaluated as a promising basis for further systematic advances in the Romany education system (2nd Report of the Committee 2009, p. 114, para I). Several projects aimed at the abolishment of the unjustified enrolment of Roma children in special schools were also put into practice, even though more action is needed to improve this language situation further. Slovakia also took measures to provide Ruthenian teacher training and research in the field, even though in general, Ruthenian still remains largely absent from education.

Conclusions

The young Republic of Slovakia, due to its historically evolved profile, faced a particularly difficult relationship with its minorities in the 1990s, resulting in a pure conflict comparable to that detailed in the initial theoretical part of this study. The oppression experienced by the Austro-Hungarian Empire and Czechoslovakia and the fear of devolution of the new entity led to heightened Slovak national self-assertion, which resulted in the state embarking on a centralized programme of nation-state building. The claims of the minorities and especially those of the most powerful group, the Hungarians, represented a threat to this integration project by opposing the state's unification interests. Slovak national self-assertion resulted in cultural and political dominance by the majority group over the minorities and associated discriminatory practices, such as the elevation of Slovak as the only official language recognized by the Constitution (Art. 6 (1), which was further enhanced by the implementation of the State Language Law. This configuration of mismatch between the interests of the majority and the minority has provoked an immanent conflict, which is difficult to solve. So, despite EU initiatives to trigger compliance through conditionality, merely formal rule adoption had been reached until the time of accession. It is therefore not surprising that the relationship between Slovakia and the EU overall is considered to have been the most difficult of any candidate state in the pre-accession period (Brosig, 2010, p. 398). Formal rule adoption in the field of minority language rights was accomplished by adopting the Charter for Regional or Minority Languages and passing laws, such as the Laws on the Use of Minority Languages in 1999, but a shift towards a more comprehensive minority language protection has not immediately followed.

Constitutive effects could yet be incentivized through more subtle channels, now that a level of involvement and ties have been created and intensified with domestic actors prior and after accession (Sasse, 2008, p. 855), given that the Council of Europe, the EU and the OSCE have been engaged in involving domestic actors of all levels in the implementation process. A central instrument that helped to intensify the relationship between the Council of Europe and the state authorities as well as domestic NGOs after accession is the special monitoring system designed for the implementation of the ECRML. So, the constructive dialogue between the Council of Europe with the Slovak authorities has been acknowledged in many reports and communications between the parties (see the Reports of the Committee of Experts, the Opinion of the Venice Commission). Also, the engagement of the minority parties has been explicitly supported by the EU and contributed to the opening of a public and political discourse on minority issues (Pridham, 2008, p. 380). Encouraged by such commitments, the Hungarian Coalition Party, SMK, and its successor, Most-Hid, became a crucial factor in shaping the minority rights policy in Slovakia. Playing the veto hand publicly and in government, it was the SMK which put the language issue on the agenda, and so most improvements can be credited to the period of the SMK participation in the coalition government from 1998 to 2006 (McDonagh, 2011, p. 14), and also to the Most-Hid participation in the Radičová government from 2011 till spring 2012, when the two new amendments of the State Language Law and the Minority Language Law were released and other measures such as the implementation of a grant system that allowed minority newspapers to disseminate were undertaken. A special institution, the Deputy Prime Minister, contributed much to the enhancement of the minority language issue by actively participating in its policy formation. Several recent commitments by the Slovak government indicate Slovakia to be on a 'pro-active track' towards heightened engagement in protecting and promoting the minority language policy in Slovakia in line with international demands, even though, especially in the National Council, party politics still represent a considerable constraint to more improvements in implementation. Due to the new Smer domination in the government, there is once again the risk that positive initiatives will get overshadowed by party politics in the upcoming legislation period.

Notes

[1] As in the case of Slovakia, if a minority becomes part of the ruling government coalition, it becomes very likely that the minority issue will not be neglected.

[2] Legal Country Study Slovakia (EURAC), p. 5.

[3] These data are retrieved from Gramma (2006, p. 7), however the numbers do vary according to the source referred to.

[4] Legal Country Study Slovakia, p. 8.

[5] *Ibid.*, p. 8.

[6] Preamble of the Slovak Constitution: 'We, the Slovak nation [...].'

[7] Slovak Constitution (Art. 34 (1))

[8] The Treaty on Good Neighbourliness and Friendly Cooperation of 1995 specifies the rights of the Hungarian minority in Slovakia and those of the Slovak minority in Hungary. It comprises extensive rights, such as the right to use one's native language in private and public life and the right to participate in the official decision-making process. In the aftermath of the signature of the treaty, the bilateral relationship between the two states has fluctuated; it became most strained in 2009, when Slovakia released its State Language Act without Hungarian involvement, and in 2010, when Budapest decided to grant Hungarian citizenship to its kin minorities.

[9] *Ibid.*

[10] 'The 1998 elections led however to a new coalition government, including representatives of the Hungarian-speaking minority, and to a more positive approach to the protection of minority languages.' (1st Report of the Committee of Experts, 2007, pp. 4–5).

[11] The Council for National Minorities and Ethnic Groups is a governmental advisory and coordination body for the area of minority policy and for the implementation of the European Charter for Regional or Minority Languages.

[12] Legal Country Study on Slovakia, p. 21; see also Györy, 2011, p. 5.

References

Advisory Committee on the Framework Convention for Protection of National Minorities, *Third Opinion on Slovakia*, adopted on 18 Jan. 2011, GVT/COM/III(2011)001.

Beneš Decrees No. 33/1945. [online] Available at <http://wintersonnenwende.com/scriptorium/english/archives/whitebook/desg89.html> (Accessed 03 Dez 2011).

Börzel, T.A., and T. Risse (2000) 'When Europe Hits Home: Europeanization and Domestic Change', *European Integration online Papers (EIoP)* 4(15) [online]. Available at: <http://eiop.or.at/eiop/texte/2000-015a.html> [Accessed 12 Dec. 2010].

Boysen, S. (2011) 'Präambel', in S. Boysen, H. Peter, C. Langenfeld and D. Richter, (eds), *Europäische Charta der Regional–Oder Minderheitensprachen. Handkommentar.* (Zürich/St. Gallen: Dike Verlag), p. 41.

Brosig, M. (2010, July) 'The Challenge of Implementing Minority Rights in Central Eastern Europe', in *European Integration*, 32(4), pp. 393–411.

Chudžková, A. (2011) 'Minorities in Political Discourse' in Minority Policy in Slovakia – Critical Quarterly, 4, pp. 10–12.

Commissioner for Human Rights (Thomas Hammarberg) (2011) CommHR/EB/sf 108-2011, Strasbourg, 24 Nov.

Deputy Prime Minister of the Slovak Republic for Human Rights and National Minorities (Rudolf Chmel) (2011) Comm. 16248/2011/PPVL, Bratislava, 16 Dec.

De Varennes, F. (2000, May) 'Minority Rights and the Prevention of Ethnic Conflicts', *Working paper for the Commission on Human Rights*, 6th Session, Asia-Pacific Centre for Human Rights and the Prevention of Ethnic Conflict (Perth).

Dimitrova, A. (2010) 'The New Member States of the EU in the Aftermath of Enlargement: Do New European Rules Remain Empty Shells?', in *Journal of European Public Policy*, 17(1), pp. 137–148.

EU (1997) 'Commission's Opinion on Slovakia's Application for Membership of the European Union', DOC/97/20, Brussels, 15 July, p. 22.

EURAC (2008–12) Legal Country Studies on Slovakia, in *Practice of Minority Protection in Central Europe* (MIMI research project), Institute for Minority Rights of the European Academy of Bozen-Bolzano (EURAC), Bozen-Bolzano.

European Charter for Regional or Minority Languages (ECRML). [online] Availabe at: <http://conventions.coe.int/treaty/en/Treaties/Html/148.htm> [Accessed 20 January 2012].

European Commission for Democracy through Law (Venice Commission) 'Opinion on the Act on the State Language of the Slovak Republic', (Opinion no. 555/2009), adopted on 15–16 Oct. 2010, Strasbourg.

EU Commission's Opinion on Slovakia's Application for Membership of the European Union, DOC/97/20, Brussels, 15 July 1997.

European Commission (1999) 'Regular Report on Slovakia'. Available at: <http://ec.europa.eu/enlargement/archives/pdf/key_documents/1999/slovakia_en.pdf> [Accessed 10 Oct. 2011].

European Commission (2001) 'Regular Report on Slovakia'. Available at: <http://ec.europa.eu/enlargement/archives/pdf/key_documents/2001/sk_en.pdf> [Accessed 10 Oct. 2011].

Finnemore, M., and K. Sikkink (1998, Autumn) 'International Norm Dynamics and Political Change', in *International Organization*, 52(4), pp. 887–917.

Gažovičová, T. (2011) 'Minority Languages in Political Discourse', in *Minority Policy in Slovakia—Critical Quarterly*, 4, pp. 12–15.

Giddens, A. (1979) *Central Problems in Social Theory: Action, Structure and Contradiction in Social Analysis* (London: Macmillan).

Goldstein, J., and R. Keohane (1993) 'Ideas and Foreign Policy: An Analytical Framework', in J. Goldstein and R. Keohane (eds), *Ideas and Foreign Policy: Beliefs, Institutions, and Political Change* (Ithaca, NY, and London: Cornell University Press), pp. 3–30.

Gramma, G. S. (2006) 'Language Policy and Language Rights in Slovakia', *Mercator-Working Papers 23* [online]. Available at: <http://www.ciemen.org/mercator/index-gb.htm> [Accessed 10 Jan. 2011].

Györy, A. (2011) 'The Slovak State Language Law and the Accommodation of Minority Rights: The Impact of International Organizations on the Resolution of Language Disputes', Master's thesis submitted to Central European University, Department of Nationalism Studies, Budapest.

Katzenstein, P.J. (1996) 'Introduction: Alternative Perspectives on National Security', in P. Katzenstein (ed.), *The Culture of National Security. Norms and Identity in World Politics* (New York: Columbia University Press), pp. 1–32.

Kemp, W. (2002) 'Applying the Nationality Principle: Handle with Care', in *Journal of Ethnopolitics and Minority Issues in Europe*, 4, pp. 1–17.

Kizilkan-Kisacik, Z. (2010) 'Europeanization of Minority Rights: Discourse, Practice, and Change in Turkey', *European Diversity and Autonomy Papers (EDAP) 1* [online]. Available at: <http://ww.eurac.edu/edap> [Accessed 20 Feb. 2011].

Kratochwil, F. (1993) 'Norms vs. Numbers, Multilateralism and the Rationalist and Reflexivist Approaches to Institutions, A Unilateral Plea for Communicative Rationality', in J.G. Ruggie (ed), *Multilateralism Matters: The Theory and Praxis of an Institutional Form*. (New York: Columbia University Press), pp. 443–474.

Mayrgündter, T. (2012) *Erosion im Demokratischen Frieden: Innerstaatliche Ethnische Kriege. Eine Neue Theorie*, series: Universitätsschriften Politik, vol. 182 (Baden-Baden: Nomos).

McDonagh, E. (2011) 'Embracing the EU Political Authority after Accession: Differentiated Compliance with EU Rules in Slovakia', *Working Paper in International Studies 2*, Centre for International Studies, Dublin City University.

Pridham, G. (2008) 'The EU's Political Conditionality and Post-Accession Tendencies: Comparisons from Slovakia and Latvia', in *Journal of Common Market Studies*, 46(2), pp. 365–387.

Report of the Committee of Experts on the Application of the Charter in the Slovak Republic, adopted on 23 Nov. 2005, ECRML (2007) 1.

Report of the Committee of Experts on the Application of the Charter in the Slovak Republic, adopted on 24 April 2009, ECRML (2009) 8.

Risse, T. (2001) 'A European Identity? Europeanization and the Evolution of Nation State Identities', in M. Green Cowles, J.A. Caporaso and T. Risse (eds), *Transforming Europe: Europeanization and Domestic Change*. (New York: Cornell University Press), pp. 198–217.

Risse, T., and K. Sikkink (1999) 'The Socialization of International Human Rights Norms into Domestic Practice', in T. Risse, S. Ropp and K. Sikkink (eds), *The Power of Human Rights: International Norms and Domestic Change* (Cambridge: Cambridge University Press), pp. 1–38.

Sasse, G. (2005) 'EU Conditionality and Minority Rights: Translating the Copenhagen Criterion into Policy', *EUI Working Papers RSCAS 16*, pp. 1–21.

Sasse, G. (2008, Sept.) 'The Politics of EU Conditionality: The Norm of Minority Protection During and Beyond EU Accession', in *Journal of European Public Policy*, 15(6), pp. 842–860.

Schimmelfennig, F. (2001) 'The Community Trap: Liberal Norms, Rhetorical Action, and the Eastern Enlargement of the European Union', in *International Organization*, 55(1), pp. 47–80.

Sedelmeier, U. (2008) 'After Conditionality: Post-Accession Compliance with EU Law in East Central Europe', in *Journal of European Public Policy*, 15(6), pp. 806–25.

Wendt, A. (1987, Summer) 'The Agent-Structure Problem in International Relations Theory', in *International Organization*, 41(3), pp. 335–370.

Wiener, A. (2004) 'Contested Compliance: Intervention on the Normative Structure of World Politics', in *European Journal of International Relations*, 10(2), pp. 189–234.

The Role of NGOs in Promoting Minority Rights in the Enlarged European Union

CHRISTOPH SCHNELLBACH, ANDRÁSSY UNIVERSITY BUDAPEST

ABSTRACT *In the field of minority protection, several concepts have been utilized to explain domestic change – like policy transfer, norm diffusion and emulation – to name only a few. But how and why have some EU policies been transferred and others not? Why do accession countries introduce antidiscrimination laws but at the same time undermine individual or collective minority rights in the (post-) enlargement process? When looking for variables of successful EU conditionality in the field of minority policy, the role of non-state actors and advocacy group influence is often neglected in the Europeanization literature. Thus, the article examines and compares the impact of NGO advocacy in the EU enlargement process with a focus on Roma policy. EU enlargement shows that compliance with EU norms can be enforced through transnational advocacy networks (TANs), lobbying on behalf of an ethnic minority. While in non-discrimination, a causal relationship between the advocacy of intermediary institutions and policy reform can be detected, NGOs seem to have less influence on special minority rights. Moreover, the emergence of TANs formed around the issue of the Roma demonstrates that advocacy groups appear to substitute other 'norm entrepreneurs' like kin states or minority parties.*

Introduction

Despite a steady increase of advocacy groups that are active in the European Union, only a few studies have analyzed their influence on the enlarged EU's policies (Beyers et al., 2010; Greenwood, 2009). The impact of 'enlargement waves' on the system of advocacy group interaction has been examined at the EU policy level (Blavoukos & Pagoulatos, 2010). However, as it is hard to measure agency, only little systemic empirical evidence has yet been gathered on the effect of NGOs on policy outcomes.

EU enlargement is often described as a 'top-down' process of Europeanization, but there is also a 'bottom-up' component of the interaction between non-state actors and the EU system of governance. This process includes uploading preferences by state and non-state actors onto the EU system of interest representation. The question remains when – and under what circumstances – do advocacy groups in the field of minority protection actually exert leverage at the national or European level? The EU enlargement process offers a special insight to the multi-directional relationship between non-state actors, governments and international organizations. After introducing a theoretical framework for the assessment of conditions of influence, two case studies are presented along the established analytical model.

Theoretical Perspectives on Advocacy Group Influence in EU Minority Policy

EU enlargement policy in the Central and Eastern European Countries (CEECs) has generally been described as predominantly a policy of political conditionality. By using that strategy, the EU sets its rules as conditions that the CEECs have to fulfil in order to receive EU rewards – from financial assistance to full EU membership (Schimmelfennig & Sedelmeier, 2005). The protection of minorities is one of the political criteria established in the Copenhagen summit in 1993. It is, however, subordinate to the other political conditions, namely the 'stability of institutions' criterion – guaranteeing democracy, the rule of law and human rights.

EU conditionality has different effects on CEECs – depending on which norms in the hierarchy of minority rights are being addressed. Different levels of minority rights address different issues, from basic rights like non-discrimination to special rights such as autonomy. Compliance is inversely proportional to the 'quality' of minority rights. In antidiscrimination policy, compliance in CEECs remains relatively high even after accession, as it is based on internal EU standards and policies. However, due to a lack of experience in dealing with ethnic minorities, the EU has difficulties to provide distinct policy models for the improvement of the situation of the Roma. Roma policy affects both anti-discrimination and special rights. In the field of special minority rights, the EU has to refer to other institutions outside the scope of its own conditionality policy, namely the OSCE and the Council of Europe. The adoption of one of the central international documents in minority protection, the Council of Europe's Framework Convention for the Protection of National Minorities (FCNM), was referred to as a precondition for accession in the EU Regular Reports.

Building on the existing literature on the determinants of advocacy group influence and further studies on policy change, three clusters of determinants can be distinguished: (1) the structural conditions of influence, including existing norms in minority protection and the decision-making procedures of the governmental actors; (2) the degree of interest convergence between NGOs and decision makers at the outset of the negotiation process; (3) the characteristics of the NGO advocacy itself (e.g., resources and strategies).

Norms: Structural Conditions of Influence

Structural conditions, such as existing EU norms in human rights and minority protection within the political system of the EU, affect NGO advocacy (Ram, 2010, p. 207). Norm promoters – including civil society organizations (CSOs), international non-governmental organizations (INGOs) and transnational advocacy networks (TANs) – operate in the given political opportunity structures, which can enable or disable them to exert influence. At the European level, those actors need some kind of organizational platform from and through which they promote their norms. Sometimes these platforms are constructed specifically for the purpose of promoting the norm (such as those promoting human rights, environmental norms, ban on land mines, etc) as are many international NGOs and the larger TANs of which these NGOs become a part (Keck & Sikkink, 1998). In post-Cold War Europe, a minority rights regime has evolved enabling NGOs to form a TAN around the single issue of minority protection.

Promotion of democracy and human rights has traditionally been on the EU's agenda, internally and externally. For a long time, however, minority rights and anti-discrimination policies were not an area of direct EU competence; rather they were left to the discretion and attention of national governments and other international actors. With respect to minority policies, the legal and political framework changed significantly after the end of the East–West Conflict. This changed situation was reflected in the introduction of the Copenhagen Criteria in 1993. Still outside the scope of the *acquis communautaire*, the 'respect for and protection of national minorities' was enshrined at the European Council meeting in June 1993 as a condition for accession. The European Commission has since then monitored the compliance with this criterion but has not established a legal mechanism compared to the Council of Europe. In order to ensure movement towards the conditions for accession, the European Commission submitted annual Regular Reports. These reports emphasized the importance of dealing with human rights issues concerning minorities, and supported national projects financially through the PHARE programme.[1]

Although minority protection became a norm on the EU's external policy agenda, the internal policy was still marked by a significant disjuncture shown by the absence of minority rights in primary law. The Treaty of Amsterdam, in force since May 1999, added non-discrimination to the EU's catalogue of founding principles. Article 13 of the Treaty established a legal basis to combat discrimination on the grounds of racial or ethnic origin, religion or belief, disability, age and sexual orientation. With the Employment Equality Directive (2000/78/EC) and the Racial Equality Directive (2000/43/EC), this set of principles defined by the two acts was put into practice.[2] As it stands, EU non-discrimination law prohibits discrimination on the grounds of racial origin, ethnicity and sex across the areas of employment, access to goods and services and access to welfare services. However, discrimination on the grounds of religion or belief, disability, sexual orientation and age is prohibited only in the area of employment. In 2000, the EU proclaimed the 'Charter of Fundamental Rights of the European Union', which explicitly singles out 'membership of a national minority' among the grounds of discrimination to be prohibited. Despite opt-outs from Great Britain and Poland, the Charter noted the importance of increasing protection of minority rights and has now the same legal value as the European Union treaties. Moreover, the Treaty of Lisbon (in effect since December 2009) finally included the 'rights of persons belonging to minorities' to the founding values of the union in Article 2 of the Treaty on European Union.

Besides these legal developments, political institutions play a decisive role in the degree of advocacy group influence on policy outputs. The scope of influence depends on the decision-making procedure. The key institution in the enlargement process – the European Commission – is not directly elected and therefore not depending on constituency interests. At the same time, the lack of electoral oversight may increase the officials' receptiveness to advocacy groups as the inclusion of organized civil society in policy making constitutes a contribution to legitimizing institutions' decisions and assuring smooth implementation of policies (Charrad, 2010, p. 56).

To this end, the unique system of multi-level governance in the EU with its complex policy making and legislative procedures offers a wide range of opportunities for NGO advocacy. The vertical and horizontal division of power and the multiplicity of power centres increases the number of potential access points for societal actors. Even in the enlargement process, NGOs have a variety of options to pursue their aims and to exert influence on policymakers, from the local to the European level. Nonetheless, the intertwined institutional structure and the consensus-building decision making culture leads to a lack of transparency – giving leeway for governmental actors to block advocacy groups' input.

Interests: Degree of Interest Convergence

Influence identified in policy outcomes is depending on the degree of interest convergence between NGOs and decision-makers at the outset of the negotiation process. Given the complex and pluralistic nature of the EU environment and the vast number of NGOs wishing to engage in European level policy-making, many advocacy groups have formed umbrella networks according to their sectoral interests. NGOs which are able to build advocacy coalitions with other organizations that share their interest are more likely to influence policy outcomes (Michalowitz, 2007, p. 135). Advocacy coalitions enable groups to set up EU wide interest organizations and to develop TANs (Keck & Sikkink, 1998). Those TANs can be temporarily formed around single issues – sometimes focussing exclusively on the cause of minority groups.[3] This was the case when domestic or international NGOs working in the field of human rights were complemented by local organizations, grassroots activists and informal associations of independent experts. In the process of EU enlargement, some NGOs from CEECs have maintained a network of individuals and organizations that were in contact across states borders and joined existing Brussels-based networks – or set up their own representations.

Moreover, the membership of both NGOs and public actors in the same advocacy coalition is even more important. If governmental actors have an interest in their demands, it is more likely that NGOs can put forward their agenda. EU states' interests in minority protection in CEECs are mostly connected to security issues and migration. A mixture of 'hard' and 'soft' security concerns in the post-Cold War period informed a push for internationalisation of minority rights. After the collapse of the Soviet Union, the EU promoted human rights and minority protection externally as a way of ensuring stability in post-socialist countries. Consequently, EU's growing concern in minority issues emerged vis-à-vis neighbourhood countries with potential for ethno–regional conflict amidst multi-faceted transition processes (Sasse, 2005, p. 2).

Advocacy: Resources and Strategies

Another determinant for successful advocacy group influence can be found in the agenda content and the properties of the NGOs. Two factors are distinguished here: advocacy group resources and strategies.

Advocacy group's endowment with resources furthers their capacity to influence policy outcomes. Resources of NGOs include money, legitimacy, political support, knowledge, expertise and information. Advocacy groups may exchange their resources for political influence with the aim of maximizing their own utility. In this rational-choice exchange perspective, advocacy groups' capacity to supply – and decision-makers' demand for – resources mutually determine the influence they may gain over policy outcomes. In the enlargement process, decision makers in the EU were highly dependent on information of societal actors operating in the accession countries. Especially bureaucratic actors like the European Commission need reliable information from NGOs for their monitoring reports. The EU's alleged democratic deficit may also cause greater demand for participation of civil society, which is seen as an opportunity to legitimate European governance (Charrad, 2010, p. 29). In the political system of the EU, advocacy groups that are well endowed with resources are expected to be particularly influential which can lead to a mutually beneficial and sometimes even 'symbiotic' relationship between public and private actors.

NGOs may also use their resources to alter public actors' beliefs, ideas, cognitive frames and preferences. In the field of minority policy, NGOs are more likely to opt for arguing than bargaining, with arguing aimed at changing the beliefs and preferences of decision-makers. Information is not used in exchange for influence, but to convince public actors. It can also be directed in order to change the framing of an issue in public debate:

> In this perspective, resources are also important, but what matters is not a group's overall endowment with resources, but whether the groups can come up with the right ideas at the right time, which change decision-makers' or the public's interpretation of an issue. (Dür, 2010, p. 113)

Advocacy group·influence is finally determined by their strategies. To maximize influence, NGOs have to employ their resources effectively given the opportunities provided by the institutional structure, the characteristics of the issue, the preferences they advocate, and their past strategies. The EU's complex institutional system and the variety of potential access points make it harder for NGOs to pick the most effective strategy. By learning how to use opportunity structures effectively, NGOs may increase their influence on public actors in the EU political system. NGOs use two major approaches to advocacy with different tools and instruments: direct policy influence and capacity-building in advocacy. Each approach involves a mix of methods. Direct policy influence aims at changes in policy, legislation, or procedures, as well as their implementation. It uses lobbying, campaigning, education, consultancy, ligitation and awareness raising. Capacity building, on the other hand, aims at developing the capacity of other groups and organizations to influence policy themselves. Methods include supporting and strengthening grassroots NGOs, networks and movements, as well as facilitating debates between policy-makers and citizens or advocacy groups (Bokulić et al., 2006, p. 96).

Taken these factors (norms, interests and advocacy) together, NGO influence on different areas can be discussed systematically. As a starting point, anti-discrimination serves as the basis for EU minority policy. NGOs have been quite active helping to develop a non-discrimination framework working on all three levels: polity, policy and politics.

Making NGO Influence Work: The Anti-discrimination Framework

In anti-discrimination, the circumstances for effective NGO advocacy gradually improved since the latter half of the 1990s as the legal non-discrimination framework of the EU was being expanded (see above). NGOs and human rights activists were framing anti-discrimination issues in a way that fit into EU's normative agenda. Anti-discrimination was a powerful condition, because it was legally backed by the introduction of non-discrimination rules in the *acquis communautaire*. Therefore, the requirement to adopt anti-discrimination legislation belongs to both forms of conditionality – political and *acquis*. It falls under the scope of *acquis* conditionality, since it includes the transposition and implementation of EU law. In addition, it also affects the political criterion to 'respect and protect minorities'. This duality is reflected in the structure of the Commission's Regular Reports, which address both non-discrimination and special minority rights issues in the chapter on political criteria, but exclusively refer to non-discrimination issues in the *acquis* part under the chapter on 'social policy and employment' (Schwellnus, 2009, p. 34). As the case of antidiscrimination illustrates, both forms of conditionality – hence a combination of legal and political pressure – are necessary for the effective implementation of EU norms.

Interest convergence with policy-makers at EU level was generally high, especially towards influencing those CEECs with larger Roma populations, because the discrimination of Roma was of particular concern to the EU. The EU's ambition to develop non-discrimination rules was connected with its interest in improving living conditions for Roma in their resident countries.

In the enlargement process, the information gathered by NGOs was an indispensable resource for EU policy-makers. The major monitoring missions of the EU were highly dependent on information collected on the ground. For instance, the Open Society Institute (OSI) provided expertise concerning the implementation of the EU directives. The European Union Monitoring and Advocacy Program (EUMAP) criticized Hungary for not introducing a unified law in anti-discrimination and that and the task of challenging cases of discrimination in the courts is primarily shouldered by NGOs (OSI, 2001, pp. 222–224). In 2003, the newly-elected Hungarian government adopted a law on equal treatment and the promotion of equal opportunities, which brought Hungarian legislation in line with the EU directives. Facing a lot of pressure from non-state actors, Hungary managed in the final stage of accession negotiations to completely transpose the *acquis* in this critical area. In Slovakia, advocacy group influence is even more obvious, as in 2001, a comprehensive anti-discrimination law was drafted in collaboration with a Slovak NGO, the Independent Centre for Legal Analysis (OSI, 2001, p. 442). However, due to veto players in the governing coalition, the anti-discrimination law was passed just shortly after EU accession in May 2004 (Schwellnus, 2009, pp. 37–38).

After accession, the institutions of the EU concerned with monitoring human rights and anti-discrimination in member states continued to work together with NGOs. In its activity report 2007–2008, published by the Directorate General (DG) for Employment, Social Affairs and Equal Opportunities, the European Commission refers to a win–win situation between private and public actors:

> Equality and non-discrimination non-governmental organisations (NGOs) play a dual role in combating discrimination. First, they often provide direct support and advice to victims of discrimination and those most at risk of unfair treatment. They also use their on-the-ground experience to provide invaluable input to anti-discrimination policy at all levels. European level cooperation with NGOs and NGO networks is mutually beneficial in both of these areas. (European Commission, 2009, p. 13)

In the implementation process, the Racial Equality Directive required member states to establish or designate 'equality bodies' – with a range of tasks to promote equality, including providing independent assistance to victims of discrimination. In its attempt to monitor the implementation of the directive, the European Union Agency for Fundamental Rights (FRA) relied on information from alternative sources, including NGO reports. NGOs had an impact on putting the directive into practice, with respect to the introduction of equality bodies and sanctions related to cases of ethnic or racial discrimination. According to the annual report of 2008, Hungary and Slovakia are in the group of EU states with functioning equality bodies (FRA, 2008, p. 24). Although in 2007, the number of sanctions was rather low in Hungary and Slovakia, the mere existence and severity of such sanctions can be taken as an indicator for the status of implementation of anti-discrimination rules.

At the national level, 10 years after the adoption of the Employment Equality Directive and the Racial Equality Directive in 2000, legislative activity remained ongoing in some EU countries (e.g., Czech Republic, Romania, Slovenia and Spain). This is the result of efforts from public and private actors to simplify, strengthen and consolidate existing national legal frameworks. The EU has also increased the pressure on member states to implement the directives by launching infringement procedures. Due to these factors, by the end of 2010, equality bodies were introduced in all EU member states (FRA, 2011, p. 84).

The cases of anti-discrimination and equal opportunity policy, or the establishment of equality bodies, are examples of initiatives in which advocacy groups have exerted influence at the EU level. In anti-discrimination policy, emerging EU norms clearly met with a high degree of interest convergence between public and private actors. Moreover, NGOs could provide critical resources to decision-makers. Regarding the adoption of non-discrimination measures, most notably EU directives, the type of influence from non-state actors mainly concerns legislative reforms. This situation enabled NGOs to pressure governments alongside international actors such as the European Commission – which has been quite reluctant in human rights issues from time to time. In the Commission's view, national governments are primarily responsible for developing and implementing policies to protect fundamental rights, tackle discrimination and promote social inclusion. NGOs for their part offered a variety of activities to support the implementation of these directives. Whereas the formal adoption of anti-discrimination legislation as a result of concerted EU and NGO pressure can be considered a success, the results regarding the implementation of legal rules are so far mixed. Due to the persistent effort of numerous NGOs, the post-enlargement implementation of anti-discrimination rules has been managed in a relatively short time in CEECs, despite still existing shortcomings.[4]

Implementing Minority Rights

As discussed above, non-discrimination is the major backdrop for EU norms and protection incentives. The following section addresses two subtypes of minority rights: equal opportunities and special minority rights. The first type mainly derives from the EU *acquis* and is discussed here in light of the Roma case, which is very illustrative. The second type addresses 'special minority rights'. These rights concern positive discrimination towards minority group members – either individually or collectively.

The Case of the Roma

An estimated population of 9–12 million Roma live in Europe, with over half a million in at least five EU countries respectively (Romania, Bulgaria, Hungary, Slovakia and Spain). With the accession of 10 CEECs in 2004 and 2007, the Roma became the largest ethnic minority in the EU.[5] The absence of a kin state and the socio-economic discrimination in many countries makes them one of the most vulnerable ethnic minority groups in Europe. It is disputed, however, if the Roma share a collective identity. While some scholars argue that Roma have never been a cohesive transnational minority, others put forward that interests of Roma are determined by their common identity as an oppressed, persecuted and marginalized group (McGarry, 2010, p. 158). The 'construction' of an ethnic group identity among Roma in Europe is complicated as they are widely dispersed without any universally accepted organization or leaders representing their interests. [6] At the European level, Roma are not politically united due to their linguistic and communal diversity, but this does not preclude the formation of shared interests through a number of NGOs who speak on their behalf.

The relevance of transnational organizing structures of representation for Roma across Europe has become more pronounced since the 1990s due to a number of reasons. The international political community increasingly focussed on Roma in Central and Eastern Europe (McGarry, 2010, p. 137). Induced by the growing media coverage and the work of international NGOs like Human Rights Watch and Amnesty International, knowledge about their discrimination and poverty became more widespread. At the same time, international institutions including the EU became more receptive to the prescriptions of (international) NGOs. For EU leaders, addressing the poor living conditions of the Roma in their home countries was seen as a mean to promote 'soft' EU security interests by forestalling Romani migration into Western Europe. This concerted effort by European institutions was also targeted to support emerging EU norms for the protection of human rights, including antidiscrimination laws.

As a consequence, in the latter half of the 1990s, the interest of EU institutions in the situation of the Roma increased dramatically, resulting in numerous conferences, resolutions and programmes on the Roma (Guy, 2009, p. 24). In the EU enlargement process, candidate states were repeatedly criticized for the mistreatment of their Roma populations and urged to reform legislation, establish institutions, and address negative social attitudes and discriminatory practices. In CEE countries with large Roma populations (Bulgaria, the Czech Republic, Hungary, Romania and Slovakia), measures to combat Roma discrimination were identified as a short-term priority in the 1999 Accession Partnerships and repeatedly demanded in the annual Regular Reports. Without having an internal policy on minority issues, the improvement of the situation of the Roma became a priority in EU conditionality. The EU policy on Roma was therefore mainly developed in the context of enlargement, where it worked as a catalyst and merged with other issue areas like the development of legislation on anti-discrimination.

This constellation offered novel opportunities for NGOs in the field of minority protection and Roma rights. It is not so clear, however, to what extent single NGOs and TANs formed around the issue of the Roma perceived EU conditionality as beneficial. The relationship between advocacy group influence and EU conditionality seems to be rather ambivalent as Romani activists:

> ... believed that the international political context of EU enlargement had indeed a positive impact on their position... in many cases they also pointed to the difficulty of turning the pressure exerted by the EU into an effective tool of Romani mobilization. (Vermeersch, 2006, pp. 198–199)

Furthermore, with growing attention in the context of EU enlargement it was feared that if the Roma issue was held responsible for hindering EU accession, widespread negative stereotypes against the Roma would be reinforced.

In the literature on EU enlargement, NGO influence is traditionally underestimated in the system of European governance. For a long time, international organizations merely reflected state preferences as they are comprised of state representatives and therefore widely exclude minority communities from negotiations on minority protection. Against this backdrop, NGOs have acquired significant attention in international institutions over the last decades. Although state actors still seem to be the main players in the field of minority protection, issues concerning Roma are increasingly pushed forward by intermediary actors. In an effort to co-ordinate governmental policy on Roma, an unique initiative is presented by the Decade of Roma Inclusion (2005–2015), which involves not only governments (the 12 participating countries are Albania, Bosnia and Herzegovina, Bulgaria, Croatia, Czech Republic, Hungary, Macedonia, Montenegro, Romania, Serbia, Slovakia and Spain) and international organizations, but also NGOs.

However, the lack of interaction between international organizations and Romani communities has led to questionable results for the Roma. The EU's 2004 report

'Roma Situation in an Enlarged Europe' points out that Roma face more serious difficulties than the rest of the population in the fields of education, employment, housing and health. The report states that there is a 'lack of capacity, understanding and professional expertise to deal effectively with the complex and multi-dimensional nature of the problem' (European Commission, 2004, p. 16). There is a vast gap between the policy level and the operational reality through the relative absence of Romani grass-root and stalagmite mobilization in the transnational political context. Thus, it is hard to detect shared interests as there is hardly a 'legitimate' Romani voice in international organizations.

A number of NGOs started to overcome the lack of interest representation, as there have been many efforts to channel Roma voices into international organizations. For instance, the European Roma Rights Centre (ERRC) has consultative status with the Council of Europe, as well as with the Economic and Social Council of the United Nations. Transnational organizing structures of representation are crucial in fostering interaction between Romani activists and advocates, and the communities they represent (McGarry, 2010, p. 138). Ultimately, the success of the advocacy group influence is dependent on its ability to bridge the gap between Romani communities and governmental actors.

Political opportunity structures offer a variety of access points which the TANs utilize to articulate their interests: 'Significantly, while international organizations are the site of advocacy and mobilization it is often member state governments which are the primary target of transnational activism' (McGarry, 2010, p. 139). That is because Roma are usually citizens of the CEE states in which they reside, meaning that tangible improvements in their situation cannot be addressed exclusively in the transnational political environment. However, interest convergence between private and public actors often goes beyond the domestic political context, which makes transnational organizing structures of representation necessary. But what are – and who defines – Roma interests?

The activities, publications and public statements of transnational NGOs reflect on those interests considered most relevant for Roma. They must be distinguished from domestic interests of Roma because some are more transnational in orientation such as the standardization of language or migration issues. The focus here is laid on those organizations which have been active on the European level. As part of their strategy, those (international) NGOs have developed their own methods and established links with Romani populations, local grassroots actors and those recognized as Romani leaders in CEECs.

One leading NGO in the area, the Budapest-based ERRC, was established in 1996 as an international public interest law organization focussing exclusively on the human rights situation of the Roma. In the context of EU enlargement, the ERRC has conducted research on the human rights situation of Roma and produced a number of reports on behalf of European institutions, including the aforementioned report 'Roma in an Enlarged European Union'.

In combining legal and political activities with advocacy on all levels, the ERRC has been especially engaged in inducing domestic political actors to uphold international norms. In the past 15 years, the ERRC has been contributing to setting a legal framework in Europe for the rights of Roma, particularly through the Council of Europe and the creation of jurisprudence at the European Court of

Human Rights. This, in turn, has had a significant impact on state-level jurisprudence, legislation and policy. The ERRC was instrumental in giving content to the existing legal framework and state obligation to investigate, identify and prosecute violence against the Roma minority and the segregation in schools. Especially the latter case shows that the practical impact of a court decision on systemic rights violation is not always so apparent. The case of *D.H. and Others v. the Czech Republic* (No. 57325/00) is an ample illustration of this lack of implementation. Despite a strong and unequivocal ruling by the European Court of Human Rights in 2007 that the tracking of Romani children into schools for children with 'mild disabilities' was illegal discrimination, the practice of segregation persists in the Czech Republic (among many other CEECs including Hungary and Slovakia). In response to the lack of government action to give effect to *D.H.*, ERRC has established a coalition around this issue with the Roma Education Fund, OSI and the NGO 'Together to School' – which has been very active since its founding and provides a model of NGO cooperation on Roma issues. However, although some steps have been undertaken by the Czech government to address the situation of access to education for Romani children, the efforts by local and international NGOs, mainly within the framework of the 'Together to School' coalition has de facto not significantly 'changed the situation on the ground' (Gall & Kushen, 2010).

ERRCs role in the accession process has chiefly been to produce progress reports timed to coincide with the periodic review of accession states progress toward meeting EU standards. At EU level, ERRC main contact points for lobbying are the European Parliament and the Commission. ERRC works closely together with friendly Parliamentarians to hold hearings and briefings on Roma rights issues of concern. For officials who are writing reports on Roma issues, ERRC provides background information, comments and criticism. Within the Commission, the preferred access points are DG Justice and – to lesser extent – DG Employment.[7]

During the enlargement process, the aforementioned OSI's European Union Monitoring and Advocacy Program published monitoring reports highlighting a number of minority and Roma issues. EUMAP witnessed a substantial evolution in the capacity of local Roma civil society to conduct advocacy. Through the involvement of local experts in preparing the reports and the combination of national and international advocacy, the programme has aimed from the beginning to ensure that its monitoring reports have a real social and political impact.

Another player on the 'NGO market', the European Roma Information Office (ERIO) has developed into an international advocacy organization focussing exclusively on the Roma cause. As a part of the NGO network European Roma Policy Coalition (ERPC), ERIO supported the development of an 'EU Strategy on the Roma Inclusion', which is expected to be channelled into a new EU policy instrument.[8] However, the implementation of the EU strategy for Roma is still subject to discussions between various actors at the EU level.[9] Moreover, advocacy coalitions with EU institutions can also be seen in the collaboration of organizing events such as the EU Roma Summits in September 2008 and April 2010 or the conference 'Roma Access to Political Participation' at the European Parliament in April 2009.

Special Minority Rights in Hungary and Slovakia

Concerning special minority rights, advocacy group influence on norm implementation is much harder to detect. Major legal improvements in minority rights at EU level were achieved after the accession of the 10 CEECs.[10] Special minority rights are provisions that go beyond equal treatment and non-discrimination. Those measures are especially relevant for ethnic and national minorities in the EU like Hungarians in Slovakia or the Russian minorities in the Baltic States. In contrast to the Roma communities, they are in most cases represented by political parties and/or kin states. For example, a minority rights model focussing on special, group-differentiated rights has been endorsed by Hungary in the early 1990s. It has proven to be inadequate, however, for socially and economically marginalized groups such as the Roma.

In the enlargement process, the EU had less leverage in areas of weak EU competence such as special minority rights. The case of political representation of minorities in Hungary illustrates this: the Regular Reports frequently referred to the introduction of guaranteed seats for minority representatives in the Parliament (European Commission, 2002, p. 20). EU conditionality had limited effects, although the constitutional right to participate in the sovereign power of the people as a 'constituent part of the state' (Art. XXIX Hungarian Constitution) has been discussed for almost two decades.

The demand for political representation has been supported by an array of NGOs, but the Hungarian government has not yet taken on the issue. Opportunity structures for NGOs seem to be limited, as EU leverage is minimal in the area of political participation, which belongs to collective minority rights.

The Slovak language law is another illustrative example for the interplay of norms, interests and NGO advocacy. The restrictive state language law of the first post-socialist government under Vladimír Mečiar was supplemented by the law on minority languages in 1999. With this law, the constitutional protection of minority languages was taken into account as it allowed the use of minority languages in the public sphere in areas with at least 20 percent minority population. The external stimulus in this case was extremely high because the language law was the last hurdle before the opening of accession negotiations with the EU. Then prime minister Dzurinda (1998–2006) was in a 'sandwich' position between the external pressure from the EU and the domestic political opposition. The pressure from the inside consisted in the fact that the Premier had to find the greatest possible consensus among the ruling parties. The Hungarian Coalition Party (MKP) – supported by many NGOs – called for further regulation in favour of minorities and thus was against the proposed law. However, Dzurinda was able to pass the law and therefore to meet the requirements of the EU and to keep the same domestic veto players in check. This example shows once again how the influence of the EU interacts with internal political pressure. In 2009, a controversial language law – mandating preferential use of the state language – was passed by the incumbent Fico government (2006–2010), which led to a setback in relations to Hungary and the EU respectively. This was only possible due to the decreasing EU leverage after enlargement – which in turn also undermined the efforts by numerous minority-friendly NGOs.

Conclusion

What does all this tell us about the influence of advocacy groups in the EU policy process? In our two case studies (Roma policy, special minority rights), three clusters of determinants were analyzed: Norms, interests and advocacy. Policy reform in CEECs was to some extend triggered by transnational advocacy of NGOs. The actions of international organizations and NGOs were mutually reinforcing, as was shown in the case of EU enlargement policy. Conditionality applied by EU's Copenhagen Criteria was crucial in creating new opportunities for advocacy – even if minority protection was the weakest political condition for accession. Facing accession states' room to manoeuvre while interpreting these vague conditions, NGOs for their part stimulated international actors to step up their monitoring activities. This constellation is most obvious in anti-discrimination and Roma policies – to a lesser extent also in special minority rights.

In Roma policy, the EU does so far not provide special norms apart from the existing anti-discrimination *acquis*. The intermingling of Roma policies with the non-discrimination *acquis* helped to establish opportunity structures for TANs lobbying on behalf of the Roma. Framing the Roma issue in a way that met with EU's agenda in combating discrimination and fostering human rights, advocacy groups achieved to exert considerable influence on EU institutions. Roma are now on the political 'radar' of the EU more than ever before. The case study has shown that resources of NGOs can be extremely valuable for states and international organizations. These components helped NGOs to optimize their strategies in the EU policy process and work efficiently towards their objectives: 'The utility of TANs lies in their capacity to empower local Romani communities through training and funding (OSI–RPP) and their ability to induce domestic political actors to uphold international norms including anti-discrimination and anti-racism (ERRC)' (McGarry, 2010, p. 160).

Furthermore, TANs such as the European Roma Policy Coalition (ERPC) are more likely to influence directional issues than single organizations. The proclaimed aim of the 'Coalition' is to promote and strengthen EU and national action aimed at the social inclusion of Roma in Europe. The EPRC, consisting of a variety of minority-NGOs, has been especially active in the adoption of an EU Framework Strategy on Roma Inclusion which was endorsed by EU leaders in June 2011. The EU seeks to improve the lives of Roma people by presenting a European structure to support the work of member states, based on their national strategies involving local and regional authorities.

Despite successes on policy and legal issues, the emergence of TANs on the international scene has not been matched by significant political representation. This is partly a result of weak Roma parties on the domestic political scenes and the lack of a Romani 'kin state'. NGOs have been trying to fill this gap and found a wide range of access points in the EU multilevel system. These findings corroborate a 'triangular' model of transnational advocacy, 'with the EU as the primary target of the advocacy and the international NGOs (INGOs) taking the lead with only modest Roma support' (Ram, 2010, p. 202).

Increasing the pressure on accession states in the EU enlargement process, NGOs lobbied the EU to include certain issues concerning the Roma in the Regular

Reports. The case of Slovakia shows how interest convergence between NGOs and the government can be crucial for advocacy group influence.

In the post-enlargement period, however, NGOs have lost the useful and effective tool of EU conditionality with regard to the new member states from CEE. In the meantime, countries joined the EU while substantial problems with Roma communities remained. The EU stance on CEE minority rights led to certain continued policy expectations within the EU and triggered internal EU developments. Significant international attention to the Roma has not automatically resulted in major improvements in the lives of most Roma. Despite policy reform on the international and domestic level, Roma still suffer from widespread discrimination and marginalization in EU member states (European Commission, 2010). As the example of Hungary shows, even the existence of functioning anti-discrimination bodies and a unique system of special minority rights have not considerably improved the situation of the Roma in recent years.[11]

In special minority rights, norms are mostly derived from other European organizations such as the Council of Europe and OSCE as the EU has just begun to develop a legal framework for minority protection. Interest of NGOs in promoting special minority rights are often diverging those of single EU member states. Member states can undermine NGO advocacy for minorities in intergovernmental institutions. Moreover, collective minority rights are mostly directional issues and can touch upon very sensitive questions of state organization. It is therefore not surprising that in the mid-term perspective, advocacy group influence remains rather low in that specific area.

Notes

[1] The PHARE (Poland and Hungary: Assistance for Restructuring their Economies) programme, originally created in 1989, is one of the three pre-accession instruments financed by the European Union to assist the applicant countries of Central and Eastern Europe in their preparations for joining the European Union.

[2] Drawing on the successful implementation of the 2005 Framework Strategy against Discrimination and the 2007 'European Year of Equal Opportunities for All', the Commission adopted under its renewed social agenda a non-discrimination package in July 2008.

[3] It is important to distinguish between international advocacy organizations and representative organizations. TANs usually do not aim to *represent* ethnic constituencies but to *advocate* on their behalf.

[4] As the monitoring reports of the EU Agency on Fundamental Rights show, these implementation issues are not confined to the CEE area but can be detected equally in 'old' EU member states.

[5] The term 'Roma' is commonly employed as an umbrella term for a number of groups including Roma, Sinti and Travellers.

[6] There are two long-standing organizations giving voice to Roma in the transnational political context – the International Romani Union and the Roma National Congress – but as their centralized hierarchical leadership is widely detached from Romani communities only few Roma recognize them as legitimate representatives.

[7] Interview held by the author with ERRC representatives on 31 May 2011 in Budapest.

[8] Cp. European Parliament resolution of 31 January 2008 on a European strategy on the Roma, P6_TA(2008)0035.

[9] The European Parliament is in the 'driving seat' in the negotiations. However, input also comes from the European Commission and minority-friendly EU member states. For instance, the creation of an overall policy framework concerning integration of Roma was one of the Hungarian EU Presidency's (January–June 2011) priorities.

[10] Before enlargement, the EU has been reluctant to introduce minority rights in primary law, also due to a lack of interest convergence between NGOs and decision makers at the European level. While NGOs were lobbying for special minority rights, single EU member states could easily block those efforts. France and Greece have been quite opposed to minority rights in the past, which made it almost impossible to find a consensus in this section of EU's human rights policy.

[11] The elected 'National Gypsy Self Government' is regarded as the official partner for discussion matters related to the rights of Roma. The influence of advocacy groups is limited in Hungary as they were not directly engaged in the self-government system.

References

Beyers, J., Eising, R. & Maloney, W.A. (Eds) (2010) *Interest Group Politics in Europe: Lessons from EU studies and comparative politics* (London, UK: Routledge).

Blavoukos, S. & Pagoulatos, G. (2010) 'Enlargement waves' and interest group participation in the EU policy-making system: Establishing a framework of analysis, in: J. Beyers, R. Eising & W.A. Maloney (Eds) *Interest Group Politics in Europe: Lessons from EU studies and comparative politics*, pp. 45–63 (London, UK: Routledge).

Bokulić, S., Bieber, F., Biró, A. & Cheney, E. (2006) *Minority Rights Advocacy in the European Union: A guide for NGOs in South-East Europe* (London, UK: Minority Rights Group International).

Charrad, K. (2010) *Participant or Observers in European Governance? Civil society lobbyists from Central and Eastern Europe in Brussels* (Baden-Baden: Nomos).

Dür, A. (2010) How to assess power and influence in EU politics, in: J. Beyers, R. Eising & W.A. Maloney (Eds) *Interest Group Politics in Europe: Lessons from EU Studies and Comparative Politics*, pp. 110–128 (London, UK: Routledge).

European Commission (2002) *Regular Report on Hungary's Progress Towards Accession* (Brussels: European Commission).

European Commission (2004) *The Situation of Roma in an Enlarged European Union* (Brussels: European Commission).

European Commission (2009) *EU Action Against Discrimination – Activity Report 2007–08* (Luxembourg: Office for Official Publications of the European Communities).

European Commission (2010) *Roma in Europe: The implementation of European Union instruments and policies for Roma inclusion (Progress Report 2008–2010)* (Brussels: European Commission).

FRA – Fundamental Rights Agency (2008) *Annual Report 2008* (Vienna: European Union Agency for Fundamental Rights).

FRA – Fundamental Rights Agency (2011) *Fundamental Rights: Challenges and achievements in 2010* (Vienna: European Union Agency for Fundamental Rights).

Gall, L. & Kushen, R. (2010) What happened to the promise of D.H.? *Roma Rights No. 1: Implementation of Judgements*, pp. 39–44.

Greenwood, J. (2009) Institutions and civil society organizations in the EU's multilevel system, in: J. Joachim & B. Locher (Eds) *Transnational Activism in the UN and the EU*, pp. 90–100 (Oxon: Routledge).

Guy, W. (2009) EU initiatives on Roma: Limitations and ways forward, in: N. Sigona & N. Trehan (Eds) *Romani Politics in Contemporary Europe*, pp. 23–50 (Houndsmills: Palgrave Macmillan).

Keck, M. E. & Sikkink, K. (1998) *Activists Beyond Borders: Advocacy networks in international politics* (Ithaca, NY: Cornell University Press).

McGarry, A. (2009) Round pegs in square holes: Integrating the Romani community in Hungary, in: T. Agarin & M. Brosig (Eds.) *Minority Integration in Central Eastern Europe. Between Ethnic Diversity and Equality*, pp. 258–277 (Amsterdam and New York: Rodopi).

McGarry, A. (2010) *Who Speaks for Roma? Political representation of a transnational minority community* (New York: Continuum).

Michalowitz, I. (2007) What determines influence? Assessing conditions for decision-making influence of interest groups in the EU, *Journal of European Public Policy*, 14(1), pp. 132–151.

OSI – Open Society Institute (2001) *Monitoring the Accession Process: Minority protection* (Budapest: OSI).

Pridham, G. (2008) Status quo bias or institutionalisation for reversibility? The EU's political conditionality, post-accession tendencies and democratic consolidation in Slovakia, *Europe–Asia Studies*, 60(3), pp. 432–454.

Ram, M. H. (2010) Interests, norms and advocacy: Explaining the emergence of the Roma onto the EU's agenda, *Ethnopolitics*, 9(2), pp. 197–217.
Sasse, G. (2005) EU conditionality and minority rights: Translating the Copenhagen criterion into policy, EUI Working Papers 16.
Schimmelfennig, F. & U. Sedelmeier (Eds) (2005) *The Europeanization of Central and Eastern Europe* (Ithaca, NY: Cornell University Press).
Schwellnus, G. (2009) Anti-discrimination legislation, in: B. Rechel (Ed.) *Minority Rights in Central and Eastern Europe*, pp. 32–45 (Abingdon: Routledge).
Vermeersch, P. (2006) *The Romani Movement: Minority politics and ethnic mobilization in contemporary Central Europe* (New York and Oxford: Berghahn Books).
Vermeersch, P. & Ram, M. H. (2009) The Roma, in: B. Rechel (Ed.) *Minority Rights in Central and Eastern Europe*, pp. 61–74 (Abingdon: Routledge).

Index

Note: Page numbers in *italic* type refer to *tables*
Page numbers followed by 'n' refer to notes
Abdulatipov, R. 46
activists: Roma 121, 122
administrative capacities 10–11
advocacy 117–18
Agarin, T. 65; and Brosig, M. 1–5; and Regelmann, A-C. 4, 59–77
Amir, N. 93n, 94n
Amsterdam Court of Justice 85
anti-discrimination 118
Arib, K. 82
autonomy: non-territorial 45–9, *see also* national-cultural autonomy
Aydin Düzgit, S. 33

Ballin, E.H. 93n
Barnett, M.: and Finnemore, M. 11
Barrett, S.M. 30, 32
Bauer, V. 46
Beneš Decrees (1945) 103
Bennett, A.: and George, A. 19
Beréni, J. 74n
Blavoukos, S.: and Pagoulatos, G. 113
Börzel, T.A.: and Risse, T. 99
broadcasting language restrictions: Turkey 26, 28, 29
Brosig, M. 4, 6–23; and Agarin, T. 1–5
Brubaker, R. 59; *et al* 44
Brunsson, N. 42, 43–4
Budryte, D. 68

Campbell 44
Čaplovič, D. 72
Central and East European countries (CEECs) 11, 24, 31, 59–61, 114–26
Charter of Fundamental Rights of the European Union (EU) 115
children's rights 82
Chmel, R. 107
Civic Integration Act (2007) 86
Commissioner for Human Rights 107

Committee on the Elimination of Racial Discrimination (CERD) 4
compliance 6–23, 41, 114; conditions 19; costs 10; criticism 20–1; definition 15; domestic mechanism 83–5; domestic politics 30–1; law observance 30; literature 6–8, 15–16; management 11, 16; measurability 15; mechanisms 8–15; pull 86, 90; research 14, 19–20; soft mechanism 86–8; studies 15–16; variables 19; worlds 30–1, *see also* norms
conflicts 97; pure 97, **98**
Connor, W. 45
constructivism 7, 10, 11–12; reflectivist view 12, 14–15, 16–17; rise 14
Convention on the Elimination of Discrimination Against Women (CEDAW) 80, 81–3, 87, 88, 90, 91n, 93n; network 82
Convention on the Elimination of Racial Discrimination (CERD) 4, 91n, 93n
Convention on the Elimination of Racial Discrimination Concluding Observations (COs) 78–90, *83*, 91n; dialogue 86–7; Dutch government 88–90; expert members 86–7; (in)effectiveness 80–1, 88–90, 91n; media coverage 85; quality 86
Convention on the Rights of the Child (CRC) 80, 81–3, *83*, 91n, 92–3n; coalition 82
Copenhagen Criteria 37n
cost-benefit calculations 9, 14
Council of Europe (CoE) 5, 100
courts: Amsterdam Court of Justice 85; European Court of Human Rights (ECtHR) 85, 89–90, 93n, 94n; European Court of Justice (ECJ) 90; ICERD 84–5; Netherlands Supreme 81, 93n
Csergo, Z. 59
Cyprus 33
Czechoslovakia 103

Dagestan 56n
deportation 103–4
Diaconu, I. 94n

Dimitrova, A. 61
discrimination 115
domestic compliance costs 9
domestic cost-benefit calculations 9
domestic costs model 10
domestic preference approach 9
Dür, A. 117
Dworkin, R. 17–18
Dzurinda, M. 71, 124

Employment of Minorities Act (Wet SAMEN 1998) 84
enforcement 11–12, 15, 16
equality 45
Erdoğan, R.T. 34, 36
Ericsson 43
Estonia 61, 64, 65–6, 68–70, 73; accession agreements 67; EU pressure 67; government 69–70; language law 68–9; legal frame 66; minority-friendly legislation 68–9; multiculturalism 69–70; nationalization policies 68; post-Soviet political transition 65
ethnic minority: identities 96–7; rights 99, 101, 120–4
European Centre for Minority Issues (ECMI) 5
European Charter for Regional or Minority Languages (ECRML) 72, 98, 100–2, 106–8; approach 98; importance 102; legal frame 102
European Commission against Racism and Intolerance (ECRI) 81, 89, 92n
European Commission (EC) 32–3, 67, 116, 119, 122; Racial Equality Directive 119
European Council 32–3, 61, 62
European Court of Human Rights (ECtHR) 85, 89–90, 93n, 94n
European Court of Justice (ECJ) 90
European Parliament (EP) 71, 126n
European Roma Information Office (ERIO) 123
European Roma Policy Coalition (ERPC) 125
European Roma Rights Centre (ERRC) 122–3
European Union Agency for Fundamental Rights (FRA) 119
European Union (EU) 5; accession 3, 59, 60, 62–4, 67, 73–4; Charter of Fundamental Rights 115; conditionality 31–3, 37, 62, 64, 98–9, 101; decision-making 17; developments 24; enlargement 1, 8, 42, 60, 113–14, 124; external evaluation 42; integration 60, 71, 73–4; membership 3, 60, 61, 62–3, 99; monitors 61, 67; policy-making 60–4, 73; pressure 67; Slovakia integration 71; and Turkey 26–7, 32–6
European Union Monitoring and Advocacy Program (EUMAP) 118, 123
Europeanization 99; Slovakia 66–7; societal 99–100
Eurozone 2
Ewomsan, K.D. 94n

Falkner, G.: *et al* 19, 25, 30–1, 37; and Hartlapp, M. 16; and Treib, O. 31
Federal Consultative Council on NCA Affairs (Russia) 48, 55n
federalism 49–54
Felice, W.F. 80
Fico, R. 107, 124
Filippov, V. 52
Finnemore, M.: and Barnett, M. 11; and Sikkink, K. 101
Fomichenko, M. 45, 49
Framework Convention on the Protection of National Minorities (FCNM) 1, 48
Friis, L.: and Murphy, A. 61

Gall, L.: and Kushen, R. 123
game theory 97; conflicts 97; zero-sum 97
George, A.: and Bennett, A. 19
Germans 103–4
Giddens, A. 98, 101
Good Neighbourliness and Friendly Cooperation (1995) 104, 110n
Gramma, G.S. 103, 104
Gramsci, A. 42
Grigoriadis, I. 28
groupism 44–5
GÜN TV 29
Gypsy *see* Roma

Hakimi, M. 92n
Halki seminary 26, 37n
Hall, P.: and Taylor, R. 44
Hallik, K.: and Pettai, V. 69
Hartlapp, M.: *et al* 19, 25, 30–1, 37; and Falkner, G. 16
Hay, C. 11
High Commissioner on National Minorities (HCNM) 65
human rights 90–1, 100; Commissioner 107
Hungarian Coalition Party (SMK) 67, 71–2, 109, 124
Hungarian university (Slovakia) 72
Hungarians 66–7, 103–4, 110n; deportation 103–4
Hungary 118, 126n
hypocrisy 43, 45, 53, *see also* systemic hypocrisy

INDEX

identities: ethnic minority 96–7; supra- 34, 36
implementation 21n, 30; research 30–2; trap 2
Ingram, H.: and Schneider, A.L. 43
internally displaced persons (IDPs) 26, 37n
International Convention on the Elimination of Racial Discrimination (ICERD) 78, 79, *83*, 87, 91n, 92n, 94n; courts 84–5
international non-governmental organizations (INGOs) 115

Kelley, J.G. 8, 62, 68
Kirch, A.: *et al* 68
Kizilkan-Kisacik, Z. 99–100
Kratochwil, F. 14, 98–9
Krommendijk, J. 4, 78–95
Krook, M.: and True, J. 13
Kurds 29, 34, 35
Kushen, R.: and Gall, L. 123

language 51–2, 66, 102–10, 124
Language Law (1920) 103
Larrabee, F.: and Tol, G. 35
Lausanne Peace Treaty (1923) 27, 28, 37n
law 17–18; integrity 17–18
Legal Country Study Slovakia (EURAC) 105, 110n
Liaras, E. 35
Lindgren Alves, J.A. 87
lobbying: NGOs 82–3, 85–6
Loveman, M.: *et al* 44

McGarry, A. 120, 125
management 11, 16
Mätlik, T. 74n
Mayrgündter, T. 4, 96–112
media 85
Meron, T. 94n
Minority Language Act (1999) 67, 72, 107, 110
mis-fit approach 9
Moravčik, J. 67
Most-Hid 106, 107, 109–10
Movement for a Democratic Slovakia (HZDS) 66
multiculturalism 69–70
Murphy, A.: and Friis, L. 61
Muslim world 87

Nash equilibrium 97
National Gypsy Self Government 127n
National Minorities Culture-2011 programme (Slovakia) 108
national self-assertion 96–7, 109
national-cultural autonomy 45–9, 54, 55n; finance 47; functions 47; law 46–8
Netherlands 78–9; Amsterdam Court of Justice 85; *Employment of Minorities Act* (Wet SAMEN 1998) 84; government 80–1, 83–4, 88–90, 93n, 94–5n; government officials 79–80, 83, 88, 92n, 93n; history 94n; International Commission of Jurists (NJCM) 93n; Landelijk Bureau Rassendiscriminatie (LBR) 93n; parliament 83–4, 93n; Supreme Court 81, 93n; treaty laws 85
non-discrimination 11
non-governmental organizations (NGOs) 46–7, 48–9, 80, 82–3, 85–6, 93n, 113–28; advocacy 117–18; capacity building 117–18; influence 118–20; international 115; lobbying 82–3, 85–6; market 123; representatives 88
norms 7; actors 13; adherence 9; adoption process 9; application 15; behavioural approach 101; constitutive function 99; development 17; domestic 15; enforcement 15; implementation 2–4, 41–2; international 13; legal 2; preference congruence 9; quality 12–13; reflexive approach 101; regulative rules 98; structural conditions of influence 114–16; validation 12, 14, *see also* compliance

one state-one nation 96–7
Oran, B. 28, 34
Organization for Security and Co-operation (OSCE) 65–6, 67
Osipov, A. 4, 41–58
Özbudun, E. 34

Pagoulatos, G.: and Blavoukos, S. 113
Pain, E. 49
Parlando 91–2n
partnership: privileged 33
persuasion 13
Pettai, V.: and Hallik, K. 69
Poland and Hungary: Assistance for Restructuring their Economies (PHARE) programme 126n
Polat, R.K. 35
policies: implementation 21n, 30; instrumental 43; symbolic 43
positivist research methodology 19
post-communist states 61–4
privileged partnership 33
Prosper, R. 86–7, 94n
protection 1, 100

Qualitative Comparative Analysis (QCA) 20

Racial Equality Directive (EC) 119
Radio and Television Supreme Council (RTÜK) 29
Ram, M.H. 125

INDEX

rationalism 8–10, 12, 14, 20–1, 64
Raustiala, K. 91n
reform: Slovakia 70–1
reforms: Turkey 26, 28–9
Regelmann, A-C.: and Agarin, T. 4, 59–77
Regular Report (1999) 105
repression 104
rights: children's 82; ethnic minority 99, 101, 120–4; human 90–1, 100, 107
Risse, T. 12; and Börzel, T.A. 99; *et al* 13
Roma 103, 104, 118, 120–3, 125–6, 126n, 127n; activists 121, 122; interests 122; language 108; National Gypsy Self Government 127n; policy 125; population 120
Ropp, S.: *et al* 13
Ross, C. 5
Russian Federation 45; Constitutions 47, 50–1, 55n; criticism 45; diversity management 41; ethnic policies 53; ethnic statehood 52; Federal Consultative Council on NCA Affairs 48, 55n; federalism 49–54; government 53; languages 51–2; legislation 45–6; public officials 55n; regional governments 52; titular ethnic groups 48, 49, 51–2, 55n

Sakha 51
Samoilenko, O. 45, 49
Sasse, G. 62
Schimmelfennig, F. 21n, 33, 99; and Sedelmeier, U. 8, 61
Schneider, A.L.: and Ingram, H. 43
Schnellbach, C. 4, 113–28
Schwellnus, G. 118
Scott, J. 44
Sedelmeier, U. 8, 10; and Schimmelfennig, F. 8, 61
Setu 51, 56n
Sikkink, K.: *et al* 13; and Finnemore, M. 101
Slovak Spectator 71, 72
Slovakia 61, 64, 66–7, 70–3, 96, 102–10, 118–19, 124; accession agreements 67, 70; coalition 110n; Constitution 103, 104; deportation 103–4; EU pressure 67; European integration 71; Europeanization 66–7; government 70–2, 108; history 103; Hungarian university 72; HZDS 66; language 66, 103–6, 124; Most-Hid 106, 107, 109–10; national integrity 105; National Minorities Culture-2011 programme 108; reform 70–1; repression 104, *see also* Hungarians
Smer 107
Snidai, D. 10
socialization 13–14, 99–100
society 44

Soviet Union 45 *see also* Russian Federation
Stamatov, P.: *et al* 44
State Language Law 66, 72, 104, 106–8, 110
systemic hypocrisy 41, 42–4, 54; hidden transcript 43, 44, 45, 53, 54

Talst, M.: *et al* 68
Tarasov, A. 45, 49
Tatarstan 51, 52
Taylor, R.: and Hall, P. 44
Thornberry, P. 94n
Tol, G.: and Larrabee, F. 35
Toshenko, Z. 52
transnational advocacy networks (TANs) 115, 116, 125, 126n
transposition 15–16; legal 15; neglect 31
Treaty of Amsterdam (1999) 115
Treib, O. 15; *et al* 19, 25, 30–1, 37; and Falkner, G. 31
Trianon Treaty (1919) 103
True, J.: and Krook, M. 13
Tuisk, Y.: *et al* 68
Turkey 24–40; accession process 32; broadcasting language restrictions 26, 28, 29; EU demands 26–7; EU membership 32–6; EU roadmap 27; government 28, 33–6; Halki seminary 26, 37n; IDPs 26, 37n; implementation 25, 29–30, *30*, 37n; improve protection 27; Justice and Development Party (AKP) 28, 33–6, 37n; Kurds 29, 34, 35; legal adoption 28–9; non-Muslims 26–7, 28, 36; observations 25–30; pro-Kurdish Democratic Society Party (DTP) 35; public service broadcaster (TRT) 29, 36; Radio and Television Supreme Council (RTÜK) 29; reforms 26, 28–9; supra-identity 34, 36; village guard system 37n

uniformity 97
unity 97
Use of Minority Languages (1999) 105

Vachudova, M.A. 62
Valentei, S. 52
Venice Commission 106
Vermeersch, P. 121
veto players 10, 14
village guard system: Turkey 37n

Walser, M. 6, 21n
Wendt, A. 14
Wiener, A. 7, 101
Wilders, G. 85
women 81–3, 94n

Yilmaz, G. 4, 24–40

Zorin, V. 46
Zwingel, S. 12